# No Coincidences Only Miracles

*A little book about everyday BIG miracles*

SHIRLEY ANNI NJOS

ISBN: 1482338645
ISBN-13: 9781482338645

# DEDICATION

This book is dedicated to
Tiffany and Monika.

With all my love.

# CONTENTS

# ACKNOWLEDGMENTS

Writing my autobiography has been both healing and cleansing. I have been empowered by this act of grace. To me, the concept of empowerment is this: Empowered people use, in a constructive and positive way, that which is in their immediate environment to craft an ever-changing reality – ME. This has been my journey.

Without my husband, Eric's full support and belief in me, I might not have written this book. I feel blessed and honored to have such an amazing man who has cheered me on from the very beginning, listening to my endless chatter recounting the past. Eric, YOU are my dream come true – I love you!

Thank you to my editor, Cara Sands, for taking the time to listen to my voice and then preserve my meaning through the most brilliant editing. Cara, your skills are unmatched, and I'm grateful for the outstanding contribution you have made to my happiness. Your faith touched my heart.

I want to humbly acknowledge my loved ones in Spirit that came into my consciousness, awakening my soul and filling me with words of love and memories.

Two of the greatest reasons I decided to write my autobiography are Tiffany and Monika, my adored children. I hope and believe that sharing my life so extensively will serve as something both my daughters will treasure.

After recently losing my own mother, I wished so much that I had more knowledge about her life. I wanted to learn about so many more of her experiences, be able to view more photographs – anything at all! As it was, I knew of only a few major events, and of course, the life we lived together through our shared experiences.

# INTRODUCTION

I believe we are all "Spirits," having chosen this human experience here on earth in order that we learn lessons of unconditional love, not only for ourselves but also for others. As I write my book, I feel very strongly that I am being guided by Spirit, not yet knowing how much I will tell or exactly what I will say. I do know one thing for certain: You won't get bored reading my very, unique life story. I'm hoping to make you laugh and cry, talk out loud, and most of all, leave you feeling happy and blessed for the life you were given. This thing – entity – we call "life" is truly a creation of what you put into it. Throughout my life, I would tell myself: "DARE TO LIVE" and boy did I! Looking back, it's clearly evident I've lived my life mostly without fear and in "THE MOMENT," always keeping faith and hope close to my heart while sporting my big smile through it all.

*"No one comes to you by accident and there is no such thing as coincidence. Nothing occurs at random. Life is not a product of chance." ~ Neale Donald Walsch*

I was born Shirley Anni Glassing on January 19, 1948 in Frankfurt, Germany to my German mother Ilse Glassing and never having known a father. I also had a half sister, and together, the three of us spent our lives surviving post-war. It was a struggle for my mother as we were extremely poor, but I never knew this at the time, since she was an immaculate woman. With the little we had, she kept the tiny space in which we lived, spotless. And speaking of this, the three of us lived in one small room where we ate, slept and bathed. There was a toilet in the hallway for all tenants to share. Food was very scarce, consisting mostly of sugar-bread and pork-fat bread and much of the time, my mother wouldn't eat, in order that she be able to feed us. At times we had hot soup, which was a huge treat because hot meals were rare.

My mother was a thin woman with movie star looks, weighing no more than 100 pounds. For much of her life, she learned to eat for survival and never for pleasure, maintaining this practice until the day she died.

There were times my sister and I walked by the nearby Army base and spotted chewing gum along the wall that GI's had chewed and spit out. We would have a competition who could find the most pieces that still had some sweet taste left in them, this becoming a little game to occupy our hungry minds. I recall bombed buildings all around where I lived and, often I played inside them. In fact, there was a bomb still lodged on the top of our building that never detonated. I wasn't fearful about it, but as a child, did fear that at any time and without warning, more bombs might fall from the sky. And so, I developed the habit of constantly looking up.

There were times that I was locked in the cellar for behaving badly and yet I don't remember what I could have done to deserve this frightening punishment. Since I would scream and cry all the way down to the cellar, my mother couldn't carry me. Instead, she would enlist the help of a young, male neighbor and he would carry me while my mom accompanied him. I was left alone in this pitch-black cellar for what felt like forever. I remember seeing bats, rats and coal all around. Yet, to this day I don't know how much of what I saw was real or imagined. Through the years I never asked my mother about this because I didn't want her to feel ashamed of her behavior. I have never held any bad feelings towards her about this awful experience, because I truly felt she was acting out of frustration, having to raise two children as a single mother in that time period. I know better than to think she was acting maliciously, which she was not.

I barely had any toys. In fact, all I remember of my possessions is a tiny matchbook-sized doll, a bag of marbles, paper and a pencil for drawing and my most-cherished plaything – a pair of roller skates that came with a key to tighten them to my shoes. And yet, I viewed myself as having been a happy child.

To help you better understand my story as a young girl growing up, I'll shed a little light about my mother. As a youngster, her life was mostly a sad one, and yet she too was one of the happiest people I have ever known. She loved life, despite having lost her father at age 11 to the Nazis, as her father was a German Jew. One day, the Nazis came, killing him in front of their home. My mother ran outside as she could hear her mother's screams. Lying dead in the middle of the street was her father; her mother, hovering over him, weeping. My grandmother, seeing my mother, screamed at her to get back inside the house. The Nazis didn't kill my grandmother – she was saved because she was German.

This wasn't the only brush my mother had with Nazis. One day when my mother was 12 years old, the Nazis came to her school and yanked her out of class. Terrified, she was taken to a concentration camp where they stripped her and shaved her head, leaving her bare on a cold, straw-covered floor. The Nazis then killed her best friend in front of her because she said something wrong. Struggling to survive in the camp, my mother made a decision that saved her life: She managed to escape by sliding her skeleton-thin body under a fence and running through fields to get home. When she finally arrived at her neighborhood, she found her house had been bombed. In a stroke of luck, signs including a list of names had been posted on how to find family members. And in that moment, my mother's horror gave way to her being reunited with her mother.

My mother has been a truly wonderful example to me in so many ways because of her positivity and strength. I made an equally excellent choice in choosing her as a mother, while still in Spirit form. Despite the difficult life she had lived, she taught me to reaffirm that life is good and that even so-called bad things are only temporary conditions. She also taught me to trust and believe in myself and to never give up hope. And through her fine examples, she supported all of my decisions throughout my life.

I love my mother with all my heart and soul, fully knowing that we are connected through eternity because life *is* eternal. Someday I will see her again and what were once tears of pain will flow as tears of joy – an experience far greater than the tears I shed when my mother crossed over to the "light" on November 5, 2011.

In my own, unique way, I summarize Suzane Northrop's words:
There are lessons here on earth that cannot be learned elsewhere. Each of us has been given the correct vehicle: We choose our parents; our parent

siblings (or not); our sex and our cultural foundation upon which to grow in the perfect way for our soul's journey. And while for reasons unexplained, some souls choose a shortened lifetime, they are all working within the framework of divinity.

My own life's journey, which started out with all odds against me has proven that anything is possible. Sometimes I have viewed my path as an impersonator "bluffing my way through life." And yet, by believing in myself, thinking in a most positive manner and taking action by following my dreams has manifested my present reality – one that I consider "My Little Miracles."

# 1 MY UNUSUAL BIRTH

I've known many people who complain about their upbringing and family life in general. Personally, I would have had every reason to feel "unwanted," and justified to have serious "father issues," never having experienced the privilege of a real dad. And yet, on the contrary I didn't feel this way at all, unaware this wasn't the norm. I credit my mother, since her love for me equaled that of two parents – maybe three!

*We do pick how we enter the earth plane, even choosing our parents.*

I will begin by going back to Germany, when my mother was only 21 years old. Her best friend wanted her to go on a blind double date. As she didn't have a babysitter, my nine month-old sister was brought along. Later that evening, she found herself alone in a room with her date, but she wasn't nervous, as her friend was in the room adjacent to hers. As the evening wore on, my mother, aware that she needed to put her daughter to sleep, attempted to leave. Her date – a full 10 years older than her – blocked the door, stating, "You're not going anywhere!"

Panic crept into my mother and she screamed for help, praying her friend would hear her pleas. No one came to her rescue, and, amidst cries from her baby daughter, she was raped.

Back in 1948 Germany, abortion was unheard of. And so, my mother's perpetrator sought "underground" assistance to get her an injection to abort the fetus – me. My mother, struggling with one child, agreed. She was given the shot and yet she did not abort, as she was injected into the vein. It did, however, cause my mother to suffer from temporary paralysis, and even though she was offered another shot, she refused.

It's difficult to believe my Spirit chose this type of inception, and yet it did. While I'm ecstatic to have been born, my grand entrance on earth had been marred by my mother's awful suffering. Despite all this, I was loved beyond belief and made to feel special. No one could walk by me without complimenting my mother on my smile and "adorable" dimples. I ended up being one of five siblings, yet it was no secret that I was her favorite child.

I believe life is a gift, and we exist here to learn and assimilate specific lessons. Our biggest lesson is the complete understanding and expression of unconditional love. Hand-in-hand with this is forgiveness, both for us and for others. Although never knowing him, for this reason, I have forgiven my birth father.

# 2 LEAVING GERMANY FOR LONDON

I recall my mother dating a very handsome German man whom I adored, because he used to carry me on his shoulders while taking me for long walks. From memory, he resembled a young Paul Newman. I believed he loved my mother and was ready to commit to her and her children. By contrast during another time, my mother met and dated an American GI whom I didn't like at all. My mother, wanting the best life she could imagine for us, hoped one day to move to America. Thus, a choice was made out of security instead of love, and she married this man. While I understand her decision, it seemed like a huge sacrifice, and at a young age I learned my first and most powerful lesson: What mattered to me most was love and being in love. Ultimately, only this would ever make me happy.

The marriage took place just before we left Germany. Moving to America sounded like heaven; with the potential for greatness in this new life almost unimaginable. The first stop in this journey was London, as my stepfather was assigned there. A suggestion was made that my mother and him move first, leaving my sister and myself in an orphanage until after they were settled. My mother balked at the idea, refusing to leave without her children. If she hadn't refused, I believe I would have never seen my precious mother again.

Together, we left Germany for London in 1957. Our lifestyle changed dramatically, with one wonderful memory of hot water being accessible via a tap in the wall to fill a big and beautiful bathtub! Compared with my mother boiling water on a stove for a once-a-week bath in a little silver bucket, this "exotica" was to die for! I had never seen so many separate rooms, complete with an upstairs, downstairs and a lovely lush garden. I enjoyed sitting on our windowsill on foggy and rainy days, staring at the greenery. For hours, I sat in this meditative state.

I made friends quickly and started school immediately, wearing a green

3

and yellow uniform with a tie. I didn't know any English, aside from the song, "How Much is that Doggy in the Window" thus needed a crash course in order that I pass my studies and keep my friends. I listened to British ladies chatting away on street corners, and recall their words sounding like gibberish, yet I learned the language well, thanks to my teachers and other children. In less than one year I was speaking fluent English, complete with an adorable German accent which I have since largely lost.

I made a new best friend that lived a few doors down and visited with her often. Together, we would listen to records on her record player. One day she showed me a new album with a terribly handsome man on the cover. His name was Elvis Presley and immediately, I knew I was in love. When his voice poured out from the little machine, cupid further hit me. From that very moment I was forever changed, as Elvis became an inseparable part of me. I dreamed and dreamed of one day, moving to America so I could meet Elvis and be with him.

My life consisted of many chores, one of them being taking the big family bag of laundry and riding the double-decker bus to the Laundromat on Rainers Lane. Although sitting on the lower level would have been easier, given the huge bag I was dragging, I insisted on riding on the upper level and loved it. While the laundry was being washed, I recall wandering off to my favorite candy store, where there was a seemingly endless selection of treats. I never had any money with me, but did carry a little pearl bag that I used to fill with candy. For many minutes and on several occasions I stood there, choosing my selections. The storekeepers saw I was filling my bag and yet, must have overlooked it.

Many evenings were spent nibbling on candy while watching my favorite show, "Cheyenne" on the small black and white television in my bedroom. I remember Clint Walker with his deep, soft voice saying, "Hi I'm Cheyenne, Cheyenne Body." I would fantasize that he was my father, versus my stepfather, whom I considered a constant intruder on my bliss.

All in all, life in London was enjoyable. I loved the British people, although I didn't quite understand their slapstick humor, coming from a more serious Germany. And yet, I never lost my dream of one day, moving and living in America, forever.

# 3 AMERICA HERE I COME! AND, MY SUICIDE ATTEMPT

The day finally arrived when my stepfather was stationed back in America. I was so happy I could have jumped "across the pond" for joy, although I knew I would miss my dear friends. We arrived in New York in 1960, and drove across the country to northern California, stopping for one week to visit with his family in Ohio. Our brood included my older half-sister, a half-brother born just before leaving Germany, a new half-sister born in London, and myself.

We arrived at my stepfather's mother's house, and were greeted by twin brothers bearing delicious, homemade maple ice cream. I had never tasted anything so decadent in my life. That, and peanut butter – another first – kept my taste buds craving the salty, creamy treat, to the point where I ate peanut butter by the spoonful until I could barely swallow.

The twin brothers gave me money, promising to take me shopping at Sears & Roebuck. Excited beyond words, I dragged my four year-old brother outside, asking a neighbor for directions to the store. And off the two of us went, without any adult accompaniment.

While walking on the main boulevard, we were approached by a man who from the get-go, made me very uneasy. As he talked, I felt a "red alert" go off and sure enough in an instant, he tried to grab my arm. I reached for my little brother's hand, squeezing so tightly he started screaming. Thinking on my feet, I agreed to meet the stranger at a certain time later that evening, and between my promise and my brother's cries, was very likely saved from a kidnapping.

I cannot begin to describe the terror I felt. I wanted so badly to run to the next house for assistance, but was afraid to, thinking that America was filled with very, bad people. What a welcome to this new country!

5

One week later we were back on the road to California. I saw palm trees for the first time and fell in love with their beautiful appearance. Looking at them, I felt free and open, unlike the big cities I was used to living in. We arrived at the base in San Rafael, having been given temporary housing and was struck by its immediate filth. Us kids remained outdoors while my mother worked miracles, transforming a dirt den into a dollhouse. We lived there for a short while until a nice two-story home was made available to us.

And thus, at the ripe old age of 12, my early teenage years began. The reality of who my stepfather was became apparent, as I was given one pair of shoes, one black, tight skirt and two blouses. I was instructed that if I wanted more clothes beyond what was given, I would have to work for them by babysitting. Dinners consisted of Rice-A-Roni, and other macaroni and cheese products. And yet this didn't bother me, as I was still a kid. I recall Sundays being the worst day of all because he attempted to force me to attend Sunday school. My mother, practically an atheist herself, knew this wouldn't wash and saved me from this torture.

My mother would cook her "Sunday meal," consisting of steak with gravy and rice. What would have been a treat turned into a culinary nightmare, my stepfather cutting away the fat from his steak and serving it to me and my sister while saying grace. While he was cutting his meat, I was gagging on fat and mastered the skill of spitting the gristle out of my mouth and into my lap. As my plate would appear empty, I would be excused and running to the bathroom, would flush the fat down the toilet.

Every night my sister and I would be tasked with doing the dishes and washing and waxing the kitchen floor. Everything would have to pass the "white glove inspection" by my stepfather and when I say the floor was spotless, I mean this in a very literal sense. Luxuries were reserved for him and him alone, as were candy and sodas, while we were never allowed any.

Even on the holiest of confectionary celebrations, Halloween, we weren't allowed to go trick or treating because he considered it "begging." In a bizarre ritual, he instructed us to hand out one single piece of candy (a corn kernel) to visiting children to ensure he himself wouldn't get "tricked." One year, we found our front lawn "toilet papered," out of retaliation.

His extreme stinginess embarrassed me; angered me, and eventually, nurtured an incredible generosity in me later in life.

As I hadn't made enough money to buy myself a new pair of shoes, they eventually developed holes. I was told to place duct tape over the holes, which I did throughout my school days. My friends kept asking what the shiny stuff on the soles of my shoes was, and eventually I forced myself to tell them. Fortunately, my friends just laughed without judgment, and I laughed with them. My mother ironed in order to earn the extra money I needed to purchase some necessities and enjoying my alone time with her, learned to iron very well myself.

I was put on restriction for weeks over the dumbest of things. Once, I forgot to put a new toilet paper roll on. The penalty for that was a one-week restriction. Another time I didn't close the bread bag tightly enough. That garnished me another week's restriction. And on one fateful afternoon, some of my friends set up a tent on a grassy area of the base, in order to share stories. It was all harmless fun until my stepfather found out I was in a tent with boys included. I was hit non-stop, and vividly recall the curlers flying out of my hair.

From that moment onward, my mission was to get out from under this man's roof. Little did I know at the time, this opportunity would come sooner than I could have ever imagined.

At 15 years of age, my best friend in high school, Bobbie Powell, informed me she was no longer a virgin. I asked her all about sex because I met an older boy out of school, 20 year-old Bob Raccio. Nobody knew I was seeing him, as I sometimes skipped school to spend the day with him. One day Bob told me that if I "don't give in to him" on our next date, he would break up with me. I couldn't bear that thought. He explained that as a man, he had "man's needs" and that I was just a little girl that needed to learn how to please him. I believed all this hogwash because I was innocent and because I was crazy about him.

On the "big night" I made up an excuse that I was spending the evening at Bobbie's house (which I often did in order that I could be with Bob) and unceremoniously, he drove us up to Cherry Hill, a favorite amongst couples and named this by no coincidence. It was here I lost my virginity and recall wondering several times that night what all the fuss was about.

Bob was in the Coast Guard Reserve and was leaving the next day. In his absence, I missed my period. I was getting increasingly scared that I might be pregnant but reminded myself that it was only one time and people don't get pregnant the very first time they have sex. When Bob returned home I shared my potentially ominous news. Many weeks later, my stomach had a slight, but obvious bulge to it and while still in grade 10, I was with child.

Bob and I decided I should try to lose the baby. First, Bob punched me twice in the stomach, but was unsuccessful in terminating the pregnancy. I finally confided in my older sister, with a promise that she would never utter a word to my mother or stepfather. One day she climbed on top of the couch and jumped on my stomach but my baby was resilient and it thrived.

My final plan was clearly desperation talking, and came from a 15 year-old who wasn't even allowed to date: I would try to kill myself. I shared my plan with Bobbie and to my surprise, she responded by telling me she wanted to kill herself too. We planned our demise – we'd catch a Greyhound bus to southern California and then take an overdose of sleeping pills. The bus would arrive at its destination, along with two, dead high school students.

On what was supposed to be the final day of my life, with my mother under the impression I was sleeping at Bobbie's, we left the base and made our way to the bus stop. It was a chilly night and shivering, we each took a bottle of "Nytol" as well as some pills to help curb motion sickness. I figured the more the merrier; with us becoming "more dead" as we increased the amount of chemicals in our bodies. At one point, I looked up at the stars and wished them goodbye, yet as the evening got colder, sleep became impossible. By 5:00 a.m., completely disorientated we each made our way home, as clearly our attempt at death evaded us.

My mother, although surprised to see me home so early didn't question me when I stated that Bobbie's family went to church and I didn't want to attend with them. We sat together on the couch, watching the little ones play with their toys. Suddenly the room filled with dozens of spider webs, complete with tiny white bugs. There were bugs in my mother's hair and I began to scream. I told her what I was seeing, and in an attempt to convince me that this wasn't real, she wiped the floor with her hands to show me her hands were clean. As clear as day, I saw the webs and bugs sticking to her hands, and realized I was experiencing hallucinations from ingesting all those pills.

Looking back, I believe the cold weather was what saved our lives. I am blessed beyond words that for whatever reason, the bus never showed up.

*There is no such thing as coincidence.*

# 4 MY VERY SAD PREGNANCY

It wasn't long after my suicide attempt that I was standing in the kitchen next to my mom, totally oblivious that my growing stomach had become evident. Form-fitting outfits weren't helping. My mom, in her soft voice, looked at me and asked, "Shirley, are you pregnant?"

She caught me off guard, and at that moment, I looked into her kind green eyes and knew I could no longer lie about my pregnancy. With a feeling of pure relief I answered, "Yes." She hugged me and told me I needed to go upstairs and tell my stepfather.

I was past the point of being scared, so I went upstairs, my mother close behind. She waited outside the door in case I needed her intervention. And, with a short introduction, I told my stepfather as fast as I could that I was pregnant. The look of shock and anger in every muscle of his face made me wonder if he was going to strike out (he didn't). My mom entered the room after I dropped the news, and immediately, out came THE question from both their mouths: "Who is the father?"

I never thought twice about my answer. Of course I would protect Bob, who at 21 years of age could face jail time. So I lied and told them after consuming a copious amount of alcohol at a party, I found myself pinned down by a young blond boy whom I had never met. And then I passed out.

My stepfather immediately made arrangements for me to move to a home for unwed mothers. And, as I protected the father of my unborn child, he protected his reputation. Neighbors were told I went to visit relatives for the summer. About one week later, I was driven to San Francisco to a home where I would stay until I gave birth. Visitors were restricted to those approved by my mother. In fact, initially, she was the only visitor I ever received. During one such visit, feeling lonely and removed from family, I confessed the identity of the father. I needed to see

Bob and needed her permission. She told me she never believed the story I initially shared, and gave the okay for Bob to visit.

Bob came up as often as his schedule would allow. He would take me out for the entire day. I complained I felt trapped; as if I were imprisoned, and so those lunches, kisses and cuddles always bestowed upon me were much craved – and appreciated. Besides, I felt it was okay to fool around a little, as I did love him. My mother also made great efforts to spend time with me, getting up very early in the morning and taking long bus rides to my new residence (she didn't drive a car). We enjoyed wonderful times, going out for Chinese food and sharing good conversation. But the remaining days were spent cooped up, as we were not allowed outside the home much in the absence of our approved guests.

I spent the remainder of my pregnancy in a room with four other girls, I being one of the youngest in the home. We spoke a lot about our babies amongst each other, learning I could spend as much time with my baby as I wished, while still in the hospital recuperating from giving birth. I thought this was a fantastic idea and decided this would be my exact game plan. Time with my baby would be short, however, as we were told that once our babies were born we wouldn't be seeing them again. The residence I was housed at supplied babies to an adoption agency, and while I would have three days to experience motherhood, once out of the hospital, my baby would be taken away and never held by me again.

On October 6, 1964 I gave birth to the sweetest looking baby boy I could have ever imagined. What I wasn't prepared for was an instant feeling of overwhelming love. While I held him, fed him and stared endlessly at him, I suddenly had no idea how I could ever survive without him. He smiled constantly, and I saw my dimples in his tiny face. I knew in my heart of hearts I could never let this precious baby be adopted. Somehow, I would find a way to keep him.

I expressed my resolve to my mother and to my delight, she committed to helping me in any way(s) that she could. We both cried together and on that day, I never felt closer to my mother. We informed the lady from the adoption agency I would be back in a few days and that I had chosen to not release my baby for adoption. As I prepared to leave, through many fresh tears I dressed him in his tiny outfit, telling him that mommy would be back shortly to take him home – for good.

A few days later, my mother's friend Lottie offered to drive us back to pick up my son. My mother had opted not to tell my stepfather, leaving this revelation for when my tiny bundle made his arrival on the front steps of our home.

Joy spread across my face as I saw my son again, whom I named Steven. And then, in what felt like seconds, the four of us were on our way back home. We concocted all sorts of scenarios of what my stepfather would say, or what expression his face would hold when he saw little Stevie. Lottie tried to lift the mood by joking about the shocking entrance we were about to make, but underneath it all we were a little afraid of my stepfather's reaction.

The story told to my young brother and two little sisters was that while on vacation, I saw an adorable baby and just had to adopt him. Because of their young ages – seven, five and three – they believed what they were told. My stepfather was speechless for two days, and so was I for another reason: Bob had asked me to marry him and naturally, I said yes, knowing it was the most wonderful solution for my young son, and in fact, for us all.

The permission form bore my mother's signature to marry as I was underage, and in a little chapel a few days later, members of both families witnessed our wedding vows. I formed an immediate bond with my in-laws, and they invited the three of us to live in their home in San Rafael. They encouraged us to save money, promising to match whatever we saved in order that we be able to buy our own home. But as we were young and needed our independence, shortly we moved out and into a small apartment.

During my first visit home to my mother, she opened the door with a black eye, not wanting to tell me the truth of what had happened to her. I didn't need an explanation: This was the consequence she paid for standing by me.

Bob got a job as a laundry deliveryman, and sometimes he brought Stevie and me along with him in the truck. Unfortunately, his salary wasn't enough to care for a wife and child. Stevie needed post-birth aftercare and check-ups, and luckily I learned of a service called "Planned Parenthood." I took him there on a regular basis and while there, met other young mothers.

It was then when I first noticed Stevie wasn't progressing at the same rate as other babies. He was much smaller and had the appearance and characteristics of a newborn. Thinking he would catch up with others of his age, I didn't worry about it.

Bob now had a new job at McGraw Hill Book Company and given my responsibilities, went to his company Christmas party solo. Late that night when Bob came home, I noticed some red smudges on his collar. It didn't take long for him to confess he had "been" with a female co-worker, long after the celebrations died down.

How could this happen, I wondered. Bob was married to ME! Bob took me for naive (which clearly I was), and explained that all men cheat. But no sooner had I thrown my wedding band out the window, I started sobbing, begging him to never leave me. Bob reassured me he never would, and we continued our lives, with me regularly checking his shirt collars for evidence of other women until I tired of this ritual.

When Stevie was about nine months old I received a phone call from one of the doctors from Planned Parenthood. I agreed to meet with her the next day. While Stevie was sleeping and Bob, at work, she came to our apartment. It was there she informed me that Stevie had been diagnosed with cerebral palsy. Thinking it was something temporary, like measles, I expected her to outline a course of treatment. She wasn't finished: Stevie was also mentally retarded.

With my heart becoming heavier by the microsecond, I was told that it was unlikely my son would live past five years old. After ushering the doctor out, I ran into my baby's room and witnessed a beautiful sunbeam of light shining down on him. In this light he glowed, truly resembling an angel while my eyes shone with tears as I tried to make sense of his diagnoses.

My mother made a suggestion that Stevie be put in Sonoma State Hospital so he could be properly cared for. Although I hated her in that moment, it took about a week to recognize that something needed doing. Bob and I made an appointment to visit the facility, but what I saw there was shocking. Tiny, deformed children were crawling on the floor. Others made alien-like sounds from their cribs. Needless to say, I was completely traumatized. We left there, with me vowing to Bob I would never, ever release Stevie to such a facility.

Fast-forward six months, I found myself on the telephone with Sonoma State Hospital. They called to let me know there was an opening for Stevie, if I wanted it. I never did remove him from the waiting list, as I sensed things were about to get a lot worse. And they did. Stevie wouldn't swallow his food, and cried for hours on end. It was extremely difficult to cope with his specialized needs, and at the tender age of just 16, I knew his care had become unmanageable.

The drive back to the hospital would be one of the most painful memories I would ever relive, over and over. I clung to my baby, knowing full well I would never see him again. What would his life be like without his biological mother? I sobbed the entire time, with Bob asking me at intervals, "Why are you crying? I thought this is what you wanted!" I despised his attitude and honestly, it sickened me that he couldn't understand what I was feeling.

Stevie had a small fan club in the form of his nurses, at the moment of his arrival. They decided to keep his crib next to the nurses' station as they clearly favored my beautiful Stevie with his "Gerber baby" appearance. For the next year, Bob's mother and I made weekly trips to visit Stevie, and this eased the pain for a short while. But as time moved on, so did the directions my life took, and it became more and more difficult to visit.

At age 21 I moved to Lake Tahoe, marking the end of ever seeing my son, Steven. When he was around 10 years of age, a truly wonderful older couple adopted him. He was loved and cared for well, and as far as I am aware, he might still be alive today.

Even now, 47 years later I still love and remember my first child vividly. There are moments that remind me of him, making me weep in a way only a mother could express.

# 5 THE AFFAIR BOB ASKED ME TO HAVE

When I was 18, Bob and I moved to a fancy apartment and bought a new sports car. We held weekly poker games at our new pad, even purchasing a professional poker table, complete with commercial-quality chips with our surname engraved on them. A regular group of guys came over to play poker with us three times a week, at first, with me only watching and learning. But within a year, Bob felt I was ready to play with the boys.

I recall this being a memorable and exciting night for me, as I had finally earned my status as a "chip-carrying" member of the poker club. And wouldn't you know it, the first time did I ever show my worth – by winning a couple of hundred dollars and being the big winner of the night!

I worked at a factory named Fairchild Semiconductor, where I did some work on an assembly line and enjoyed flirting with one of the bosses. Horst Muenzenberg, a cute German guy was looking mighty fine to me, especially as Bob had told me several times he wanted me to go out with other guys. Although I convinced myself I only wanted Bob, sometimes I thought of Horst in ways other than just employee and boss. My fantasies were further stimulated when Horst invited me to work in his department, away from the assembly line, and doing much more skill-intensive duties. Indeed, when it was just the two of us in the lab, the attraction we felt for one another got a little steamy.

I couldn't wait to share this latest development with Bob, thinking he would be very pleased that I finally had some interest and desire to be with someone else. But Bob went crazy when he heard!

I was completely confused – isn't this what he wanted?

By now, the attraction between Horst and I was undeniable, and on a couple of occasions, we snuck off at lunchtime to his house to have sex. But with me being married, and Horst aware of this, it didn't quite feel right. From then on, we stuck to harmless flirting.

Bob and I had a love of music, and he introduced me to live talent such as The Righteous Brothers and Diana Ross. Elvis continued to be my favorite artist, and will remain so for life. We went to the movie "2001: A Space Odyssey" but I couldn't quite relate to it, as "2001" seemed so far away. On our way to the theater in San Francisco, we drove through Sausalito. Bob and his friends laughed at some men walking together, pointing out they were "queers."

Unfamiliar with this term, I needed it explained to me, and learned this meant men enjoying sex with one another. I had never before heard of anything so ridiculous in my life and thought they were crazy making such assumptions. I spoke up, telling them they were nuts. How could they know what one person did – or didn't do – in the bedroom? I didn't want to hear any more of their wise cracks. No one had the right to make fun or criticize another.

It was a big year for me as I was turning 21. Bob and I moved to Lake Tahoe, with aspirations of becoming dealers in the casino.

# 6 WINNING

Before the big move, Bob and I drove up to Lake Tahoe many times before my 21st birthday, and on one occasion, casino security asked me to show them my I.D. for proof of age. Despite my attempts to look more grown up, with my hair in a French bun and sporting bright red lipstick, I was busted. Bob, who *was* of age, signed papers stating he was fully responsible for me and that I wouldn't engage in any gambling.

I made friends with some of the pit bosses, with one particular boss at Harvey's Wagon Wheel promising me a Blackjack dealing job as soon as I turned of age. He advised me to get on the "list" first, as only people from inside the casino were hired in these positions. He also suggested I be a "change girl" so they could hire me. On the employment application, I indicated I was a high school graduate as this was a job requirement, crossing every imaginable body part so I wouldn't get caught.

At 21, I found myself living in Lake Tahoe as part of our "new life." I did as the pit boss advised, carrying change for three weeks until the list came out. And of course, my name was on it to be a Blackjack dealer!

I believe Spirit was on my side once again, as I successfully bluffed my way into becoming a dealer in a major casino.

I went to dealer school inside Harvey's Casino, and was paid while training for the job. We were told all kinds of stories about the "eye in the sky" watching us 24/7 from large, two-way mirrors above. If we even thought about taking chips for ourselves, well, needless to say, these thoughts didn't ever cross my mind. I learned how to deal well, without tossing cards on the floor, and since math came naturally for me, counting cards quickly and accurately was never a problem.

After dealer school, I started dealing right away. I was one hot dealer, with the cards always running in my favor. As such, the pit bosses generally moved me to the high roller tables. I made a fortune in tips, but we had to split them amongst all three shifts. Still, I made a lot of money and enjoyed the most fun and exciting job I could ever imagine having.

I gambled a little on my days off, but quickly learned what a "no-no" this was, gambling my first few paychecks away. Besides, no matter how good a player was, the house always held the advantage. A player has to make the first decision, and assuming both the house and player held the same hands, if the hand busted, the player would lose. Sometimes I would "shield" in the poker area at the Sahara, where Bob dealt poker. I was told not to win and not to lose, but to just sit in as a player until the table was full.

Once on my night off, I played poker for myself, with some of the regular, and very skilled local players. We were playing lowball and I hardly ever bluffed. I was dealt a 9-8 low in the first five cards. I stayed pat, betting and raising a lot, playing my hand as if I had a "wheel," meaning the best low hand you can get: Ace, 2, 3, 4, 5. Many of the players folded, while meanwhile, the pot was getting huge. It came down to me and one other player. He stared at me and said, "Shirley I know you don't bluff, and I believe you have a winner, so I'm folding my 7-5 low."

I usually never show my hand but feeling so victorious, I showed my 9 low. The man was totally shocked, respecting my skills and giving me credit for a grand play. Whenever I ran into him, he never let me forget about that hand. Bob was so proud of me and knew he taught me well.

I spent much of my time in the casinos, and was quite surprised when several times, I spotted Horst Muenzenberg sitting at my casino bar, looking like a lost-love puppy. I smiled and greeted him with some quick small talk, and that was that. On my days off, I also loved shopping in some of the new boutiques in Tahoe, as they carried sexy Cher-like fashions, which quickly became my style. I spent a lot of money on these clothes, and was blessed with a slim frame to carry these unusual fashions. I also loved the attention other dealers gave me when dressing as I did on my days off.

Bob and I were working different shifts and in different casinos, with me working the swing shift – meaning I got home late. We lived only about one mile away, so I took a cab home after work, as Bob was just waking up and getting ready for work himself. One night, a dealer friend living in our apartment complex saw me waiting for a cab and offered to give me a lift. Bob once again went crazy, cursing and spitting and calling me a whore! I was completely innocent and shocked he would use such language to describe me. I tried ignoring him as I got ready for bed, but Bob was still in a rage. Suddenly without warning, Bob grabbed me, throwing me out in the snow, with me dressed in only a babydoll negligee.

This was the definitive "light bulb" moment, and I vowed to save enough money in order that I be able to leave him forever. Unfortunately, I found myself stuck in the same situation a few months later. To make matters worse, Bob brainwashed me by constantly reinforcing that if I ever tried to leave, he would kill me and then kill himself. Bob counted on my naivety to keep me dependent on him, and in many ways I was, never even having sat behind the wheel of an automobile.

But one day, fate had something else in mind.

On a routine game play of "Keno" I won! I played a one dollar 8 spot and all eight numbers came up! Winning a sum total of $3333 in 1970 was a BIG DEAL.

I was rich and with my winnings paid out in cash, the world was mine. Despite my previous plans, I shared my winnings with Bob, paying off all our bills. The large chunk of money left over went promptly into savings.

I resonate very much now with triple digit numbers, believing them to be a message from Spirit. I looked up 333, having won all threes and it read: "The Ascended Masters are near you, desiring you to know that you have their help, love, and companionship." Wiser words were never spoken.

# 7 DISAPPEARING WITH GREG TO LONG BEACH, CALIFORNIA

One night while I was dealing cards, I made eye contact with a very cute guy who clearly had his eyes on me. We both stared and smiled at one another, and I couldn't wait until it was time for my 20-minute break, so we could say hello, face-to-face. Greg Kladivo was his name, and big-time attraction was what we instantly felt. He asked if I would have a cocktail with him after I got off work and giddily, I said yes.

Greg seemed very laid back, which I liked. He explained he was a longshoreman in Long Beach, and that he enjoyed going surfing every morning at the crack of dawn. Well, that sounded plain cool to me! He had baby blue, bedroom eyes, wild hair and a sexy grin. In fact, Greg was the polar opposite of Bob, who was Italian and Swedish. But Bob was handsome as well, resembling Andy Garcia with his dark hair and brown eyes.

As promised, Greg was waiting for me as I got off work and we went to the bar to have that drink. We talked for a bit and Greg asked if I would go back to his van so we could kiss. In-between the kissing and talking, I managed to spill my story about my relationship with Bob, and how I was planning on leaving him. Greg was smitten, and asked me right then and there if I would leave Lake Tahoe to go live with him in Long Beach. I said my second "yes" of the evening. The arrangement was for him to return in two weeks' time to come get me.

Greg called me every day at the casino and we anticipated the day we were going to be together. Finally, the morning had arrived for Greg to be waiting in his van in our parking lot. (Not so) patiently I watched as Bob prepared to leave for work so I could signal to Greg that the coast was clear. I recall Bob applying lotion on his body and it dawned on me this would be THE last time I would ever see him again. I wasn't exactly sad, but it was a bittersweet moment. Bob and I had been together for seven years, and at such young ages, too.

Bob finally left, and together, Greg and I threw my clothes and personal belongings into his van. I was so happy and excited. At the last minute, we decided to take the little dining room set as Greg said he didn't have one. After withdrawing exactly half the money we saved from my Keno winnings, I left Bob without any bills – and without a wife. In less than 30 minutes, we were on our way to Southern California, with me mostly never looking back.

On our journey to Long Beach, Greg stopped at a gas station and filled up his van, never going inside to pay for his purchase. I found this to be both exciting and dare-devilish, and laughed as we drove off. We ended up driving straight through as Long Beach was only about a seven-hour drive from Lake Tahoe.

Greg rented a cute little apartment for us in a beach town in Long Beach, called Belmont Shore. I couldn't help but fall in love with my new home, as the area was so quaint. It was worlds apart from Lake Tahoe, which now I feel is one of the most beautiful places in the world.

After being with Greg for a few days, I noticed other parts of his personality began to surface. One of these was that he was a poor communicator. It really bothered me, because all he would do is nod and smile at everything I said, instead of engaging in a mutual dialogue. We had our first fight and I went to sleep on the couch, hoping Greg would ask me to come back to bed with him. He didn't. I remained awake most of the night, at first, fuming mad and then, becoming sad. Eventually I decided to go to the phone booth on the corner, call Bob and tell him I'm coming back home.

Early in the morning while Greg was still sleeping, I found myself on the phone with Bob. He was elated to hear from me, telling me he had gone nuts when he returned home and found me gone. He said he visited every casino in the area to see if anyone had seen me, also asking my friends if they knew where I was. Nobody disclosed my whereabouts, even though I had confided in a couple of them. Bob even thought I might have met a European man and left with him to go back to Europe (something I had actually longed for, deep, down inside). Bob told me he would do anything for me, and asked if I would consider coming back home.

After hanging up, I called a cab to pick me up at my apartment. Finding Greg awake, I told him I was leaving, and going back to Bob. Greg pleaded over and over for me to stay. I never heard him talk so much, and whatever he said convinced me to remain where I was. Greg sent the cab back and I stayed, never calling Bob to say I wasn't coming back. The next time Bob and I had contact was about six months later, when I started divorce proceedings so that I may marry Greg.

Greg had a wonderful family that loved me as much as I loved them. His brother Dennis was one year younger than him and married to a beautiful girl named Becky. She and I became best friends. The four of us did many hilarious things together, including something we called "dining and dashing." We would visit a restaurant and when nearly finished eating, Becky and I would excuse ourselves to go to the restroom. Except we would leave instead, with the boys close in tow. It's not like we couldn't afford the bill, but rather, enjoyed getting away with our antics.

My first job in southern California was as an exercise instructor. I made up all the exercises to the music and nobody knew the difference. The ladies were all older than me and believed their bodies would morph into my slender shape, if they just followed what I taught them. Again, I bluffed my way through this job and the ladies loved me to boot!

After my divorce became final, Greg and I were married in Las Vegas. The ceremony was held in a small wedding chapel, with his parents, aunt, Dennis, Becky and Greg's two best friends in attendance. I recall having the giggles and literally couldn't stop laughing as we attempted to complete our vows. My stomach started to ache as I tried – and failed – to hold back laughter. Soon enough, Greg's family started laughing with me. I have no idea what was so funny, but it ended up being a fun and even funnier wedding.

# 8 WINNING MY CAR ON "THE PRICE IS RIGHT"

I learned quickly that living in southern California definitely had its advantages. Television game shows were one of them, with "The Price is Right" being my absolute favorite. I must have sent out about 20 ticket requests, as I was determined to get on the show and win! And that's exactly what happened.

"Shirley Kladivo, c'mon down. You're the next contestant on The Price is Right!"

I was first up and was the big winner of the day, winning a car! If a new Vega wasn't enough, I also won a set of sterling silver, a trip to Arizona with luggage, and a snowmobile! Greg immediately taught me how to drive, and within a week I had my California driver's license. It's amazing how one's independence increases, with the addition of four rubber tires and a steering wheel. And boy, did it feel wonderful.

I'm truly embarrassed to share that many more tickets arrived from The Price is Right. And wouldn't you know it, greed got the worst of me. I decided to try my luck again, only this time, impersonating my sister-in-law, Becky. I told her that if I won again, we would split the winnings down the middle.

I entered the studio in disguise, complete with a blond wig, a skycap and sunglasses. I must have looked as ridiculous as Michael Jackson did in some of his costumes, because as I moved up in the entrance line, the assistants recognized me immediately. When asked if I had been on the show before, I replied I had not. I wanted to slither away into a den, one reason being that I might face a large penalty if I was caught trying to appear more than once. But, as I was recognized and unlikely to be picked again in this century or next, we decided to stay, with Greg hoping to snag a chance to play.

The first four contestants were called, and we heard neither one of our names. But in the second round, as clear as a pin dropping on a museum floor, the announcer broke the silence with: "Becky Kladivo, c'mon down..."

For the second time in my life, I wanted to die, and if I could have twitched my nose as Samantha did in "Bewitched" to teleport myself elsewhere, I would have. While my mind cycled all sorts of scenarios for escape, my legs ran down and took me to my spot on the panel. The main model recognized me and smiling, she mouthed the word, "Hello."

Thinking fast as usual, I looked at her, sporting a confused expression on my face. If I had said hello back, I knew that I would have been busted on the spot. My troubles didn't end there, for while looking at me, I noticed her whispering something to the cameraman. As bidding started, I realized there was no way I could win anything, so I bid ridiculous amounts that I knew would make me lose. For perhaps the first time in my life, I was grateful for not winning a thing!

I had to stay until the end of taping, as everyone had to sign some forms, even for consolation prizes earned. The producers waited since I was last to sign, before confronting me. I was getting scared, turned around and spotted Greg, still sitting in his original seat. I knew I was on my own. I was asked if I was the girl who had just been on the show and won the grand prize. Smiling sweetly, I answered no, they must be thinking of my sister, Shirley, who had won last month. Their tone immediately became much friendlier, but still asked me to show I.D. as proof. In a moment of pure grace, I reached into my purse and drew out the social security card Becky threw into my bag at the last second.

The huge lesson here is never, ever be greedy and be grateful for what is bestowed upon oneself, without expecting more.

The date this show aired on television remained unknown to me. I didn't want to watch myself carry on as a fool. But, after skipping several episodes, I decided to flip it on one day. Wouldn't you know it; my lesson of greed was reinforced in that moment, as THE show was on the screen!

Since it's permitted for people to appear on multiple game shows for a total of three times, I was a contestant on "The Match Game" a couple of years later. I didn't win any prizes. I did manage to get my best friend, Linda addicted to game shows and together, we went on one called "The Better Sex." The show consisted of women bluffing men, and men bluffing women. Being the great poker player that I was, I bluffed all the guys out and won all the money for my team.

I never considered *this* to be greed, but rather reaching for, and taking hold of, opportunities.

*Life is an opportunity, not an obligation.*

Now that I was the proud owner of a brand new automobile, I was able to search for a better job. Unfortunately, I learned that the Vega was a lemon of a car, similar to the Pinto. But it did the trick – it got me to drive, and to feel more independent. I never thought I'd be sitting behind the wheel, as Bob didn't want me driving and my mom also had an extreme fear at the very thought of driving.

And speaking of mom, she adored Greg, loving his easygoing personality. Now that she had finally divorced my stepfather, we drove up to northern California to visit her often. Greg brought the sweetest little presents, and he loved cooking filet mignon steaks for her and my other younger siblings. Together, we would listen as she talked about everything under the sun, including her days at the Nazi concentration camp. Greg and I both got tears in our eyes as we listened to every word with empathy. Even though I heard the story told many times before, it was always as if I heard it for the very, first time.

I think Greg was my mom's favorite choice of husband for me, until of course, I married my current husband, Eric, who promptly earned – and kept – that title.

# 9 MY ELVIS DREAM CAME TRUE

My wildest dream since I was a little girl was to someday, somehow, see and meet Elvis Presley. One afternoon while I was listening to the car radio, I heard an announcement that Elvis was performing at the Hilton Hotel in Las Vegas. I knew this was my opportunity – I was going to go meet Elvis! Nothing on this planet could stop me now. I could barely believe that after so many years of fantasizing about him, I would finally have the opportunity to make my dream come true. I was going to at long last, lay my eyes on my Elvis. I was so excited to tell Greg and to my delight, he agreed to take me.

"Elvis Day" had finally arrived, and we found ourselves seated about eight rows back. I immediately spotted Elvis's wife, Priscilla, right up front, and was struck by how absolutely beautiful she was.

Nothing could have prepared me for what came next: Elvis – live on stage! He was slim, dressed in black and absolutely gorgeous. My heart started to beat wildly and I wondered if it would take off in flight! He was tall (over six feet) and even more breathtaking in the flesh than I ever thought possible.

Elvis's live performance was spectacular and his singing literally took my breath away. I loved his personality since he had the greatest humor. Greg admitted that he really enjoyed Elvis too, which made me happy. I knew I had to come back, so I could be seated in front, right next to the stage. From this vantage point did I have my best chance of getting a scarf from Elvis, and a little kiss he so generously gave out to several girls. This was where the action was, and to say the least, I wanted it all!

I talked to one of the ushers on our way out and asked how I could best accomplish this, since long lines started forming outside the showroom early in the day, with no guarantee of ringside seating. The usher smiled at me and told me to wait until the very last minute as there were always a few spots saved for celebrities. For this valuable bit of information, I reached into my purse and pulled out a $20-dollar bill, but he wouldn't accept the tip.

In the not-too-distant future, we made arrangements to head back to Las Vegas. This time, I was determined to get a seat next to the stage. Following the usher's suggestion, we waited until everyone was inside and voila – I was seated right under Elvis's nose! I was stunned, but not too stunned to be sitting where I was. I knew this would happen because I wanted this more than anything in the world.

In this performance, Elvis came out wearing a white jumpsuit, looking a little heavier. Rumor had it that Elvis and Priscilla were getting divorced, and this was likely taking a toll on him. But still, he was the most beautiful sight I had ever seen, and nobody in the world could match his voice. While Elvis was singing, he actually noticed me sitting in the audience. He looked directly at me, making eye contact and smiling with that sexy grin. In that moment, I completely forgot I was married and that the spousal unit was sitting with me on the other side. Elvis smiled at me a lot throughout his performance, and about halfway through the show, fate took hold of me and, absolutely entranced and totally mesmerized, I stood up, holding my arms out for him.

Elvis came towards me then, smiling in his sultry way. And with my confidence at an all-time high, I gave him a look of utter abandon. He knelt down on one knee as he laid his microphone down, and suddenly we were in each other's arms, French kissing! I was making out with Elvis Presley!

We stayed like this for at least 30 seconds. In a dreamlike state, I heard loud screams coming from the females in the audience. At most, these girls would have received a quick peck, with several of them in a row waiting their turn. But this wasn't one of those kisses, and I became totally lost in his mouth. At one point, I recall wondering how much longer this could possibly go on. I hoped, forever! But eventually, this man, whom I now learned was a fabulous kisser, pulled away, taking a dripping-wet scarf off from around his neck and placing it around mine.

In what felt like slow motion, I fell back in my seat, my head still spinning. I felt I had arrived on heaven's welcome mat. Elvis went back to center stage, smiling at me once again as he attempted to begin a song. But instead, he shook his head, grinning at me and under his breath, mouthed "Phew," as if our kiss left him "all shook up!" Elvis and I continued to smile and flirt with one another throughout the entire rest of the show.

Seated next to me was a pretty red-haired girl, who kept screaming things to me like, "Elvis loves you; you're so lucky; I wish I looked like you!"

Moments later, Elvis came back, giving me another scarf, and I thought he temporarily forgot he already gave me one. I decided to do a very sweet thing and make this girl happy by giving her the second scarf. She couldn't stop thanking me, but it was okay because I had the original scarf drenched in Elvis's sweat.

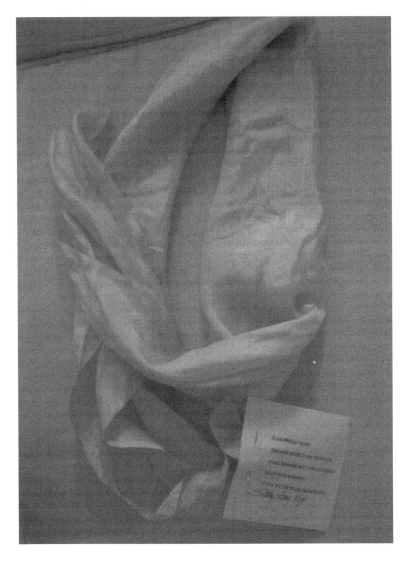

After the show ended, Greg grinned in his usual, good-natured way, but commented that from now on, I would go see Elvis by myself. He wasn't mad; he just had enough. This was unbelievable; it was a dream. And yet it was real. I had finally manifested my nirvana on earth, and even to this day, I can visualize everything as clear as if it happened yesterday. I still have the scarf Elvis gave me, after our "marathon" kissing session. Of course, it has never been washed.

For months after, I lived on cloud nine, as I truly believed in my heart I would become the next "MRS. Elvis Presley." I was more in love with Elvis than ever before, which I didn't even think was possible. In fact, I could barely function in my everyday life.

Not long after in November 1972, I read in the paper that Elvis was coming to the Long Beach Arena. This time I asked a girlfriend to go with me, who also loved Elvis. I got dressed up in a short, cream and rust-colored dress, complete with a rust suede jacket and identical-colored high-heeled shoes. Feeling exceptionally pretty, I wondered what this night might hold for me.

We arrived at the arena and wandered around for a while before we took our seats. Elvis's friend and back-up singer, Charlie Hodge spotted us and came over to talk. Charlie was funny and sweet, and invited us to hang out with Elvis and the band after the concert. He told us that a small intimate after-party was being held at the Hyatt Edgewater Hotel in Long Beach, where Elvis was staying. He said to tell security, which would be tight, that he invited us. We were both thrilled and speechless – not having the greatest seats, we couldn't wait for the concert to be over so we could go "hang" with Elvis!

Once the show was over, we drove to the Hyatt and saw that half of the hotel had been rented out for Elvis and his entourage, due to privacy concerns. We informed one of the security officers we were there by invitation, and followed up by asking which room we were to go to. Surprisingly, security not only let us through without any hassle, but also escorted us to the room Elvis was to be in.

We entered the room to see Elvis's father, Vernon, as well as many boys from the band. Also present were about seven, other beautiful young ladies. Some of the girls were just sitting on the floor, so I sat on the couch. About 10 minutes later, Elvis walked into the room and sat on the couch beside me.

W-O-W. Once again, I found myself with Elvis, and this time, we could actually talk to each other. Elvis, still charged up from his performance, was telling us all sorts of stories. I remember J.D. Sumner, Elvis's bass singer very well, because he was teasing Elvis about how he hit all the deep notes for him while Elvis was singing. Believing they were just fooling, together they demonstrated this right in front of me and everyone started laughing. Elvis also talked about his love for Ann Margaret and Hope Lange; and how Mary Tyler Moore talked too much while they filmed a movie together.

Several times when Elvis opened his mouth, I responded to what he said. He continually touched my knee, and at one point, mentioned he was really tired of eating food on the road during his tours. With my quick wit, I promptly invited him over to my house for a home-cooked meal. I was met with more laughter from Elvis and then he squeezed me again. The rest of the evening consisted of sharing stories and laughter, making it another unforgettable and intimate night with Elvis Presley.

I never mentioned anything to Elvis about our "kissing session" at the Hilton because I felt it would have sounded corny. I was sure that for Elvis, it was just another one of his fun nights. Of course, I was and I am an Elvis fan, but feel even more than that, because I'm an Elvis lover and friend. Before the night ended, Elvis gave me an open invitation to spend as much time at his Beverly Hills mansion as I wished, and was given the address and security code. I vowed to visit soon.

I picked my day to visit Elvis and inviting the same girlfriend who attended the concert in Long Beach, drove to Beverly Hills. Cruising through the ritzy Beverly Hills neighborhood, we saw many beautiful homes. Finally, we arrived at a large, white one story house – Elvis's home! I used the code that was given to me and nothing happened; nobody was home. We decided to climb over the gate since after all, we were welcomed guests, and I wanted to check out the property, having driven such a long way.

Everything was locked up, but we made our way to the backyard and under a bright sun, hung around Elvis's pool. With our feet dangling in the water, we marveled at how amazing it was to be spending time at Elvis's home, despite the fact that Elvis himself wasn't there. We hoped he might still show, but after about an hour, we resigned ourselves to the fact he wasn't coming and decided to drive back home.

After all of this, life changed a lot for me, and I never attempted another visit to Elvis's home. Elvis will live in my heart throughout eternity, and I will always adore and love him. Someday I know I will see him again, although I did hear once that nobody is famous on the other side. My experience with Elvis is a true lesson to never, ever give up on one's dreams, because dreams really DO come true. My biggest dream certainly did, which was no coincidence.

*"No Coincidence at all; only a Miracle." ~ Shirley Anni Njos*

# 10 BILL BATES – MY YOUNG TRUE LOVE

I was still married to Greg when I decided I would look for a job on the Queen Mary. I read they were hiring tour guides and thought I would be perfect for the job because I still spoke fluent German. Unfortunately, they were very strict about at least having a high school diploma, so in the end, I applied for a gift shop position. As luck would have it, they hired me on the spot. About two weeks into the job while riding on the elevator, the sweetest looking guy got on. For the duration of the ride, it was only the two of us in the car. We looked at each other, grinned, and then this sweet boy turned slowly and cusped my face in his hands. Without saying a word, he gave me the most tender kiss I had ever felt.

I remember thinking this was straight out of a romance novel, and stunned, never said a word back. The elevator door opened and with a modest smile, I got off, heading to the gift booth outside the ship's deck, wondering whom in the world he was.

It didn't take long for him to find me, and this time he introduced himself as Bill Bates. He told me he was working his way through college and said he worked as a bellman there. Bill was only 21 and I was 25, and nothing, *nothing*, like this had ever happened to me before. He was truly the cutest and most charming and sincere guy I had ever met.

From that day on, to my surprise, Bill brought me a fantastic lunch prepared by the ship's fine restaurant. I watched while he walked towards me, carefully carrying the tray over his head, and my breath was taken away. His gorgeous shoulder-length dark hair would blow in the wind as he walked – and I found him absolutely irresistible. I could stare at his big, brown eyes and chiseled jaw all day long and drink in his innocence. Strangely, I felt a close connection to him that I could not explain.

Bill made sure he visited me in my booth every chance he got, and in a short while, we became extremely close. The attraction was getting so strong that we talked about being together.

One day I agreed to see him after work and found myself driving to his tiny apartment in north Long Beach. He had candles burning when I arrived and welcomed me with an enormous warm hug. Needless to say, it wasn't long before we were intimate. Our making love felt so right; in fact, everything about him felt right and I knew we belonged together.

Being married to Greg and considering myself a "one man woman," non-cheating type made for difficult choices and decisions. But sometimes things really do just happen. And in moments like these, it's wise to remember that there is a greater purpose or a divine plan, even if we do not see the full picture as yet.

One evening Greg told me he and his brother were going to drive to Los Angeles to look at some guitars that he was considering buying. I took advantage of this opportunity and went to visit Bill, since I could not stop thinking about him. Bill was so happy when I called, but understanding all the same when he realized I couldn't stay as long as I would have wanted. Bill walked me to the car and whispered, "I miss you already babe. Please come back to me later tonight."

And although we both knew the impossibility of our situation, I answered softly, "Yes I will."

Could this possibly have been another premonition?

Driving home as to arrive before Greg, I was surprised to see his van parked in our driveway. I made my way inside, trying to think fast what my excuse would be, in order that my absence be explained. Greg, turning to look at me, asked if I would go in the kitchen so he could show me a card trick. I thought this was very strange and started feeling uneasy. I noticed Dennis, his brother, sitting on the couch, a peculiar expression on his face.

I agreed to do so, wanting to get this nonsense out of the way. Greg promised it would only take a moment. I sat down, with him dealing out cards on the kitchen table. He dealt aces and eights, which I knew meant "a dead man's hand."

I looked at him, momentarily feeling a little frightened and blurted out, "Are you crazy? This is weird. You know that's a dead man's hand!"

Greg responded, "That's exactly right. I followed you to your boyfriend's place and you're busted!"

He then calmly asked me to pack my clothes and leave immediately. I did just that. Funny, I actually felt a sense of relief and in about 15 minutes, had my things packed and ready to go. As I got into my car, I knew I would head back to Bill's house that night as he so lovingly asked me to do. Greg, on the other hand, was watching me from outside the house, his eyes glassy and his expression, sad.

I honestly felt bad that I hurt him as I did, because he was a great guy. Looking back, I now know that Greg was a rebound marriage, which held so many wonderful gifts in itself. Although Greg came to my work about a month later, asking only once if I would consider giving our relationship a second chance, I declined. Some unions are meant to be only temporary, leading one to where they need to be; where they truly belong.

There are NO coincidences in this life, and when I learned exactly how I was caught, I was blown away. Sometime later, I found out that Greg's brother's best friend, Larry, was out at a bar one night and met a girl. The girl soon found Larry's shoulder to cry on, telling him that her boyfriend was seeing a married woman who worked on the Queen Mary. Larry, after asking a few more questions, extracted a description of this woman.

It was "me" to the letter "T."

Larry, wanting to do the honorable thing, told Dennis – Greg's brother. This is how Greg learned that I was seeing Bill. Funny thing, almost 40 years later, Larry now lives in my neighborhood and is friends with Eric and me.

After leaving our matrimonial home, I drove back to Bill's house. He was sound asleep and I had to knock several times to awaken him. When he saw me at the door he must have thought he was dreaming! He couldn't believe his eyes, and the joy and surprise on his face was priceless. I was with my true love at last, and had a new home in which to live.

This was the beginning of the sweetest relationship. Although Bill didn't have much money, he treated me like a princess. Every penny he earned over and above his expenses, he loved spending on me, buying me gifts and other things I wanted. He promised me over and over that when he graduated, whether we were together or not, I would find a white 450SL Mercedes parked in front of my residence, wrapped in a big red bow.

He drove a motorcycle because as a college student, he couldn't afford a car, but at least we had my Vega. Just being together made us very happy. Bill told me I was his first true love, and I knew he was mine, too.

Bill and I soon moved out of his tiny apartment to a nicer area where I liked living. It was in Belmont Heights, not far from Belmont Shore. Our relationship was, by every definition, a sweet young love – right out of the movies.

One day, Bill saw that a new, fine restaurant in Long Beach called Charley Brown's was hiring. He said to me, "Babe, you could make a fortune there. It's such a classy place, you just belong there." I didn't like the idea of being a waitress – even a cocktail waitress for that matter – so I told him I would interview for a hostess position only.

The following day a great manager, Terry Rosentiki, interviewed me. Terry immediately told me I should also take a waitress position for exactly the same reasons Bill did. "Just try," he said, "and if you don't like it, you can move into the hostess position." I agreed, and Terry hired me that very day. I started working the lunch shift and to my surprise, loved it. Charley Brown's would change my life – FOREVER.

# 11 CHARLEY BROWN'S CHANGED MY LIFE FOREVER

When I started working at Charley Brown's, I wore the cutest green and white low-cut short, ruffled uniform. And true to what I had been told, we were treated with the utmost respect and admiration.

I made a lifetime friend there – Linda Farrow. Linda was six years older than me and immediately took me under her wing. She was planning her wedding to Dave, so our friendship consisted mainly of spending time together at work as well as on the telephone. Linda was literally the funniest girl I had ever met, and her sarcastic humor kept me laughing all day long. She intimidated many of the other girls, but we clicked perfectly, perhaps due to my own great sense of humor. She was the best in sales and sold more wine in our wine contests than anyone else. She was also a master at selling my clothes, which I no longer wanted.

Linda started calling me daily at home, just to chat. At first, I thought this was most odd, with me mainly using a telephone to hold specific conversations. Linda however, taught me how to just talk about whatever was on my mind, and as a result, I learned to love the telephone.

I also became best friends with another girl, Susan, whom was hired shortly after me and later became a Playboy centerfold. She told me she wanted to be friends because I was so well liked. But as much as she wanted to enjoy "girl nights" with me, I didn't want to spend my time with anyone other than Bill. She understood this, and fortunately, we still remained friends. After awhile, Susie transferred to the night shift to be a cocktail waitress, making more money and urging me to do the same.

One day Bill started acting strange. I couldn't put my finger on what was wrong, so I asked him. At first, he denied anything was, but guilt ate away at him and he finally confessed: He had slept with a girl that was flirting with him at his workplace.

Even after hearing his words that continued to echo in my head, I couldn't believe it. I was incredibly disappointed as we had been so happy together. And while I felt completely crushed, I also knew he hadn't been with many girls at all. Given the opportunity, he must have felt like a kid in the whole, damn candy shop! Nonetheless, I started crying and pounded him on his chest, alternating between betrayal and sadness. Bill was crying himself, apologizing and wondering why he did it at all. He swore it only happened once and promised never to stray from me again – he loved me that much. But, after wearing myself out from shouting, I told him I needed some time to think things over.

We didn't break up immediately afterward, but things between us were just not the same. And exactly one week later, I asked him to move out. Linda said I should have given him another chance, but I didn't. And while Bill moved out reluctantly, Susie eagerly moved in as my new roommate. Susie was the perfect girlfriend to hang out with. We not only worked together (I was now working nights in the cocktail lounge) but we were best buddies, both on the dance floor as well as roommates. We went "clubbing" at a nightclub called The Windrose every night after work, and loved the musicians in the band. We even went out with a couple of them for a short while. These were wild and fun times for me, and were a necessity because I never had any "single" life at all. Bill tried getting back together with me on several occasions, but even though I still loved him very much, I moved on. I was now on a different journey and yet despite this, we stayed very close friends for years with a continued love that would never die.

One night while at work, a couple of car salesmen came into Charley Brown's, asking us girls if we wanted to buy a new car – one which we could drive home that evening! I told them there was NO WAY they could sell me a car because most of my money was in the form of tips, and my paychecks were small. Their response: NO PROBLEM!

When I got off work at 2:00 a.m., I followed them one mile to the car dealership, and after a few minutes, was seated behind the wheel of a new Mazda! They told me to bring the car back the next morning so a stereo could be installed.

A few hours later I found myself back at the dealership and noticed a very handsome guy – a Don Johnson type – staring at me with the most intense gaze. He introduced himself as Klaus Fleischer, Service Manager and asked if he could help me. I noticed he had a European accent and asked where he was from. When he said Austria, we immediately started speaking a little German with one another. After my stereo was installed, he asked me on a date. I liked him and found him to be charming, but told him I couldn't because I already had a boyfriend, and swiftly left the dealership.

That very night at work, I saw Klaus sitting at the bar. He told me he didn't usually frequent bars but he had to see me. And after one cocktail he left, with a parting comment: "Woman, I would love to see you pregnant!" It knocked me flat. First, because I was 26 and totally obsessed with babies and second, because all my thoughts of late centered on actually having one!

Wouldn't you know it, Klaus was really persistent and very late the next night, came back into the bar. He ended up trying to follow me home, which made me quite uneasy. I pulled over on the side of the road and he came over to the driver's side of my car. He stated bluntly that he was just going to kidnap me. I told him to stop, go home and leave me alone because this wasn't as funny as he must have thought it was. He left grinning, with a look of confidence and triumph on his face.

Klaus came to the bar one final time, handing me a Christmas card. The envelope was addressed to "YOU" and inside were goodbye sentiments. The card, dated December 16, 1974 with its frequent misspellings really made me smile. I could hear his accent through the words he wrote: "I will miss you little tiger and if you are ever in Europe, please come and see me in Austria." With a few more sentiments about how he felt about me, he included his Austrian address and telephone number. Again, he hit a chord with me: a European man whom I always longed to be with, and his comments about a baby, and boom, Klaus Fleischer won! I telephoned him the next day, telling Klaus that I would go out with him.

Wasting no time at all (no surprise there), he came to pick me up that night and off we went to his apartment. I remember the night being very foggy, yet he drove like a maniac, almost hitting a train head-on at a railroad crossing. In a split second, my memoir could have ended here. I spent the night with him and when morning came, the first question he asked was whether I was committed. I wasn't exactly sure what it meant so I asked him. The answer he was expecting was that I would be his girlfriend and of course, I responded yes. Klaus told me he lived in Wilmington as he was attending a Deep Sea Diving School, to become a diver. Working at the dealership was only a temporary job.

With him leaving so early and me, still half-asleep, I stayed in bed for a while. During sleep, something in bed woke me up, and throwing back the covers, I found a python snake in bed with me! I launched out of bed like a rocket, ran into the living room and called Klaus at work. His voice resonated laughter and then he calmly explained that it was just a "little" python and that there was a terrarium for him. All I had to do was put the snake back inside. I thought, "Are you NUTS?" I realized he was and then, gingerly, picked up the six or seven-foot long snake, putting him back in his "bed." This was the day I learned to like reptiles.

I didn't enjoy hanging around Wilmington, because it wasn't a good neighborhood. One day, a customer at work asked if I wanted to rent his beach house. This three-bedroom home was right on the beach in Sunset Beach and as I loved the coastal areas, Susie, Al (a bartender) and I all moved in with one another, with Klaus staying over at times. It was perfect. Unfortunately, this bliss didn't last long.

I awoke one morning with the worst stomach ache I could have ever imagined. I was bleeding and unable to move. Susie came home several hours later, finding me helpless and groaning in agony. After calling 9-1-1, I was rushed to the hospital only to find out I was pregnant with a tubular pregnancy. Although it hadn't been long that I got off birth control, it came as a complete shock that I was pregnant and as such, needed immediate surgery as the baby could not be saved.

This was one of the most painful experiences I had ever endured, even more excruciating than giving birth naturally. The doctor told me if I had arrived to the hospital 30 minutes later, I would have likely hemorrhaged to death.

When I awoke from surgery, Klaus was standing over me, asking if it had been a boy or a girl. It was the last question on my mind, one that I didn't have an answer to. I recovered well and shortly after my second brush with death, both of which occurred while dating Klaus, he finished diving school and asked if I would move with him to Austria. I ended up saying goodbye to the people and job I loved at Charley Brown's and in what seemed like a flash, Klaus and I were off to Austria, Scotland and then, Malta.

# 12 MY NIGHTMARE IN EUROPE

Klaus and I traveled to Austria first, so I could meet his family. The next stops would be Scotland and Malta, where he had been promised a job as a deep-sea diver in the North Sea. He insisted on taking his pet python to give to his best friend Erich, who lived in Austria. We ended up putting the snake in a big hat box, poking holes in the box for air. With airline security nowhere near as strict in 1975 as it is now, we managed to get through. Although "snakes on a plane" were definitely not allowed, the python had its first plane ride, arriving to Austria safe and sound. Life with Klaus was never dull!

Upon arriving in Vienna, we went to his parents' home to meet his mother, father and little brother. They lived in a nice house and we visited for a few hours. Afterward, the three of us – soon to be ex-pet included – left for Erich's place. Erich invited us to stay, and trading the snake for room and board, we stayed for the week as planned, then left for Scotland.

We arrived in Aberdeen, and took up temporary residence in a bed & breakfast, learning suddenly that Klaus's job wasn't quite so certain as he had been led to believe. We strolled the streets of the city, with me dodging huge wads of spit, which covered the pebbled sidewalks. The pubs were filled with loud jolly guys drinking and conversing in their own dialect of English. They attempted conversation with us but no matter how hard I tried, or how slow they spoke, I couldn't understand a word that came out of their mouths!

Klaus was finally called to the North Sea, but never ended up diving, due to both confusion on the part of his employers, and bad diving conditions. They ended up advising him to go to Malta, as there might be stable work there.

We arrived in Malta but with money getting scarce, we barely had enough to rent a small apartment. We waited for money to be transferred to us but the money never arrived.

Malta was a beautiful and very colorful island, with nice-looking people sporting jet-black hair, blue eyes and fair skin. Unfortunately, the local fare was much less appetizing than the people, with horsemeat being a common staple. And I didn't want any of it!

Klaus was finally called for a diving job, and although he was very excited, he wasn't gone anywhere as long as he had planned. The other divers didn't like him at all, and diving conditions were very dangerous. They had been told to wait on an oil rig until conditions improved, but Klaus, being impatient and fearless, hopped into the water to complete his work. The other divers were made to look bad, as a result. Being the good girlfriend that I was, patiently, I listened to this tale day after day.

The money we were anticipating had still not arrived. Tension was building, as Klaus hadn't been called for another job. We were about as broke as we could be, not knowing what could have possibly held up the money transfer. There was no food left to eat with the exception of flour, salsa and coffee mate in our cupboards. Klaus mixed the entire lot together, baked it and ate it. Wisely, I decided to pass on this "meal," with hopes that I wouldn't starve.

We went to several different banks trying to solve the money situation, and finally to our great relief, the money arrived. To celebrate, we cooked our favorite meal, Hungarian Goulash. Still, Klaus was very keyed up about his unknown job situation, and while we should have been overjoyed to fill our stomachs, he looked for excuses to pick a fight.

Tired of trying to make this occasion joyous for two, I finally told Klaus to shut up. Out of nowhere, he became filled with rage, throwing his beautiful dinner all over me. I was numb, but didn't have a chance to process my feelings as a moment later he grabbed me and threw me against the wall. My shock increased as Klaus continued to assault me! Kick after kick; blow after blow caused me to land in the back room.

Even from this vantage point, I could feel the searing burn of his red "evil" eyes as he yelled, "Don't you DARE come out of here!" And then he slammed the door. With tears running down my face, I remained in the room in complete silence until the next day. What had I done, leaving my friends and the country I yearned so long to live in – for this?

I recall looking out the window, wanting to scream for help but I had no voice. The street was crowded with people walking past, laughing and shopping yet I had never felt so alone. Klaus came into the room at one point, telling me he took my passport away to abandon me here. And yet still, I couldn't utter a word. He terrified me with tales of me being unable to work as a foreigner, and thus, I would be reduced to someone begging on the streets. At that moment, I contemplated jumping from the third floor to the street below, hoping I would die. But my goodness from my dear mother's upbringing made me think twice, not wanting to hurt or worse, kill anyone in the process. My mother had survived a rape. She had survived the Nazis! I too was determined to survive this nightmare!

In the next, several days Klaus cooled off and attempted to talk to me, but I spoke very little. He returned my passport so I remained polite, knowing I had to if I was to survive and eventually, make it back to the U.S. I saw a body in the mirror – my body – completely black and blue. I was in terrible pain, both physically and emotionally, but was grateful my face remained intact, without any bruises. My plan was to leave this man forever and I started writing letters to my friends, Linda and Susie, asking for help.

Linda wrote immediately, suggesting she send a plane ticket for me to come back to California. Her support meant the world to me, knowing I had a best friend for life. I also received a long letter from Susie, telling me she was soon going to be featured in Playboy magazine as a centerfold! She also said she would send some money, but I don't think she realized how serious a situation I was in. She even intimated I should be one of the featured models in Playboy, as she thought I was the most beautiful woman she had ever seen. I felt something, yes, but my emotions were dark and they had nothing to do with being beautiful.

We had been in Europe for almost three months and now, Klaus too was ready to leave. Together, we started planning our trip back to the U.S.

We flew to London to catch a more affordable flight to California. Here, Klaus bought a newspaper and in it, found an ad placed by a guy who owned his own Lear jet. He was looking for three people to fly back to California with him. We thought that this would be the cheapest way home and honestly, it sounded heaven sent.

We arranged to meet this individual, and, after surveying his plane, decided to embark on the adventure. The next day, another young man showed up, ready to fly with us all. The plan was to stop in Greenland, Iceland, and Canada, with California being our final destination.

# 13 WE ALMOST CRASHED AND DIED IN THE LEAR JET

In what felt like a real adventure, the four of us took off in the Lear jet. I took an immediate liking to the pilot, who looked identical to Tiny Tim. I had no choice but to trust Klaus's opinion that this man, with the continuous dripping nose, was a good pilot. The other guy traveling with us was fun and adorable, taking obvious pleasure in telling his life story.

Up until that point, the flight had been an enjoyable experience. That is, until the pilot announced his concern about oil leaking from the wings. He stated that once we landed, he would have someone check for the source of the leak. Nobody seemed overly concerned so neither was I.

Our first stop was Greenland and although we weren't planning to stay there overnight, our plane needed checking and wouldn't be ready until the next day. The four of us shared one room because that was all that was available. And although it felt excessively awkward to be sharing a bed with Klaus, especially as we were splitting up, we all needed to sleep. And so, I went along with it.

Four days later, our stay had turned into a nightmare. Poor weather prevented us from taking off and, to make matters that much worse, one night Klaus decided he wanted to have sex. I went along with this too, as not to wake anyone up.

The morning finally arrived when we were given the clear to leave. Thus, after a lovely breakfast we took off, our serious pilot back at the controls. Time really "flew" too, as everyone was engaged in conversation. It was no surprise that I had every intention to leave Klaus, once we were back on U.S. soil. However, financial constraints made it necessary to make a few tweaks to this plan. We were going to rent a cheap apartment together, with him immediately working back in car sales. This would provide free transportation as well as some quick cash. Klaus had always been great at selling cars, being the top salesman every month. By now, his attitude had changed to one of sweetness, with him promising me an inexpensive car with his first paycheck, in order that I could work, too. I was hoping to go back to Charley Brown's.

In what felt like no time at all, we were preparing to land in Iceland. Just then, the pilot heard from someone on the radio that weather conditions over the past few days were never bad at all. The weatherman, a Communist, did this purposely to force everyone to stay longer in Greenland, putting money in the pockets of the hotel owners. We were all surprised and nonetheless, not too happy, but what was done was done.

Our pilot was looking more and more nervous, and, seconds from touch down, informed us that the landing gear wasn't lowering. He was going to try to "drop" the plane, in hopes of triggering the release of the wheels. He then proceeded to make several jolting drops and – nothing!

"The landing gear must be frozen!" he exclaimed.

Our faces each registered the concern that the other was feeling. I looked over and noticed Klaus reaching for his seatbelt and knew we were in deep trouble. The other passenger started chanting some prayers and at that moment, it dawned on me what might, or might not, come next. Yet, remaining perfectly calm, I stared out the small window of the aircraft while the pilot, on the radio, was told that another small plane would be sent to fly underneath us. Their recommendation was that he keep dropping the plane, but then another problem started to unfold: The plane was running out of fuel.

Ambulances had begun to arrive to the airstrip, preparing for what might be a belly crash landing. It was also suggested that the pilot attempt to land on a nearby frozen lake. We all took a vote. It was decided we would try to land on the airstrip.

The speed at which all this took place felt instantaneous, yet we all knew we might be experiencing our last moments in this incarnation. This organism, which we spend our physical form in, is truly remarkable, as I was like the lake – "frozen" and yet fully serene and aware.

Making one last attempt to drop the plane, we were now in the process of making the belly landing. BANG! Suddenly the other plane radioed ours, telling the pilot our landing gear had just dropped! Our relief was written in a million tiny words all over our faces, but no words were uttered until we landed safely on the ground. Then the plane shook with screams of joy!

When we embarked, complete strangers reached for us, hugging us, and I had never felt such human love in such a demonstrative way. Once again and for the last time, I experienced a "near death" episode with Klaus.

That night, everything was on the house, and we all celebrated our very lives!

This is another momentous example of why we should all live and stay in the "moment" as one never really knows what the next moment has in store for us.

# 14 UNEXPECTED AND PREGNANT WITH MY DAUGHTER TIFFANY

The rest of the journey home was drama-free. We all said our goodbyes and going our separate ways, promised to stay in touch by mail. Klaus and I found a cheap rundown apartment in Long Beach, with him immediately returning to work as a car salesman. The job was the same but the name of the dealership had changed. He did keep his promise, buying me a big, old Ford with low mileage. The car had just one elderly owner and was a reliable means of transportation. I went back to Charley Brown's and got my old job back. There were some new faces there, and I made a friend, a girl named Debby almost immediately upon returning.

Fate echoed that one night in Greenland, with me missing my period. The doctor confirmed I was indeed pregnant. The joy I should have felt I simply could NOT feel, given my commitment to separate from Klaus. Yet I wasn't depressed either, as I longed so much to have a baby. Speaking strictly for myself, I don't support abortions, and in fact this wasn't even an option. I presented Klaus with the news and he seemed genuinely happy, despite my reminder that I was still planning on leaving him.

However as the weeks went by, I became overwhelmed with the prospect of raising a child alone. But I knew I could draw on my mother's strength, for she raised not one – but two – children, under much more difficult circumstances.

It was definitely an emotional time and once again, Klaus was returning to his cruel ways. One night, he threw his wooden Birkenstock sandal at me, hitting me directly in the head. In a way it served as a necessary reminder that I had to get out sooner, rather than later.

I told some of the girls at work of my dilemma, and Debby offered to let me move in with her for as long as I needed. I was grateful and relieved, and moved in almost immediately. Debby's two young sons moved into one bedroom, allowing me the use of the other bedroom. I was assured this was no problem.

One weekend her mom watched the boys so Debby and I could go to Palm Springs. A fun time in a restaurant nightclub turned into more excitement when I met a guy named Shawn. After asking me to dance, we spent a lot of time in conversation, with me telling him flat out I was pregnant, but that I had left the father. It didn't seem to bother him at all, as he asked if he could see me again. Shawn was tall, blond, good looking and worked as an architect.

After our first meeting, he called me daily, with us making plans for him to come down when I had some time off. We had a great time together, and, out of the blue, he stated he would be happy to take over as my child's new father. My mouth dropped when I heard this, with his next statement completely blowing me away: He would also love to give my unborn child a brother or sister!

With me craving both personal space and privacy, I wanted to move out on my own. I found a tiny apartment on the beach in Seal Beach. In the days that followed, Klaus came into Charley Brown's, attempting to charm me back. Shawn also visited several times, surprising me. One night found both men in my workplace, vying for my attention. I pointed them out to all the girls; gladly they gave their opinions as to whom I should choose. I wasn't seriously considering getting back into a relationship with Klaus, at least, not for myself. Obviously, my preference was to stay with Shawn. But sometimes my thoughts would swing back and forth, wondering whether it was fair that my child would be without his or her paternal father. Maybe it was just hormones, manifesting themselves as doubt.

Klaus came in again one day, as he didn't know my new phone number, nor where I lived. He told me my mom was arriving from Denver the next day, and he was picking her up. Unbeknown to me, this was one sneaky maneuver, as Klaus realized I wouldn't be able to resist seeing my mother!

I hadn't seen my mom since arriving back from Europe and my excitement was bubbling over. The next day as Klaus promised, my mom had arrived, and our reunion was a happy one. Klaus wined and dined us both, being the master "charmer" and salesman, a role he played well. Although it wasn't mom's intention to manipulate me into returning to Klaus, that is exactly what happened. Of course he talked to her before I came over, and we both fell victim to his trap.

My mom went back home, and I allowed Klaus to move into mine. As I agreed to give the relationship another chance, I threw myself wholeheartedly into making it work. Five months into my pregnancy, I quit my job at Charley Brown's, with the manager once again telling me I was welcome back anytime. Klaus worked very hard and was more than happy to support me.

Our plans were to move to Denver, once the baby was born. Time passed quickly, and before long I was ready to give birth. Klaus stayed by my side for the entire duration of my labor, which was much longer than I care to remember. I chose to have a natural childbirth and although my contractions were extremely painful, it was finally time to push. The moment had arrived, and 1-2-3, a beautiful baby girl rocketed her way into the world. My daughter, TIFFANY and I met outside the womb for the first time, greeting one another face-to-face.

I was overwhelmed with a very special kind of love, when I held my adorable little Tiffany. So powerful this love; the kind only a mother could experience. Tears formed and fell from my eyes, witnessing this little "miracle" that arrived into my arms, a gift fresh from Spirit. In that moment, I was impressed with Klaus's tender side, as well as his show of love and support, as he stayed with me the entire time I was in labor and delivery. We took our Tiffany back home to the little apartment in Seal Beach, waiting for her one-month birthday so we could make the journey to move and live in Denver, Colorado.

# 15 ELVIS SADLY LEFT "THIS" BUILDING

Tiffany's one-month old milestone was a turning point for us all, as we made the long journey to Denver. Upon our arrival, we found a nice apartment to rent, confident that Klaus would find work selling cars. He was wrong. It was December, right before Christmas and nobody was hiring – or firing – for that matter. We had to do something and fast, so we whipped up a huge garage sale to make ends meet. Fortunately, we made enough money to tide us over until Klaus found a job. Santa delivered, albeit a little late, and Klaus found work right after the holidays, as a used car salesman. Ideal? No, but it was something.

We both loved and adored Tiffany, enjoying her more than I ever thought humanly possible. Klaus started calling her the "mommy hanger," because the only person in the world she cared about was me. For the longest time, she wasn't the least bit friendly towards her father, or anyone else for that matter. Klaus always said if anything ever happened to me, Tiff wouldn't make it. She was forever in my arms, with me taking her everywhere. And each night when she slept, she did so on my chest. I literally could never be out of her sight, which was fine by me since I loved being her mommy!

Linda and I still talked daily on the phone, since the moment we met at Charley Brown's. There was nothing she didn't know about my life, or me and was the type of friend whom would never judge; never condemn. I was blessed for her friendship. Although she was married to Dave and busy taking care of her own children, she missed having me near. My other best friend, Susie, was doing more modeling as well as making a few movies. We too, stayed in close touch.

Even Bill Bates and I remained good friends. I regularly received the sweetest letters from him, sharing how his life was going and wondering what was happening with mine. On my first Mother's Day, Bill sent me a dozen red roses. I was incredibly touched and missed him, too. I knew we would always have a very special connection.

In what seemed to be a repeat scenario, Klaus was once again, getting frustrated at not making the big money he had made in Long Beach. As such, he was becoming more difficult to live with. With yet another huge fight under his belt, I could think of nothing else, other than my desire to leave him. No matter which way I approached things, it was apparent I was afraid of him, fearing his unpredictability. How did I handle this? The only way I knew how, by making him invisible to me and saying nothing to him.

After the last detestable fight, I called Susie, who insisted I come stay with her. I told Klaus I was leaving him (again) and returning to California. Susie made a very generous offer to rent a U-Haul and come get Tiffany and me, with the assistance of her bad ass German boyfriend. But in the end, Klaus himself moved us, as the "good" Klaus made a comeback, acting really nice again. He too was ready to leave Denver, and as I had a child now, I agreed to move into a nice apartment with him in Huntington Beach, close to where Linda lived.

I was thinking about Bill again, too, and while unpacking, read a letter he wrote:

"Shirley, you're fantastic! I sent you roses on Mothers Day and the day after, I got a picture of the two most beautiful women in the world (I sent him a photograph of Tiff and me.) Thank you! You'll get roses from me all the time if I get treated so nicely in return. I think I'll frame it. I'm really interested in the long story that may send you back to Long Beach. I really want to see you again. Please write and tell me about it soon. I'm always more than interested in your life, if you'll believe me. Let me know what you're doing Babe." He concluded with, "I love you, Bill."

I loved being back home with all my friends nearby, and Susie and I spent a lot of time hanging out with one another. We went shopping, watched soap operas, and mainly spent lots of time playing with Tiff.

It was August 16, 1977. Rain fell for much of the morning as Susie and I shopped at Bullocks Department store. Tiff was in my arms the entire time as we rushed to get home to watch "All My Children." On the way out, I noticed a book display in the center of the floor. A new Elvis book had just come out, written by a few of his closest friends and ex-employees. I bought a copy, anxious to open it as soon as I had a moment.

I had told Susie about my phenomenal Elvis story before, yet on the way home, she asked to hear it all over again. I started telling her about Elvis, knowing she loved living vicariously through my experiences. I talked – and talked – about Elvis right up until I turned the key in the lock of the front door.

We made it just in time for our soap opera and quickly, I went to put Tiff down for a nap. Finally sitting down, I put on the television, hearing words that I understood in meaning, but ones that I simply could not (or would not) comprehend. Breaking news had pre-empted regular programming: ELVIS PRESLEY WAS DEAD.

Disbelief morphed into grief; panic. I was crying hysterically, not believing the solemn-faced news anchors, because it was impossible, *impossible* that Elvis had died. It wasn't real and it wasn't true. There are some emotions that defy interpretation and explanation. I felt the most intense sadness and sorrow, which pierced deep into my soul. I started to drown in my bereavement – where was Elvis? My Elvis was gone!

I know now that we shed only our "human" bodies, and that our Spirit is eternal. Elvis is alive, in Spirit form. I recently read a book written by a medium, which reassured that Elvis is waiting to greet each and every one of his fans and admirers. I have no doubt he continues to do so today.

And still, amidst the loss, I felt him. It was no coincidence that on the very day of his passing, I recounted my Elvis experiences. Being a busy mom, it wasn't something I thought about regularly, although he was a constant presence in my heart. Yet there I was, spilling minute upon minute of every moment I spent in Elvis's energy.

A few nights later, Klaus surprisingly suggested to me, "Why don't we make a brother or sister for Tiffany, because it's no fun being an only child." I agreed, and on that very night, got pregnant again.

# 16 MONIKA'S BIRTH, AND MY SERIOUS POSTPARTUM DEPRESSION

I always considered Belmont Shore to be my American home, and I wanted to live there again. Looking in the daily newspaper, I saw an ad for a small, two bedroom duplex. Rushing out to see it, I found it was ideal and rented it immediately. Conveniently, the house was closer to Klaus's job as well.

Being pregnant and living back in Belmont Shore was perfect. Klaus and I built a wooden fence around the front yard so Tiff and the new baby could play outside safely. All in all, we were pretty happy. There were other children in the neighborhood to play with, and even older kids would come over to socialize with Tiff. Naturally, she was the one always in charge. In fact, Tiff seemed to have the run of this new neighborhood.

When my mom came to visit she would always observe, "Tiff has definitely been here before," meaning, "of this world."

Tiff was mature and extremely smart for her age, learning to read from "Sesame Street" by age three. I spent all my time teaching her and gradually, she started adapting to others. She promised to marry me when she grew up, or at least move next door to me, after I explained daughters couldn't marry their mommies.

The time felt appropriate to bring Klaus's seven year-old daughter to Belmont Shore for a visit so she could spend time with us, as well as meet her new sister. She was living with her mother in New York, so this was an important step for all of us.

During my last month of pregnancy, my mom came to help me. I was diagnosed with toxemia, a blood disease requiring me to stay in bed and rest for long periods of time. I was due any day now and suddenly – my water broke.

I called Klaus to come home and take me to the hospital. We made our way to the maternity ward where once again, I chose a natural childbirth, with Klaus by my side. After several hours of labor, I was finally ready to go into delivery and start pushing. I thought once again it would be "1-2-3" and out comes baby, but nature had something different in store for us.

My baby wasn't overly eager to make her entrance into the world, so after pushing nonstop and exhausting myself more and more each time, I finally screamed, "I GIVE UP!" Honestly, I didn't care what the doctors had to do, as long as I could get relief from the excruciating pain. The experience felt literally like an old-fashioned birth, where the baby is born while the mother loses her lease on life and passes away. But everyone attempted to soothe me, urging me not to give up.

On the verge of passing out, the baby finally greeted us all. Once again, I succeeded in having a natural childbirth, and my beautiful daughter was named MONIKA, with me instantly calling her Mo.

Klaus and I couldn't wait to get home the next day to introduce Tiffany to her new sister. I remember holding Mo as I walked in the front door and, smiling at Tiffany, said, "Hi Tiff, look at what we brought you – a new little baby sister!" Tiffany was 1+1/2 years old, had never spoken a full sentence in her life, and yet in a mad and authoritative voice said, "Mommy, put that baby down!"

Shock was written all over my face as I handed Mo to Klaus, and proceeded to take Tiff in my arms. I knew that in time, she would get used to her younger sister and with luck, like and love her too. Fortunately, that's exactly what happened, but as Tiff warmed to tiny Mo, something changed in me to cause me deep fear.

The word "depression," means literally, "a depressed or sunken place." For no reason at all, I started keeping my distance from Mo, not looking after her the way I should. Tiff was never a problem, but for some reason, I couldn't connect with Mo. I felt detached from her, and from myself. I reached out to Klaus on many occasions, telling him I didn't know what was wrong with me. I was feeling strange and terribly unhappy. Out of nowhere, morbid thoughts passed through my mind, and silently I observed them in shame, praying for them to pass.

"Come on, we'll take a nice drive," Klaus would suggest, and I would feel better. But my relief was momentary, with me quickly sinking back into a place very alien and frightening. Time didn't change my feelings towards Mo. If anything, they actually got worse. The thoughts I had only been observing up until now, started turning into potential actions. Yet I didn't want to harm her! Not me; this wasn't me!

It took a very long time for me to get well. And when I did, I swore I would warn every young mother about this insidious phenomenon known as postpartum depression. There is no need to suffer for years, as I did. I believe my naturally compassionate and loving side, while doing battle with this condition, won, as I never ever physically harmed Mo in any way, shape or form. Looking back, it's exactly why I managed to keep my distance from her.

Although it took a lot of courage to commit these thoughts to paper, I wanted to express the seriousness of this temporary mental illness. To this day, it still hurts that I even had the thoughts and feelings I did, but thankfully, Mo survived it, and I love her now more than ever. Many years ago, Brooke Shields shared her experiences with postpartum depression, and how medication may help in most instances.

# 17 MARRYING KLAUS

During one of our many walks through the neighborhood, on our way to the beach and playground with our children, we saw a gorgeous, big brown house with a "For Rent" sign on it. We looked at each other, looked at the property (the house was on the beach) and thought the same thing – let's go for it! It had a large kitchen and living room, a huge dining room with a den, two bedrooms, two bathrooms, a large garage and a beautiful front yard with a tree. Our children would have more room to play as well, with the beach as their backyard. This was our dream home, and with Klaus making fantastic money as the Service Manager at the European car dealership, delightfully it became a reality.

It was wonderful having friends over in our new home. Susie had met a gorgeous male model on one of her photo shoots and quickly, he became her new boyfriend. She was excited for us to meet him, telling me there was a strange "coincidence" about him. When I asked what it was, she reminded me that years ago when we were roommates, she had bought a Playgirl Magazine. This was the sexy guy whom had been on the cover. She went on to remind me that I sketched the cover picture of him, and that she had wanted to keep it.

Of course, I remembered now! At the time I was flattered, telling Susie I was just doodling, since we had the magazine. We were both blown away, because to this day, she kept the drawing I had made. Now, she had the real guy – Bill Cable – too!

I soon met "Billy" and, just as Susie gushed, was more gorgeous in the flesh than in print. He took my breath away, and I think he was the most beautiful man I had ever seen. He looked absolutely perfect from head to toe, reminding me of Elvis when he was at his best. Billy was a talented actor, writer and model. One couldn't help adore him, as he was so gentle, kind and down to earth.

We all became best friends, with Susie and Billy often driving down to hang out with us on the beach, all weekend long. I couldn't help thinking I had an innocent little crush on him. They had fun playing with Tiff and Mo, pretending sometimes that our children were theirs, and once again, life was good.

Never once did I plan on marrying Klaus, but one weekend on the spur of the moment Klaus asked, "Why don't we drive up to Lake Tahoe and get married?" He said that as we now had two children, it would be nice for all of us to share the same last name. I agreed, and we called Susie and Billy, asking them if they would go with us to be our witnesses.

We planned our wedding trip for the very next weekend, and as we both liked emeralds, Klaus bought me a lovely emerald ring.

The week flew by and soon, we were on our way to Lake Tahoe, with our children as well as Billy and Susie. It didn't take long for Klaus and I to start arguing. I could see that Billy was very uncomfortable, so he said to me, "Why don't you and I get married, Shirley" as a way to break the somber mood in the vehicle. I knew Susie and Billy were not getting along, as Susie had a weakness for cheating with other guys. Of late, Billy was calling me, asking for advice. Billy's remark warmed me from the inside out, and we looked at each other, smiling. I guess it was at that moment when I first felt a serious "spark" between us.

We finally made it to the chapel and Klaus and I got married. When it was my turn to say, "I do," I secretly wished that I was declaring my vows to Billy. We all celebrated that night at the top of Harvey's Wagon Wheel, where I worked many years ago.

The drive home the next morning stood out as being a nightmare. Klaus was mad at something yet again. He jerked the car so violently, that it ended up in a snow bank. Tiff and Mo were quite jostled in the car, but luckily were unhurt. I was furious but kept my mouth shut because once again, Billy saved the day. With our wheels spinning and stuck in snow, Billy jumped out of the car, making light of the situation. Being very strong, he pushed the car out of the snow bank by himself, joking about it the entire time. We couldn't help but laugh, and with Klaus's mood finally dissipating, the rest of the drive home was uneventful.

# 18 DIVORCING KLAUS AND MUCH, MUCH MORE

My life was flowing pretty smoothly and at one point, had thought Klaus changed for the better. We continued to fight about his maniacal driving amongst other things, but I knew this stemmed from his desire to be a professional race car driver. Still that served as no excuse, especially as we were parents of two young children.

One afternoon, late in the day, Klaus went to the supermarket, taking 3+1/2 year old Tiff with him. I stayed behind with Mo to make dinner. When they returned home, Tiff's excitement was spilling over. Running over to me, she told me about riding with Papi (Klaus) while sitting in the open trunk of the car while the vehicle was moving and on the roadway. I started screaming, accusing Klaus of being out of his mind. His reaction proved it – he started laughing. At times, I felt just as insane for remaining in the marriage, but provided there were no other incidents of violence, rationalized I should stay, as Klaus was my girls' father.

As far back as I can remember, I told myself that I would never want to put my children through the ugliness of a divorce and the subsequent absence of a father.

As I desperately needed a creative outlet to help unwind from the stresses of the day, I created a serene space for myself in the garage for adult, alone time. I could go in there and immerse myself in my own private world, when the children were asleep at night.

I taught myself to oil paint, creating some awesome works which even Klaus thought were amazing. I was also interested in fashion, specifically, textures and fabrics that weren't customarily available in regular department stores. I loved suede and leathers, and one day while shopping for a chamois for my car, it hit me: What a great-looking ladies top this would make! I bought a few more skins to play around with in my spare time.

I really wasn't much of a sewer, but owning a sewing machine, managed to make myself an ultra-soft, chamois vest from just my imagination. It turned out really cool looking! The next thing I knew, I made Tiff an adorable little chamois vest and skirt to match my own outfit. Decked out in cowboy boots, she was a walking advertisement for "WAY TOO CUTE!"

Klaus didn't say much, but I knew he thought they were strange-looking clothes, being a conservative dresser himself. I had finally found my outlet and was having a lot of fun – that's what mattered most.

There were also phone calls to friends, something that had now become firmly rooted in my daily routine. Klaus seemed to enjoy calling me a "peasant" since the calls made me happy. He, of course, never partook in this. I recall one day asking Klaus something, but he didn't feel like any discussion and instead, suggested I call Linda. I went to the phone and did just that, telling her what Klaus had said. Red alert = BIG mistake.

The call was short as it was time to bathe Tiffany. Suddenly, Klaus came out of nowhere and stomped into the bathroom, yelling at me because of my telephone call to Linda. I told him to leave me alone. In seconds, my head and body were slammed into the floor. Tiffany, witnessing her mother being grabbed and thrown down, jumped out of the tub and soaking wet, scrambled into her bed.

Obviously, my first concern was to soothe her, and make sure she knew mommy was all right. I knew, then, that all three of us had just witnessed "THE MOMENT," where I had finally made up my mind that living in fear and violence was no longer an acceptable way of existing. I would divorce him – my mind was made up.

The next day, still sore from Klaus's display of violence yet more determined than ever, I dropped into an "Attorney at Law" office, unannounced. I hired the first lawyer I found – Scott Lands. He was superb and we became good friends as he handled my divorce proceedings. I told Klaus that night I was following through with my resolve to seek a divorce. At first, he didn't believe me, accusing me of playing out "one of my escapades," whatever that was supposed to mean. I knew he didn't think I would go through with it, but he underestimated Shirley Anni!

Still, I didn't want to take my children away from their father, so I agreed to joint custody. Klaus had been a good dad in many ways, and I didn't feel he presented any threat against them. Yet, despite my attempts to make our divorce as pain-free as possible, after meeting with a court counselor, Klaus bluntly stated he was going to get full custody of our daughters – even insinuating if it meant taking the girls to Austria with him!

I did what I mastered best, over the course of our relationship: I ignored him. Klaus knew what a fabulous mom I was and besides, no court would remove my daughters from my care. And yet, there was a niggling feeling deep down that Klaus might make good on his threats, and disappear with our children. Once again, he was underestimating me. Tiff and Mo were my entire life now, and there was no way he would ever succeed in this. I kept trying to work things out and did my best not to anger him, for without my children, I would quite simply, die.

Being the good attorney that he was, Scott asked me to gather several character witnesses who would be able to testify that I was a good mother. I had Linda and Susie, and then thought of Bill Bates. Being male, he would be another valuable witness.

I called the Queen Mary and was put through to the Bell Desk. I asked to speak with Bill Bates. The young voice on the other end of the line paused, and then asked me to hold. Someone else came on the line and asked what my relation was to Bill. This was weird! When I clarified who I was, the next words which came out of the phone receiver were like knives slashing my face: "I regret to inform you that Bill was killed in a motorcycle accident two weeks ago."

I did drop the phone then, screaming. Tiff and Mo stared at me with puppy dog eyes, as I started weeping. Tiff knew who Bill was, since she had met him on a few occasions. I had to pull myself together for my children, even though I grieved for him more deeply than I would ever express.

Later I learned that a drunk driver had hit him on his motorcycle, on his way home from work. Bill had just completed his master's degree, and just like that, was dead on August 30, 1981, at 29 years old.

One night not long after, I recall waking suddenly. I sat up in bed and, fully alert, saw a shadowy male figure slowly coming towards me. I was totally unafraid of this benevolent presence and gradually, the figure faded from view. In my conscious state, I realized this was no dream. I had never experienced anything like this "mysterious something" before. The warmth and love which exuded from this "energy" left me in awe and wonder, with no idea what had happened, or why. Now I knew as I did the math: It was the day my Bill died, and in Spirit, he came to say goodbye.

To this day, I have never forgotten, nor will I ever forget my first, true love. I know Bill is a soul mate that one day, I will see again. Bill has been around me and with me throughout my life, guiding so many of the wonderful events that have comprised my life. Love, *our* love is eternal, and this has given me tremendous peace.

Our day in court had finally arrived. The judge, predictably, ruled in my favor, with us being given joint custody of the children. Klaus was asked to move out of the family home, and that was that. It was done. Klaus moved out to a nearby apartment, which was good because Tiff and Mo could still see their father daily, freeing me up to look for a nighttime job as a cocktail waitress without needing a babysitter. Our custody agreement stipulated that Klaus would pick the children up after work, as well as take them every other weekend. Klaus seemed okay with this arrangement, so my biggest fear of losing Tiff and Mo went away, at least, for the time being.

Money became a problem again, as my rent was so unaffordable. I came up with the great idea of renting out the garage as a "beach single." It was certainly in a fantastic location, was spacious, and even had its own bathroom and private entrance. I immediately put an ad in the paper, and soon, a young girl asked to rent it. Upon moving in, she made the space her own and everyone was happy. I could continue to live here with my children, in the home we knew and loved.

Klaus still remained Klaus, and I wasn't naïve to this. One morning at 5:00 a.m., I awoke to the sounds of someone watering my yard. It was Klaus. Other times, I was shopping for groceries and saw him walking through the aisles, specifically at times he was supposed to be at work.

One weekend, on our way up to the castle in Hollywood Hills, where Susie and Billy were living, I noticed a car following us. I didn't recognize the vehicle, so I kept switching lanes to see if the driver of the car would do the same. He, or she, did. Without warning, the car pulled up alongside me and looking over, I was stunned to see Klaus smirking behind the wheel. I was completely spooked out and spent what should have been a beautiful weekend visiting with friends in complete unrest. Billy told me not to worry, as Klaus had no way of bypassing the guarded gate that led to their castle. I assumed Klaus went back home. I assumed wrong.

A trip to the Beachwood Market found Susie, the kids and me in a lurch. After shopping for some goodies for dinner, we returned to my VW bus and it didn't start. Looking under the hood, Billy, whom we called for help, saw someone had disconnected some wires. It HAD to be Klaus. I really tried to hold it together for my children, yet that very evening, saw Klaus, parked at the gate. He remained there for hours. Cuddling up with Tiff and Mo, I held them just a little closer, knowing Klaus was still outside. Thankfully the girls thought it was nothing more than a game, as they too, saw him there.

To my relief, Klaus finally left sometime during the night. And yet, I can recount many more incidents of Klaus stalking me through the years, and in different cars. He had access to so many vehicles, working at the car dealership, that I had no way of knowing if he was lurking around at any given time. It was a horrible time for me, so much so, that I seriously considered marrying a policeman in order that my daughters and I would remain safe.

I did manage to make friends with several policemen who surveyed our house regularly, but I didn't find a husband. I must have prayed a dozen times a day that Klaus would start dating and LEAVE-ME-ALONE!

Eventually, I got a job working as a cocktail waitress at The Quiet Cannon, a lovely restaurant on the water in Long Beach. It was a fun place to work, as the money was good and live bands played at the venue each weekend.

I noticed one, mysterious guy in particular, and as I walked by him, he raised his sunglasses, slowly smiling. He was sitting in with the band as their drummer for the evening. Later, introducing himself as Rico, he told me he was the former drummer for Hamilton Joe Frank and Reynolds, whose big hits included "Falling In Love" and "Don't Pull Your Love Out On Me Baby."

Throughout the night we talked and flirted. I liked Rico and he was one, hot drummer too! I invited him to stay at the house that evening, in order that he didn't have to make the long drive back to Venice Beach. He agreed to leave first thing in the morning, as my kids were being driven back by their father.

The next morning, try as I might, I just couldn't wake him. So, closing the door and hoping to hide him from Tiff and Mo, I proceeded to greet my children. This was the beginning of Rico, although his real name was Richard.

# 19 MY NEW BOYFRIEND RICO, THE DRUMMER FOR HAMILTON, JOE FRANK AND REYNOLDS

I still do not know how this happened, but Rico never left. He became my first "post-divorce" boyfriend, and looking back, am certain Spirit magically dropped Rico into my life. He was THE most spiritual soul I had ever known, and after being married to a man so devoid of spirit as Klaus was, it was exactly what the doctor ordered, in order that my own Spirit be healed.

I warned Rico about Klaus, telling him to be very careful, as Klaus was unpredictable and not to be trusted. One day, as per our established routine, Klaus arrived at the front door to pick up Tiff and Mo. Rico answered the door, dressed in his full black belt karate outfit. Momentarily taken aback, Klaus introduced himself to Rico and attempted to shake his hand. Rico refused – and he became my "instant" hero. Klaus never stalked me again, and even began dating.

Rico and I had a ridiculous amount of fun together. I went with him on some of his musical gigs, and he let me play the tambourine so I could feel as if I was a part of the band. Music was another one of my lifetime dreams, and although I would have loved to be the lead singer, I lacked a certain amount of talent in this area. So much so that I would have single-handedly (or vocally) been responsible for clearing out the patrons in the clubs!

Rico may have begged to differ, as he was preparing a video with me singing Elvis's "Are You Lonesome Tonight?" He had me wear a skin-tight black leather outfit as I sat at a small round nightclub table, draped with a black tablecloth and complete with one red rose. I knew I could do the sultry "talking part" and I could certainly look like Elvis's sister, but I would have needed to lip-sync the rest. What a beautiful dream, however! Occasionally Rico invited Danny Hamilton over, the main singer in

Hamilton, Joe Frank and Reynolds and together with other musicians, would spend hours jamming in my house. I was in absolute bliss and life was once again, a blast.

Tiff and Mo liked Rico, even though he was restrictive in terms of what they ate, being a very health-conscious individual. Both my children loved singing along while the band rehearsed, and they had a ball! I learned so much from him, despite feeling frustrated at times because of his lack of money to contribute towards our life. He told me not to worry; that everything we need would be provided for. At the time we were together, I was yet to tap into my high spirituality, so this added to my level of annoyance. Everything about me, from my upbringing to my adult life indicated that hard work was the only path to money.

It was times like these when my temper flared. I had a lot of anger inside me in general, that needed an outlet. One day I was so angry I thought I'd explode from screaming so loud. Suddenly, Rico took hold of me and gently laid me down on the floor. I became even more livid, and for about 10 minutes, bellowed while he held me down. Gradually I became totally exhausted and what he did, worked. I learned to be a calmer person from that moment forward but it took effort to keep my temper in check. Rico repeatedly reminded me that deep down, I knew of my soul's spirituality, and that this would continue to develop over time. It all sounded like hocus pocus to me, and I demanded a clearer explanation of this so-called "spirituality" from him. He'd smile in that sweet way of his, but never did elaborate any further.

He asked me one day if I would like a hit of his pot, not anything he did regularly. I told him no, that I had tried some once with Billy and wasn't a fan of it. He persisted, and finally to stop him from bugging me, agreed. After all, it was just one hit and it likely wouldn't do much, anyway.

Lying in bed, I suddenly noticed Rico and me cuddling below. How could this be, I wondered. And yet, there I was, floating above the heater in my bedroom. I was having an out-of-body experience – and was I ever pissed! I clearly remember being afraid to leave the room, (yet knowing full well that I could) for fear I wouldn't be able to find my way back. I wanted this to end – and now – so I could chew Rico out, and ask him what in the hell he gave me.

I ended up returning, without any real sense of time as to how long I was in this state. Rico was sincerely perplexed, as he swore all he gave me was a bit of pot. After recounting my experience with friends, they were convinced the drug was laced with some other substance. Little did I know at the time, this unplanned event helped me conceptualize that our bodies are our vehicles while on earth, with our essence, Spirit; a totally limitless form.

During one of my mom's visits, Rico and I took her to a gig of his on the famous Rodeo Drive. It was swanky for her, but she admired Rico's talent and always enjoyed her outings with me. We dressed up that night, with me wearing my unique chamois vest. Rico couldn't believe I actually made and designed this "piece of art," as he called it, and told me I needed to make many more items of this nature. He was blown away, as I was for different reasons. I was tickled as he liked it so much, but didn't think of it as anything particularly special, aside from the fact that I myself liked wearing it. The rest of the night was extraordinary. Owners and friends made a complete fuss over us; I received several heartfelt compliments on my vest and we dined in a first-class establishment at one of the most expensive addresses in the world.

With all the attention we got at the restaurant, wheels were turning in Rico's head. And the very next week, Rico had a plan: I was to wear my vest again, but this time, we'd go to Kelly's, the local wealthy bar. He was certain that some rich woman would want one for herself. I agreed to do so, but wasn't convinced anyone would place an order for the clothes off my back!

We walked into the restaurant, and immediately went to the bar area, ordering a cocktail. Sure enough, no sooner did I sit, when a man seated beside me complimented me on my vest. Smiling, I proudly stated that I designed and created this one-of-a-kind piece myself. "Great," he said and then asked if I could make an identical piece for his wife, as he wanted to give it as a Christmas gift.

I couldn't believe my ears, but knew this was another one of "THESE MOMENTS," and acting as professional as possible, explained the cost for this custom-made piece was $200 (a lot of money in 1981). He agreed – and wrote me a check on the spot.

Trying not to look as completely stunned as I felt, I proceeded to gather the necessary details about the man's wife, including size and body type, in order that I be able to create the perfect-fitting vest. Looking at me, he said to just make hers the same size as the one I was wearing. I thanked him for his order, and promised to call when it was ready.

Back in the car with Rico, I screamed and laughed with pure joy! I hoped I could do this again! Wait, I knew I could! This evening marked the beginning of something spectacular for me, and, thanks to Rico, a wonderful and successful life for myself.

When thinking positive and believing in oneself, anything is possible. Circumstances will gel together in life to make one's dreams come true. And yet again, another of my dreams manifested in the most glorious of ways.

I finished the vest in exactly one week, and as promised, delivered it into the man's hands. Holding the garment, he kept telling me he loved it and his wife would too, as it was absolutely perfect. And in grace as only Spirit could liberate, my first client was sent to me, boosting my confidence so I could create more beautiful designs, which I did, with absolute pleasure.

# 20 I MAGICALLY TAUGHT MYSELF FASHION DESIGN AND MADE ANOTHER DREAM COME TRUE

Rico was leaving for one week for a gig in Arizona. He insisted that while he was gone, I was to make some more designs, including an Indian top and perhaps a dress as well. I couldn't believe he actually thought I could do this. Annoyed at Rico yet again, I told him I wasn't exactly a fashion designer, and that I could make vests – but that's all. He smiled and said I was wrong.

With Rico gone, competitive Shirley kicked into high gear. I bought more chamois skins and started working right away, first attempting the Indian dress which I had always wanted, admiring the ones worn in Western movies. Worst-case scenario, I rationalized, at least I could say I tried! With some frustration and a LOT of perseverance, I succeeded, feeling so much joy I could barely put my feelings into words. The dress turned out and fit beautifully, complete with hand-cut fringe as a finishing touch.

With this project completed, I couldn't wait to create more pieces. Rico had already mentioned how excited he was about showing my pieces to select store owners. These items would form part of my very own fashion line, which I tentatively called "Feather River." I never used sketches as a starting point but rather, my creations "came together" magically, through what I now know was divine guidance.

One week later Rico returned from Arizona, and I showed him the pieces I created in his absence. He was beyond proud of me, promising to take them to Venice Beach and a few other places, in hopes of soliciting new clients and venues upon which my designs could be sold. To my delight, store owners were eager to display my merchandise, wanting to keep them on consignment. At first I was uncomfortable with this, as I

69

needed money now for a working income to be able to invest in more skins.

Jonathan's, a large store in Redondo Beach, was holding a big fashion show in a few weeks, featuring the famous dancers, The Rockettes, directly from New York to model the fashions. I brought some of my designs to show them and it was love at first sight! The owner asked if I could leave a few pieces in the store, at least, until the show. This was too exciting to pass up, and with this great opportunity I left most of my pieces there.

One order was placed immediately for the Indian dress, in a size 18. I didn't know where to start, so I bought a dress pattern, just to learn how to work with the various measurements. It was extremely difficult but I finished it – and it looked and fit great! After holding my breath, wondering if I made the dress in the correct measurements, I now boasted a new level of conviction that I could make anything I set my mind to.

I was still working nights at the Quiet Cannon as well as working all day at home on my fashion designs. Then there was me as "mommy," driving Tiff to and from school while Mo stayed at home with me. Tiff wasn't all that interested in what I was doing, as she would have preferred a more conventional mom. Mo was a real tomboy but enjoyed sitting by my side, creating little pieces of art from the scraps of leather I discarded. That, or she spent time outside, playing with her best friend, Matt.

One night while at work, there was a large party thrown by a local trucking company. A beautiful, young blonde asked me to bring more cocktails for the group, handing me a $50 tip. Aside from her looks, she had an incredible angelic "vibe" around her and this sweet woman – Gail Cooley – and I became best friends. I explained to her that I could use a blond-haired model – the polar opposite of me, sporting jet-black hair – to wear my designs to Jonathan's fashion show. She was thrilled that I asked her, telling me she had never done any modeling before. Nonetheless, she was very excited to do this with me.

We had a few days to prepare before the show. Gail came over and fell in love with my fashions, placing an order for herself. "Gailee," as I liked to call her, had a fantastic time at the fashion show. We both met some famous people and I also took several orders for dresses and tops.

At a certain point, it became apparent that I needed to dedicate a lot more time than I was to creating and marketing my fashions. Rico suggested the energy was ripe for me to quit working at my night job and stick to designing. How frightening, I thought, but how else could I manifest my dream of becoming an artist and designer. And with that, I resigned from the Quiet Cannon, on pure faith.

I started using the big window in the den, overlooking the beach, as a space to hang my designs. A lot of pedestrian traffic passed by here, and perhaps I could gain some new clients. Rico also started photographing Gail and me wearing my fashions and he took the photos with him wherever he played. I hung a copy of the pictures all over my walls, so whoever came by could get an idea as to what my fashions looked like while being worn. Things were moving along at a very rapid pace and soon, I was getting enough orders to pay the bills. I had also found a new outlet that sold a large variety of suede and leather skins in multiple colors. Gail was incredibly helpful, not only by purchasing and wearing the clothes herself, but also by attracting new clients.

I was quite literally, thanking God each day for being able to make a living as an artist.

Rico suggested we take a trip to Santa Fe, New Mexico and Sedona, Arizona in hopes of enticing new clientele. With my mom watching the kids, we were soon off on our road trip, complete with a sample set of designs and high hopes. Rico took beautiful photos of me, with the red sand hills and white Indian buildings forming gorgeous backdrops. In the end, we sold a few pieces while collecting plenty of offers for consignment but it wasn't enough to turn a profit. I charged the entire trip on my new credit card and luckily, was able to pay off the bill. We had an enjoyable time anyway, and while in Sedona, Rico asked if we could partake in our own spiritual wedding, under the star-filled canopy of the Arizona sky. Since there were no legal implications, I agreed, and together we enjoyed a very romantic evening.

After returning from our trip, I was more motivated – if that was even possible – to expand my designs. With a Southwest inspiration, I worked the intricate detail of hand beading into my fashions, making them wearable pieces of art.

Gail wanted me to think "big time," as she felt my designs surpassed even those that celebrities were wearing. She affirmed that my clothes were the most beautiful fashions created with skins she had ever seen and with that, offered me a free computer. As I didn't know what this was, or what it was used for, I politely declined.

The tenant renting the garage space was moving out. Gail asked if she could rent the space, so she wouldn't have to drive home to her ranch every night after work. I was thrilled and she ended up staying several nights a week, often taking us all out to dinner at her favorite Japanese restaurant, Suma. It was cool watching everything being cooked right in front of our noses. Gail was overly generous in every, possible way and Tiff and Mo were crazy about her.

One night, downstairs from our regular dining spot, was a new little sushi bar. Mo said she wanted to try some, but I responded in laughter, as none of us had ever heard of eating raw fish! Seeing only a couple of Japanese people there, I refused, steering everyone upstairs. Gail interrupted me, saying she would join Tiff and me in a short while, as she and Mo were going to try sushi. They both came upstairs a little later, with big smiles on their faces. Mo loved it, and I was completely amazed.

Rico was still trying to sell pieces for me, but artists aren't usually terribly talented in sales. I met with professional clothing reps who actually owned their own private plane, and they took my fashions across the country, selling them in small boutiques. They asked that I make a minimum of 10 dresses per day. Although I was making money (finally), I couldn't keep up with the production demands. With minimal regret, I finally decided they were just too "city slick" for me. I was an artist – first and foremost – and my business was beginning to feel less like an artistic endeavor and more like "factory output." I terminated their services, which made Rico happy because he didn't care much for them either.

One day out of the blue, Billy called. He was in Hawaii and confessed he had been thinking of me, knowing I was divorced. Susie and Billy were permanently split up now, and as he thought we were both single, asked if he could come by for a visit in two weeks when he was back in California. I told him I had a new boyfriend, and could hear the disappointment in his response. What this did do, however, was plant a seed in my mind. Susie and I weren't close anymore as we had a bad fight some time ago. When we were working together at Charley Brown's, she slept with one of my exes and that didn't sit right with me. But now, Billy was no longer off limits.

One month later Rico and I broke up. I thought Billy would be perfect as my male model and telephoned him, telling him of my designs. I really didn't need an excuse to see him, since it was his idea to get together with me. In truth, all I dreamt about was the two of us being together forever!

Billy came down almost immediately after I called. He took one look at me and melted in his dramatic style. My hair was very long now, and I was wearing one of my suede mini designs. He proclaimed I was the most beautiful woman he had ever seen. I had finally lost that average "mommy" look – and this moment marked the beginning of Billy and me.

Rico provided me with the greatest gifts money could never buy. Sometimes we may not realize these gifts at the time they are given to us. Looking back, I know that although he may not have contributed much in a monetary way, he was a heaven-sent force, sent to me just when I needed help the most. Rico will never be forgotten and will always be loved; he was definitely my Earth Angel.

# 21 FINALLY AT LONG LAST, MY GORGEOUS BILLY AND I ARE TOGETHER!

As soon as Tiff and Mo saw Billy again, they ran for hugs, yelling his name. Tiff was seven years old, and telling us to "just relax," she and Mo went into the kitchen to prepare a little something. A few minutes later, out came a lovely tray filled with cheese, crackers and fruit, with my two daughters acting as wait staff. It made me incredibly happy and put the biggest smiles on our faces. How adorable this was! They were both clearly happy and Billy loved my kids. In fact, aside from him picking up his belongings, Billy never left, moving in with me to all our delight. He was really happy that we were together, and made himself instantly at home.

When Klaus came to get the girls, it was obvious Billy wasn't just a houseguest. Surprisingly, the only thing he said was "Hi." This apparent acceptance made things much easier on us. Sketching Billy's picture from the 1974 Playgirl cover, years before I had ever met him was a premonition that we would be together. There are no coincidences.

Billy was genuinely excited about my fashions, as this style of clothing was right up his alley. Soon, I made him three custom suede shirts, knowing he would be a walking advertisement for me. Billy was extremely demonstrative in his affections and honestly, I wasn't used to this much "drama." But don't get me wrong, I liked it and did get used to it. His nickname for me was "Little Treasure," a name I absolutely loved.

Each day, Billy lay in the sun as he had to look his absolute best at all times, in preparation for any auditions and subsequent acting roles. He was also the first male model for Fredericks of Hollywood catalogues. Billy's true passion, however, was writing movie scripts and he wrote several.

Many of Billy's famous friends called the house, including John Schlesinger, Pee Wee Herman (Paul) and Elvira (Cassandra), who had been a former girlfriend. This new life was very different from anything I was used to, but it was exciting! Billy filled me in on the Hollywood scene, telling me that it was THE most frustrating and disappointing business in the world. He explained, you were too tall or too short; too fat or too thin; too good-looking or not, and it just went on and on. He was a very sensitive soul, which made any rejection that much, more difficult. Deep down, Billy didn't like the Hollywood life at all, telling me he always wished for a more normal life.

And normal (more or less), is exactly what I was able to provide, with him now enjoying a beach lifestyle. It was his sister's best friend, actress Linda Evans that initially talked Billy into becoming an actor, as he had talent. He was simply too beautiful of a man NOT to be in show business.

Being together felt so right for us both, that we barely spoke of Susie or Klaus. We were completely happy in our lives – so exciting and yet, so familiar. Billy was the kind of man I always fantasized about. He loved when I was totally natural and wore absolutely no makeup. He also loved when I made myself look more glamorous. Everywhere we went, we turned heads. Having Billy by my side made me feel as if I was the most beautiful woman alive, despite never having had any self-esteem issues.

Some girls are "gold diggers," but it was never my thing. And although everyone is entitled to his or her preference, for me, "pretty boys" are what made my world go round! Of course, they needed to be beautiful on the inside, as well as on the outside. I've always said when I roll over in the morning and open my eyes, the man lying beside me must draw a smile across my face. With Billy, I could never wipe that smile off!

Occasionally, Billy would go to Hollywood for an interview or a cattle call. Fortunately, he also had a regular job with his friend, Lewis that he did once in awhile – trimming trees in the valley. One day while on site, he met Christian Brando, the son of Marlon Brando. They became the best of friends.

*"Self love" must come first and foremost, in order to be able to truly love anyone else.*

Billy went out of his way to make others comfortable around him. Unfortunately, most people judged him by his appearance, automatically thinking he must be conceited. And yet, he was one of the kindest souls I have ever known. As I've always believed, when you judge another, it's the insecurity in yourself talking.

The phone rang one day. It was Christian, telling Billy that his father wanted him to go to work for a couple of months cutting some trees on Marlon's private Island, "Tetiaroa" in Tahiti. He asked if Billy wanted to come with him and help, as the job would pay well. Billy was excited about the offer and after talking about it, we decided he should definitely go.

## 22 I VISITED "TETIAROA," MARLON BRANDO'S PRIVATE ISLAND IN TAHITI – AND MET MARLON HIMSELF!

It was 1984 when Billy went off for a few months to Tetiaroa with Christian. We kept in touch mostly by mail and sometimes via telephone whenever he could get through. There was much clean up work that needed tending to, as a result of damages from a hurricane. Marlon had plans to open his private island for tourists, after the clean up was complete.

Billy was missing me a lot, and decided to ask Christian for permission if I could visit him on the island. Christian checked with his dad and it was a go. I jumped at the chance, and calling my mom, asked if she could come out for ten days to stay with my girls. No problem, and off I went!

One week later, I landed in Papeete. Marlon's young secretary, Christina picked me up from the airport, taking me back to her home. I had to wait until the next day for Marlon to arrange for a private plane to take me to his island. Christina had one of the most beautiful homes I had ever visualized. It was very secluded and entirely open, surrounded by tropical trees and the beauty of nature. She had a stream running right through her home, with a huge native tree growing through the roof. I had never seen anything like this in my life. I would have enjoyed staying with her longer, but I was dying to see Billy. Christina and I became instant friends and she was sad to see me leave. For a few years we kept in touch by mail, with the intention that I would come back and visit her again someday.

The next morning right after breakfast, Marlon called, telling her that the plane was ready for me. She took me to the airport and we said our goodbyes. I was surprised to see that it was just the pilot and I in the aircraft.

The flight was quick, and as we flew over the island, I spotted Billy waiting for me below. He was standing in the sand looking up at the plane, holding out his arms with a huge smile on his face. As I disembarked, Billy ran over, embracing and kissing me as if we were stars in a major love scene in a movie. He had clearly missed me!

A few minutes later, I looked up and saw Christian walking towards us. We were introduced for the first time. I smiled, stating it was great to finally meet him, and thanked him for allowing me to visit. He smiled back with a shy, boyish grin, and then they both took me on a tour of the island. The property was completely deserted, with the exception of the three of us, one tractor man named Johnny and the housekeeper, Ann.

Tetiaroa was an incredibly beautiful island, with its water the purest and cleanest I had ever seen. The sand was snow white, and against a backdrop of pale emerald green water, I felt as if I had just arrived in paradise.

We had an abundance of everything we needed, or wanted. Marlon had the huge kitchen fully stocked, including too many beers for the boys! If this wasn't enough, I learned we were going to kayak to some of the other islands, which all formed part of the Tetiaroa island chain.

Billy couldn't wait to show me our hut. The first thing I noticed was the bed, as it was covered with a mosquito net to protect us from getting bit as naturally, we slept in the flesh. The island was full of beautiful, cozy huts, giving us our choice of sleeping locations, but we stayed in the same dwelling night after night, loving its location.

Billy inside our hut on the first night I arrived.

With Christian and Johnny off on the tractor to do some work, Billy and I settled in for some alone time. I had arrived in a tight blue suede dress, which I had made expressly for this trip. But in this heat, I was extremely uncomfortable and anxiously wanted to change into a bikini. When I took my dress off, I couldn't believe my eyes – my whole body was BLUE! The suede dress wasn't lined and the ink bled, causing me to turn blue all over. Billy and I cracked up laughing, but thankfully, the blue slowly wore off with several showers over the next few days.

We awoke early the next morning to a gorgeous view of the water. Gazing out at this breathtaking sight, Billy spotted who he thought was Christian in the water. As it appeared he might be in trouble and in need of assistance, Billy took the kayak out to where Christian was.

Billy's suspicion was correct: There was too much wood in the boat, and it tipped over, dumping Christian into the water. There were several small sharks in the vicinity and Billy pulled him to safety. Later this story was re-told in The National Enquirer. Welcome to my first day in paradise!

*Terrifying Nightmare in Shark-Infested Wate...*

Marlon Brando's son Christian was nearly killed by ravenous sharks while swimming off the coast of his father's South Pacific island near Tahiti late last year. Here, exclusively for ENQUIRER readers, 27-year-old Christian vividly describes his nightmare at sea.

## Brando's Son: 7 Savage Man-Eaters Circled Closer As I Slapped the Water Wildly

By CHRISTIAN BRANDO

"Don't let me die in this watery grave! Don't let these sharks rip me apart!"

That urgent prayer ran through my mind over and over as I treaded water in the ocean 100 yards from shore — completely surrounded by huge, hungrily circling sharks.

Each time one of those horrible monsters closed in on me, I shouted at it with all my strength and slapped the water in its direction.

That was all I could do to keep those ravenous devils away from me. I was trapped, and there was no place to go.

How could I have gotten myself into this fix, I wondered.

That morning one of my father's employees, Johnny, and I had been towing a barge loaded with logs from a smaller island to the main island, where they would be used to rebuild my father's hotel. It had been destroyed by a tropical storm earlier in the spring.

But we'd overloaded the barge, and it began to sink.

I told Johnny to stay in the boat while I swam to the main island, about 200 yards away, to get help. I didn't want to cut the barge loose and risk having it swept out to sea.

I dove overboard and started swimming. After I'd gone about halfway to the main island, I ...

LUCKY Christian Brando (left) and the pal who saved his life by shooting one shark give thumbs-up signal

MARLON BRANDO

Each time a shark came closer, I'd slip under the water and yell with all my might. They stayed about four feet away from me.

I kept spinning around trying to watch all of them at once, afraid one would attack. I'd been treading water for about 45 minutes and was getting exhausted.

Then suddenly I heard a purring sound, like the humming of a bee. I looked around ... and saw an outboard motorboat heading straight toward me.

The sharks scattered as the boat drew nearer — and I saw the face of my friend Bill Cable. He had spotted the barge with his binoculars, realized there was trouble, and came out to help us.

Just as I swam toward the boat a shark darted toward me. And as I threw myself in the boat, Bill grabbed his spear gun and fired at the monster. A spurt of blood came gushing out and all the other sharks ripped the wounded one's body apart in a feeding frenzy.

I was afraid to tell my fa...

... ed its head out of the water and I was horrified to see row after row of razor-sharp teeth staring me in the face.

"One bite from those teeth and I'm a goner," I thought.

Once the other sharks ...

of mad wolves. I wouldn't have a chance.

Terrified, I slapped water at the closest one. Then I remembered a trick a Tahitian native told me about. He said if you shout underwater it frightens a shark ...

---

While I was on the island, Billy and Christian basically stopped working, and the three of us went exploring for hours at a time. It was obvious Christian was a little jealous, because Billy was the lucky one to have his "woman" with him on the island. Sometimes we told one another scary stories while sitting outside in the pitch black of night. Then we'd observe the silence, relieved at the peace that resonated in the air.

During the day, I watched as the boys did a lot of spear fishing. Once, Billy showed off by climbing a coconut tree, picking one so I could drink its fresh milk. The main island was my favorite, but I also enjoyed our kayaking trips to Bird Island. As the name implied, there were thousands of beautiful birds there.

I was told it was a tradition in Tahiti to go topless, and it felt fabulous to do so on this private island in the middle of nature. When it was just Billy and me, I always went topless, but one day out of nowhere, the tractor pulled up with Johnny and Christian on it. Naturally, they both saw me, and smiled, gesturing a friendly howl. I blushed, not like anyone would have known as I was more tanned then I had ever been in my life!

The only working phone on the island rang. It was Marlon. He told Christian he was coming out the next day to check on everything. The strange thing was, he never showed up, nor did he call back even though we all anxiously awaited his arrival.

One person that did show up was Christian's stepmother, Tarita, from the film "Mutiny on the Bounty." She said she wanted to cook a big Tahitian feast for all of us and we were looking forward to this home-cooked meal.

When she arrived, she brought her beautiful young daughter, Cheyenne, as well as her handsome young son, Teihotu – Marlon, being the father of both children. The day turned out fantastic, and we enjoyed a feast fit for kings. It was awesome to have some of Christian's family on the island. I had never seen Mutiny on the Bounty and thus, wasn't star struck. As far as I was concerned, they just represented some of Christian's Tahitian family. I had truly hoped to meet Marlon on this trip, as I was a big fan of his movies.

The ten days passed quickly and soon, it was time to go home. Billy was miserable, and asked if I would extend my stay. Christian wanted me to stay as well, tempting me to call my mother. I couldn't, as I had to get home to my children, whom I was missing. I also knew there were many design orders awaiting my attention.

The same, small private plane arrived to take me back to Papeete, where I would catch a jet back to California. Billy could barely let me go, openly crying when I left. And I cried, too.

This was truly a "once in a lifetime" dream-come-true experience, something I could have never "dreamt" of.

I arrived back home to find a big sign outside my house – "WELCOME HOME MOMMY" – which my mom and the children had put up in honor of my return. Tiff and Mo were standing beneath it, jumping up and down, waiting to greet me with hugs and kisses. Paradise was amazing, but I was so happy to be home with my children.

A few weeks later, I went to the airport to pick up Billy, as well as drop Christian off at his home. Or so I thought. I arrived at LAX – International Flights, and parked my car to go inside the terminal. As I anxiously waited for the boys to arrive, I felt someone very near, studiously checking me out. I had no intention of making eye contact, but the person didn't leave. I finally turned to look him in the face, and saw MARLON BRANDO.

He quickly looked away, as he must have felt busted. I tapped him on the shoulder and smiling, I said, "Hi Marlon, I'm Shirley, Billy's girlfriend. I had no idea you would be here to pick up Christian." Marlon smiled back, saying it was nice to meet me and asked how I enjoyed my stay on his island. I told him how much I had loved it and thanked him.

Marlon then asked me what I did for a living, and I told him. He was very interested in my Indian-style designs, and asked if I had any photos with me. I was thrilled, and as I always carried a small portfolio of pictures in my bag, showed him my designs. To my delight, he was extremely impressed. He said he'd like me to design an Indian vest for him and I responded it would be my pleasure! Just then, the boys arrived and were walking towards us.

I was so happy to see Billy again. Suddenly, I noticed the many eyes staring at us. Marlon wanted Christian and him to get out of there, fast, and as they were leaving, invited Billy and me over to his house for Thanksgiving dinner. Although I had other plans for us, I wasn't going to turn Marlon's invitation down. Therefore, Billy and I followed Marlon and Christian to Marlon's home. We stayed for about an hour, and while I was there, got his measurements so I could later design a very special Indian vest for "THE" Marlon Brando.

Several weeks later, Billy delivered the vest to Marlon, since he was heading to Los Angeles. Guess what? Marlon loved it!

# 23 MY NEW "FOREVER BEST FRIEND" MEGSY

I decided that since my business was doing so well, I needed a new car that would spell "success." Into the dealership I went, buying myself the car of my dreams, a brand-new 1984 Mercedes! I hoped and prayed I would continue to be able to afford the payments, but as it turned out, my fears were unfounded. In fact, I made double payments and paid my car off in just a couple of years.

This car purchase came about in a strange way, as I had my heart set on a red Mercedes. However, as soon as I arrived at the dealership, I spotted a white one and just had to have it! I didn't look at any other cars. And now, reflecting back to the years with Bill Bates, who constantly promised me a WHITE Mercedes, I know he was with me on this day. There is no such thing as coincidence!

I was so in love with my Mercedes that I actually kept it until 2009. It was a sad day when I finally said goodbye to what felt like an old, reliable friend.

One afternoon while working on a new design, I heard a knock on my back door. Standing there was an adorable, smiling young girl with wild hair. She was so very pretty and unabashed, asked why those hot clothes were hanging in my window. Laughing, I explained they were my designs and that I made them for a living. Still smiling and clearly wanting to see more, she simply said, "Hi I'm Megan." With that, I invited her in to take a closer look. At 36 years of age, I took an immediate liking to this 19 year-old.

Talking nonstop, she told me she had just moved across the street, as she was attending Long Beach State University. She was from Sacramento, but had spent time in Hawaii, where she met a guy named Cheyenne, who accompanied her back to the mainland. She asked if she could try on some of my designs and I said yes, figuring that although she probably couldn't afford them, there was no reason why she shouldn't have a little fun.

*You can never judge a book by its cover and thankfully, I never have.*

She was seriously excited about all the clothes she tried on, and loved every single piece. We were laughing and having fun while she admired herself in various outfits. I thought she would make a fabulous model, if nothing else, as she looked stunning!

After she was done, I assumed she'd leave and go home. To my surprise, she started asking how much certain outfits were. After I quoted the prices, she ordered three custom outfits! I wondered how this 19 year-old cutie could afford these. Within a few moments, she was off to the bank and back, returning with a pile of cash, which she enthusiastically handed over as payment. We talked and laughed for a few more hours and then she went home.

I had made another "best friend" for life. We spoke almost every single day, and visited each other a lot because she lived so close. Tiff and Mo met Megsy and they both loved her too, as she was so bubbly and full of life.

One day she came over, bringing Mo a huge shopping bag of healthy snacks from Trader Joes, so Mo could learn that healthy foods could be delicious too. Mo was a typical, chunky little kid, someone that Megsy could relate to from when she was a child herself. It was the sweetest, kindest gesture and it absolutely melted my heart. This was the sort of person Megsy was – and still is.

Megsy had a huge crush on Bon Jovi and wore a big button with his face on it. At the time, I didn't know who this was, but joked they could be girl/boy twins – after all, they had the same fantastic hair!

I still saw Gail, but she had moved out as her dad passed away. Now living in Santa Barbara, Gail had also gotten married. I did drive up to see her but did so less and less as time was becoming scarce. I missed her a lot but was so thankful Megsy came into my life when she did. Now, I had another best friend, including Linda, whom I talked to on a daily basis.

Megsy literally became addicted to my fashions, ordering one outfit after another. One day while her parents were in town visiting, I had the pleasure of meeting them. Her dad told me they were both delighted that their daughter had me as her friend, and were no longer worried about her living alone in Long Beach. Her dad is a powerful criminal attorney in Sacramento, and was the kind of father that I could only have wished for. For the first time in my life, I had observed a close bond between a father and daughter, making me realize how wonderful having a dad like that must be for Megsy.

Even though there was a significant age difference between us, it never felt that way to either Megsy or me. We were simply best friends and I called her father, "Pop." I'm proud to say Megsy is still my best friend today.

More proof that Spirit is ageless, with only our human bodies defining us.

Billy often told me he would marry me someday, and that he planned on having only one wife in this lifetime. Naturally, that wife would be me. This time I responded, "When?" At that moment, he asked, "Will you marry me?" Smiling from ear to ear, I said a resounding, "Yes!"

When I told Megsy that Billy proposed to me, she suggested we should get married in Tahoe, offering us the use of her cabin. Megsy adored Billy, telling me that he reminded her of Cheyenne. We were really moved by this and one month later, Billy and I drove up to Lake Tahoe to "do the deed!"

# 24 BILLY AND I GOT MARRIED

Billy and I decided on a very low-key wedding, as it was much more intimate and romantic. We had matching "moon face" rings created for us, and I designed what we wore for our little ceremony. I made Billy a white leather, pirate-style shirt, and black tight leather pants. As for myself, I wore a beautiful white leather dress, complete with an all-lace white front, tapering to a "V" right down to my belly button. Our outfits were stunning.

On August 13, 1985 we were married outdoors in a tranquil spot overlooking the lake, with two white doves at our feet. We said our vows, kissed, and the doves flew away. It was bizarre, but at the same time, added a magical touch to our wedding. I couldn't help but wonder how exactly they arrived there, because I didn't think that "actor" doves existed! In our hearts we both felt it was a special blessing.

After the ceremony, we dined at a fabulous restaurant, right on the lake. We spent a few more days at Megsy's cabin, enjoying the myriad of beauty and nature. Then, as Mr. & Mrs. we drove home, happy and at peace.

Not long after we arrived back home, work responsibilities kept us busy.

Billy landed a small part as a cop in Pee Wee Herman's Big Adventure. When the movie played in the cinema, we couldn't wait to take Tiff and Mo. Billy's part in the movie came up, and Tiff got so excited she yelled, "Look Billy – it's YOU!" People in the theater turned and smiled. Thankfully, his part wasn't bigger or we might have been mobbed!

I received a call from the owner of an Orange County Magazine, as she had seen my work in stores and asked me to custom design several dresses for her. She was a fantastic new client and we became close, with her ordering a couple of beautiful, long suede dresses every single week. For me, business was great. I wish I could say the same thing for Billy's career, as he had so much talent to offer.

As time went on, Billy seemed to get more and more moody. He was frustrated he wasn't getting enough work, and we started fighting a little. I was a busy mommy, a busy wife and a busy designer – someone who didn't have time for complaining or whining. It seemed to me that Billy was constantly competing with my daughters for attention and that really bothered me too. Honestly, there was plenty of me and more than enough love to go around!

There were times I became so angry at his behavior that he would leave the house and stay with his friend, Dave in Hollywood, for a couple of days. Inevitably, he'd call the next day, telling me how much he missed me and that he wanted to come home. This was becoming a recurring pattern, but I gladly welcomed Billy back because I really did love him.

What I didn't understand was his extreme moodiness, as I was doing such a fine job of handling the finances and household responsibilities. I loved my work, and was never bothered being the so-called "breadwinner." It wasn't an issue for me, but I know it was very much an issue for Billy.

Then, he would get a little work – and, just like that – Billy would be happy as a lark again. Did I regret marrying him? Never. I just hoped and held onto faith that our lives would be brought back into balance in the near future.

# 25 "ALMOST FAMOUS" FOR MY DESIGNS

The owner of the Orange County Magazine had a proposition for me, so we met for dinner at a restaurant called Mastro's. Here she asked if I would be interested in going into business with her. She would be the primary financier and I would supply my time, talent and designs.

I was careful when it came to business decisions, not wishing to race headstrong into the wind, so I took a couple of days to think about it. I felt this had the potential to be a big opportunity so I agreed to her terms.

We started a small manufacturing company, calling ourselves "FANFARONE" – her idea. I hired seamstresses and pattern makers. We bought several industrial sewing machines and stocked up on suede, leathers and other supplies. And so it began. I worked in the factory every day, along with a secretary we hired. She stayed home, making phone calls for contracts and true to her prediction, started receiving several great ones.

One day she called, excitedly telling me she managed to land the BIG one –Nordstrom was now a client of ours! Time for celebration!

"Baby you made it!" affirmed Billy, genuinely happy and proud of my accomplishments.

The very next day she called again, telling me she was coming to the factory that night after closing. She wanted to talk and although I detected something "not quite right" in her voice, had no idea what this could be about. She showed late that night, and with few words, bluntly stated, "I'm done and I don't want to do this anymore." Figuring I heard wrong, I asked her to repeat herself, which she did.

"How could you do this to us, when we just got the biggest contract ever?" I shouted back. "How could you suddenly pull the rug out from under me for no reason at all?"

No response. She then told me it was time for me to leave, and that we were done.

I had never before witnessed such cold, bizarre behavior from her, and cursing, left the factory. I cried during the whole drive home, stunned and not making sense of what just transpired. Thankfully, Billy was home when I opened the door, and in his typical warmth, soothed me as I continued to cry hysterically. I felt his arms around me as he kept telling me he would think of something.

And he did.

A new day – the same conundrum. I called Megsy, and she came over right away, bringing her new, German bodybuilding boyfriend. The four of us rehashed what had happened the night before and discussed the contract that was signed by us both. How could she leave me with nothing when this was a stated partnership?

Billy called his sister's longtime friend, Max, a high-powered attorney on Rodeo Drive. He was the same guy who handled Jim Morrison's (The Doors) case, many years back. His power came in handy in a MAJOR way, since immediately, she played her next hand – suing me for millions of dollars! I wanted a sewing machine and half the stock we had acquired – she wanted my flesh.

When the four of us went back to the factory, taking one industrial machine and half the skins, (because technically half of them were mine), shocked, she threatened to call the police. I knew there was nothing the police could do, but Max advised me to sit there, and not do or remove anything from the premises. He said I was still a partner and that I was within my rights to be there.

She started to fume. I was right: The police didn't do anything, other than smile at me. For a couple of hours I did exactly as I was directed – sat and waited. Finally, she gave in, telling me to take half the product and leave. Megsy, the German bodybuilder, my reassuring husband and my bewildered self finally finished loading up, and so it ended. I affirmed then and there I would NEVER go into business with anyone again.

I remained friends with one of the girls from the magazine, who later told me the owner was jealous of me. Apparently that was her plan all along – to take ownership of my designs and dump the very talent who created them.

I went back to my own designing, now having more materials than ever including a professional sewing machine, and built my business.

# 26 WOO HOO! I BECAME A "MOVIE STAR"

When the owners of our home suddenly complained about me sub-leasing the garage as a single, we had to move. And although we found another nice home in the area, Billy and the girls were never as happy there as in the Claremont home.

Klaus bought a big dog for Tiff and Mo, and met a new girlfriend who moved in with him. He started asking if he could keep the children at his place more often. Since they loved their dog (who lived with Klaus) and seemed happy enough with the idea, I never objected. Better to keep the peace than rock the boat, especially with someone as unpredictable as he was.

Tiff was now 11 and Mo, 9. I knew in my heart that all the frequent shuttling back and forth between his home and mine had to come to an end one day, as they got older.

In less than one year we moved again, to another place in the Peninsula. It was a much smaller apartment and everyone was happy with the arrangement. I bought a futon for the girls to sleep on, giving Klaus their bunk beds as they were now spending most nights with him. Our home however, was cozy and came complete with an ocean view. I set up my sewing machine, looking out over the water.

The year was 1987. One day the phone rang – Christian Brando was on the other end of the line. He wanted Billy to accompany him on a trip to Italy to act in a film. The Italian producers wanted the name "Brando" in their film, due to the associated star power. Problem is, Christian wasn't an actor, and really didn't want any part of "the biz." He figured if he could get Billy a role in the movie, he himself, would give acting a try.

Billy and Christian were practically brothers, and he trusted Billy to coach him in the skills of acting. Being a Brando, you would think he would have asked his dad instead!

Billy was over-the-moon excited and left for Los Angeles to meet with the team. He came home, telling me they gave him the part of a Cabineri, a cop. He said he was leaving immediately with Christian for Italy.

I was excited too – and a little jealous. Ever since I was a young girl and saw a Shirley Temple movie, I wanted to be a movie star. The time came for him to leave, and less than an hour before he was out the door, I suddenly told him I wanted to go too! I gave him some of my modeling photos to bring with him and then said in my most authoritative voice: "Tell the producers I am a well-known actress here in the U.S." Billy knew I was serious and I reminded him that I CAN act! Billy chuckled and said he would try, but to not count on anything.

I wasn't sad when I took him to the airport because I had high hopes for myself. I was always thinking positive and believed I had a good chance of getting a role in this film.

Two days later the phone rang, direct from Rome, Italy. Billy was on the other end, asking, "Are you ready, treasure, because you have a part in the movie!" I screamed louder than I thought I had lungs for, and danced around in delirium. I thought I would pass out from happiness! Laughing, Billy told me to get ready, because flight arrangements were being made as we spoke. He was as happy as I was, and then threw in another perk: They were flying me to Italy, first class!

There was no time, nor place, for self-doubt. The last thing Billy said to me was an affirmation that I always believed I could act, and this was my chance to prove it.

I called Klaus to make sure he could keep the girls for the duration of the summer, as I would be gone. No problem, he said. A discussion ensued about his wanting to take the girls for a grand sea voyage, via a boat he had purchased. Their excitement allayed my concerns and I gave them the okay. Next, I contacted my mom, Linda, Megsy, Gailee and anyone else I could think of, to share my amazing news. Everyone was so thrilled for me, which added to my joy. Before I left, Tiff and I went shopping in the Beverly Center, a swanky mall in Los Angeles. We had a ball, splurging as if we were filthy rich.

Almost immediately after receiving the call from Billy, I was on my way to Rome.

Laura Fuino, an ex of Christian's, picked me up at the airport. She was instrumental in arranging all this, as the producer was a close friend of hers. Laura was a beautiful, young actress and we became instant friends. On the drive to the studio, she filled me in on the details of the film, including the role that was to be mine. The film, "La Posta in Gioco" or "The Issue at Stake," was based on a true story about a political assassination, which occurred in the small southern, Italian town of Nardo. Christian was to play the killer, and I, his girlfriend. Billy was the policeman, and Laura, the sister of the woman that would be assassinated. This was all sounding pretty exciting to me!

Upon arriving at the studio, I saw Billy looking proud as a peacock, for making all this happen for us. He was delighted to have been instrumental in helping a major dream of mine come true, and was also grateful I would be spending the three months of filming with him. It was fantastic to see Christian again, as we hadn't seen one another since spending time together on his dad's island.

He smiled and embraced me, saying, "Can you believe this Shirley, we're gonna have some more fun here." I smiled, and hugging him, agreed wholeheartedly.

I practiced embracing the "movie star" aura with the cast and crew of the movie, then met with the producers and directors. They were extremely pleased when they saw me, and I hoped they were picking up the "vibes" I was so diligently attempting to radiate.

With the producer heading to Nardo to "take care of business," Billy, Christian, Laura and I were to stay in his gorgeous, high-rise loft. The four of us toured Rome, enjoying the sights and sounds of the city. We dined in fine restaurants. We had already been paid good money, and were now given a per diem, as well.

When the week was over, a driver picked us up to take us to Nardo, a six-hour drive to southern Italy. Upon our arrival, we couldn't help thinking it looked like a small ghost town. It was afternoon and the townspeople closed shop for a couple of hours to rest; a custom of theirs.

We were given a choice of either staying in a beautiful Italian villa, or the main waterfront hotel in town. We chose the villa, loving the cozy, yet luxurious accommodations.

The next day we all went to meet everyone, and to see where some of the filming would be taking place. When the scripts were handed to us, I felt as if the dream I had been enjoying over the past, few days suddenly became reality. I was deeply happy, and identified with being an "actress," something which went far deeper than just "acting."

As filming wasn't officially scheduled to begin until the following week, we spent time meeting many of the town's local people. Several knew about the upcoming filming and were excited to meet us, thinking we were big, American stars. To them, we were celebrities, knowing well of the great Brando name. Despite playing a killer, they were thrilled to meet Christian. Billy somehow "became" Clark Gable's son, with his tall, dark and handsome looks and Hollywood last name being "Cable." Meanwhile, with Laura and me so glamorous and looking like sisters, we were compared to Italy's most revered actress, Sophia Lauren. It was hilarious, and at the same time, unbelievable.

We studied our lines daily and in no time at all, filming commenced.

My first scene placed me in a restaurant with Christian. I had only a few lines, aced them and boy did it feel good! In-between each of our scenes, there was a lot of waiting around. In what took three months of filming seemed to pass by in just minutes of actual screen time.

The bulk of my role consisted of an interrogation scene. After only three takes, I received applause from both the director and cameraman, having played the part so well, and in so few takes.

After completing my set work, I left. Billy was waiting outside the door, after hearing the applause. He hugged me profusely, so proud of what I had done. I COULD act, and did.

Although this was all very exciting, I was thinking about my Tiff and Mo, more and more. I missed them terribly and even tried sending for them at one point. But each time I tried, I could never get through on the phone. The producers understood my desire to share this incredible experience with them, as they would have loved all this, too.

We received notice of breaking for two weeks, with no filming, and I jumped at the chance to fly home to see them. Billy and Laura stayed behind, and with Christian accompanying me, flew back to the U.S.

Upon arriving in California, I learned my children were with Klaus in Colorado. Confused, I bought another plane ticket and flew to Colorado immediately, arriving at my mom's house as she knew where they were. Klaus brought the girls over, telling me he had taken them there since he was looking into some business. Constantly dabbling into new ventures, I didn't give his explanation much thought.

After a wonderful week with my mom and the girls, I flew back to California, in order that I catch my flight to Italy to commence filming.

Christian and I made the tabloids on several occasions, with rumors of us having an affair. We all laughed about the press. In truth, Christian was enjoying his choice of local girls while Laura hung out with Billy and me much of the time. Whenever Billy and I quarreled, Laura and I would go for long walks through the town, only to be followed by young boys on scooters. And while they did their best to flirt with us, Laura learned an arm gesture, which came in handy – the Italian equivalent to giving someone "the finger."

Billy had played Tarzan once in a movie, and the local town photographer, after finding a photo of him in "costume" blew it up to poster size. Everywhere we went, Billy was now referred to as Tarzan, given that his poster was displayed in the window of the shop!

It literally got to the point where we couldn't go anywhere in public without being mobbed for autographs. Crowds of people gathered outside our villa, day and night. I would hear my name called repeatedly, as did Billy, Christian and Laura, asking that we come outside. For this reason, we decided to relocate to the beautiful, waterfront Hotel Riviera in Nardo. It would offer us more privacy, something we desperately needed.

One day, the producers told us to get ready and pack, as we were leaving for Cannes, France as part of the promotion for the film. If I thought this adventure couldn't get more surreal, I was wrong!

We arrived in Cannes, its elegance and beauty so tantalizing to the senses. We learned we would be staying in the same hotel that Princess Diana was occupying at the time. Settled into what were likely the swankiest accommodations in the city, we were given the green light to order whatever we wished. Room service was soon bringing us Cristal Champagne by the bottles, expensive caviar and everything else we could think of. No wonder the total bill for the four of us was over $4000 for the weekend!

Even our promotional commitments were exciting, with lots of paparazzi following us. Christian, being a Brando, answered most of the questions. And, just as we were getting ready to leave, we caught a glimpse of Princess Diana getting into her limousine. First to feel like a princess and next, to spot one. It was the perfect conclusion to our whirlwind in Cannes.

Upon returning to Nardo, filming began again, with Christian and me sharing a bedroom scene. Being this close to him, I could feel his nerves radiating, especially as Billy was standing just off-camera, watching. In the spur-of-the-moment, I grabbed the covers and pulled them over both our heads, flashing my boobs! This proved to be the ultimate ice breaker, and the three of us laughed any tension away.

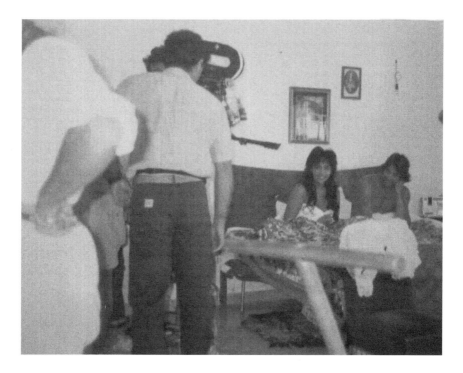

The last scene took place in a disco, lasting a full 16 hours in the smoke-filled club.

And then, the film was a wrap.

A huge after-party was thrown for us as well as several smaller parties during our last few days in Nardo. During one particular party, wealthy locals opened several wine bottles from their cellars, most being over 100 years old. We were also served more courses of exquisite cuisine than we could count. I felt honored they would do this for us, and graciously drank the indescribably delicious liquids, while sampling as many foods as I could.

Many of the Italian folk were genuinely sad to see us leave. They told us we were family now, and welcomed all of us back to Italy anytime we chose, offering us huge villas in which to stay. We told ourselves this would be a destination we would all visit again one day. As we departed, all I could think of was that I had just lived a once-in-a-lifetime experience, manifesting yet another huge childhood dream of mine.

We drove back to Rome, and stayed again in the producer's place for a couple of days before flying back to California.

Once back on American soil, I left my fame behind and reverted back to my best role ever – as MOTHER – excited beyond words to reunite with my children.

# 27 KLAUS TOOK MY CHILDREN

When the fame and adoration I experienced in Italy wore off, it did so as unceremoniously as pulling off an outer layer of clothing. I was home and the only thing on my mind was seeing my children.

It didn't take long for me to learn that Klaus was remarried, and had moved to Vail Colorado with my two daughters.

The superficial hollowness I experienced, walking off the plane and back into reality was nothing, *nothing*, compared to the wretched grief, and then fury I experienced, learning this news. Shock made me cry my eyes out; letters in the mail from Tiff, complete with her own tears, asking that I come and get her made me want to snap Klaus in half.

*In the animal kingdom, a mother will kill to protect her children.*

I prepared to hop on the next plane to bring my children home. First, I called Tiff – thankfully it was she who answered the phone as I had no intention of speaking to Klaus, nor his wife, as nice as she had seemed from past encounters. I told her not to worry, and to not warn her father I was coming.

To my immeasurable relief, Tiff sounded fine, happy to hear my voice. Then, in what hit like another shock blast, she proceeded to tell me about an amusement park with water slides, asking me to send money for goggles. She wanted to stay there, for now.

Confusion clouded my reasoning. I thought she was miserable and wanted to come home! I talked to Mo and she too sounded fine. But Mo was always the quiet one, relying on her older sister to take the lead.

Confronting Klaus was useless, since I still feared he would simply disappear with my children. His new bride was a young German girl, who I felt would likely be glad to live in Austria with him and the girls. My only hope was to tread lightly and "sneak" my children out from under his grip, in some sort of surprise attack. Maybe later the courts would have to get involved, but I worked hard to avoid dragging the girls through painful custody battles. In my heart of hearts, I knew even legal tactics wouldn't work with Klaus. Nothing would stop him!

My strength came from the resolution that Tiff and Mo's happiness was my first priority. As such, I decided to wait a short while to see what developed.

Tiff and I talked on the phone regularly, and she loved writing me letters. I became more content, knowing they were both happy. Before long, I sent for them to come for a visit.

I picked them up from the airport, and was immediately showered in hugs and kisses. I distinctly noticed how pale they had gotten, no longer living in sunny California. As they got in the vehicle, they both exclaimed, "Oh mommy I love this car, because it smells like you!"

That moment was so telling, and so bittersweet, that it hurt – a lot. I pulled myself together and shared stories and laughter on the drive home. We had great fun, yet the sadness seeped back in, knowing they were soon leaving. I thought about asking them to stay with me, but I didn't want to add more confusion to their little minds.

As quickly as they had arrived, they were gone. I sought solace in the comfort of Billy's arms, where I spent much of my time crying. I missed them so much, and yet an answer to this very sad situation seemed unclear. I wondered at times, if there even was "an" answer.

In part, to compensate for my loneliness, I started designing again, throwing myself into my work. Several months later, the solution that had escaped me for so long had just materialized. I was talking to Tiff one day, when she told me that Klaus was thinking about moving back to California. The restaurant he had opened in Vail wasn't turning a good profit. Naturally, I was thrilled, and shortly thereafter, they moved back to San Pedro, California.

Tiff and Mo had a new baby sister, and I knew Tiff felt responsible for the little one. I designed a tiny, suede baby outfit for their new daughter, and personally delivered it. It was my way of showing that all I wanted was for everyone to get along, for the children's sake.

Klaus enrolled them in school almost immediately, and I suddenly became a weekend parent. We did a lot of fun things together, including taking outings to shopping malls, purchasing things the girls needed and wanted. Even though our time was reserved only for weekends, it became quality time for us all, as every moment was filled with love.

I believe to this day that my attitude is the ONLY thing that made this arrangement work. Although Klaus meant what he said in court about taking my children away, I never let this affect my dynamic with them.

When I drove them back at the end of the weekend, no one ever came out to say hello. Sometimes, I thought I saw a curtain move ever so slightly. I did notice my girls looking nervously at the house, each time I pulled into their driveway. I would always ask if everything was ok and they always responded with a "Yes."

Over time, Tiff and Mo became quieter towards me, making excuses why I couldn't pick them up on a particular weekend. I was starting to sense rejection, and the pain, a frequent companion, came flooding back. I knew Tiff always liked the idea of having a "Leave It to Beaver" type of family, which I certainly wasn't able to provide. Still, I was the best mom, putting my children first out of love, and only love.

I often looked back, wondering if I should have taken Klaus to court for full custody of the girls. But I knew we would have suffered a far worse outcome, as the potential for Klaus to disappear to Austria was always a major concern. Amidst the difficulty of the situation, I acted in the very best way I could.

*There are no wrong decisions. There are only lessons in this lifetime.*

I was seeing the girls less and less, as the excuses kept piling on. Finally, I just had enough, telling Tiff and Mo that my door would always remain open for them. If they wanted to see me, all they had to do was call and I would come pick them up.

I felt as if Klaus had succeeded in completely breaking me. I had done everything possible to keep my children in my life, so much so that more often than not, I felt I was dealing with the devil.

My mom was angry with me for telling the girls what I did. But it's hard to walk in another person's shoes; in fact, it's impossible. All the while, my children were innocent victims. God only knows what was brainwashed into their trusting little minds.

The beautiful thing about life is no matter how difficult the path may be, it always takes us back to where we belong.

## 28 MY VERY OWN BOUTIQUE IN BELMONT SHORE AND SADLY, MY DIVORCE FROM BILLY

While driving through town, I noticed a "For Rent" sign on one of the shops. Everything about the storefront looked perfect: It was small, the name of the street was appropriate to my business (Park Avenue) and I liked the vibe in the area.

When I told Billy, he wasn't at all enthusiastic. First, I didn't have any business experience and second, a beach town in his opinion wasn't the best location to sell upscale, one-of-a-kind suede and leather designs. Although he raised good points, I ignored him. I knew, as in everything I had done up until this point, I could "learn on the job," so to speak. I had enough confidence in my creations to be able to adapt to my client base, and design suede bikinis and associated accessories as well.

I telephoned the landlord of the shop and struck a deal which I felt was fair and affordable. I already had enough stock to fill the small shop, so I signed! Billy helped me decorate and load up all my fashions, and together, we decided which pieces should be displayed where. Some of the designs were hung smartly on the walls and it looked simply amazing! I purchased a mannequin for the window and hired a company to build a green awning with my company name, "SHIRLIANI" on it – a combination of my first and middle name.

Gail was really excited for me, and offered to throw a Grand Opening party at my new shop. I was thrilled and thankful, and with everyone I knew invited, many of my friends would have the opportunity to meet one another for the very, first time.

Megsy invited her friend, "Dr. Ben Casey" from the 1960's television show. We all got a kick out of meeting him. I invited actress Judith Light, from "Who's The Boss" as she was both a friend and customer of mine. She actually chose to wear my designs on the cover and inside pages of the Orange County Magazine. I truly adored her for doing this, and had my new friend and "new" owner of the magazine to thank!

Although Judith had promised to attend the party, at the last minute something came up and she couldn't make it. She did send me a beautiful bouquet of flowers along with a lovely note. All in all, everyone enjoyed a fun evening and we ended by going to 555 Restaurant, an elegant venue in downtown Long Beach.

As I rightly predicted, it didn't take long for me to teach myself all about business, even arranging for credit card transactions. Everything was truly taking off now, and the store attracted many curious pairs of eyes, as my fashions really made their mark. I was receiving several new custom orders, and was also selling fashions off the racks.

Surprisingly, Klaus brought the girls over to see me one day, having heard about my shop opening. He commented, "Good job! It's nice to see you're not a loser after all!" I believe he thought he paid me a compliment. But putting his words aside, it was wonderful to see my children – albeit for only a few, short hours. And I felt the loss again, stronger than I had in awhile.

The store made me busier than ever, and Billy was really missing me at home. We weren't getting along much of the time anyway, as I was becoming extremely irritated with him. What made it hard was that I loved him; yet, was well aware that I was basically at the end of my rope, period!

My anger towards Billy began to spill over and, one day, the rope let go, with me screaming that I was filing for a divorce. It was the very thing I had promised I would never do. All I heard from him was, "No way!" With my words tearing him up inside, he left to stay with Lewis, in the valley.

I asked Megsy to get some simple do-it-yourself divorce papers, as she was working for an attorney part-time, while still attending school. With some hesitation, she brought them to me. I completed them promptly and mailed them to Billy, for his signature. He was fuming and refused to sign them, throwing the document in a drawer and forgetting about its existence.

A short, while later, Billy called me again, asking if he could come home.

The truth is I always missed him when he was away. But there was a definitive pattern to his behavior: He would come home and I'd be happy for a few days, then the pattern of "misery" would start all over again. Lying around and smoking pot whenever he could get his hands on it, he would start complaining about his life and about Hollywood. What mainly depressed him was that his own scripts weren't selling, and he felt several had simply been ripped off.

Billy became what I would call a "dead weight." After awhile, he would succeed in bringing me down with him, at a time when I was fighting to stay happy myself in the absence of my children. On the flip side, we had many amazing moments together, but now, the "being together" was precisely what was making things worse! When I realized this, I knew there was nothing else I could have possibly done to help save our marriage.

On the heels of yet another fight, I became determined to get Billy to sign the divorce papers. With a second copy ready for him to sign, I purposely became as obnoxious as possible, screaming about everything under the sun. Amidst the verbal diarrhea, I also screamed at him to sign the divorce papers. With me holding them directly up in his face, one fraction of time found him weak, and he signed the papers – and left.

Unexpectedly, I myself felt as if my life was spiraling out of control. I became depressed, very not "me," and honestly, don't know what I would have done if not for the comfort of my dear friends.

Linda and Megsy remained there for me, as always. They, along with my mom, tried to offer me solace, with reminders that one day, I WILL have my girls back when they are of the age to leave their present home. My response was always the same, telling them that although I was well aware of all this, it didn't serve as medicine for the pain and despair I was feeling NOW. Even Billy reminded me over and over that my girls would be back with me before long.

Billy and I had been through A LOT over the years, and, amongst other things, he served as my trusted security blanket. With him gone, I felt – for the first time in a long while – alone. We shared the craziest love, and, despite our divorce firmly in the works, he never stopped calling to tell me how much he loved and missed me – never.

Billy often went to Hawaii for what he referred to as "getting well." While there, he stayed at Uncle Bob's, a dear friend of his, dined only on tuna and regularly worked out on the beach. Upon returning home, he always felt better. During any "down time," he was on the phone with me. I honestly don't remember when our divorce became final, because we were still participating in our old patterns of "getting back together and leaving again!"

My business managed to do very well over the course of the year I ran the shop and I even hired help. I myself, however, was in a place of confusion, in the absence of my kids. And in this headspace was when Billy asked me to move to Hawaii with him.

This move had always been a dream of his, as his dad owned several acres of property on Kona. Billy used to promise he would build a house there for us someday. Accepting this as yet another, new phase in my life, I closed my shop and planned for my move. "555" was the place where my initial celebration began, as a shop owner, and in spiritual terms, 555 means "a major change is upon you."

And indeed, it was.

# 29 I WAS MOVING TO HAWAII UNTIL...GEEZ!

The year was 1988. I rarely saw my girls now but knew they would come visit me in Hawaii. So, with my shop officially closed, I agreed to move to Kona with Billy, and marry him for the second time!

I surprised Tiff and Mo not long before, with a trip to Maui. The three of us had a fabulous time, basking in the sun and enjoying private tours of the islands with our guide, Kimo. He definitely outdid his hospitality, taking us on a free, scuba diving trip, and we maintained a friendship even after returning home.

Once again, the prospect of having me back in his life on a permanent basis made Billy over-the-top excited. He rented a U-Haul and moved my industrial sewing machine, fashions and all my personal belongings to Lewis's house. When we were done, I surveyed what used to be his living room and realized that every, last bit of space was filled with my "stuff!" The plan was to live at Lewis's until Billy earned enough money for our move to Hawaii. Honestly, this sounded like a much, simpler life, and exactly what I needed right now. As I settled in, I didn't do any designing, but did go on several cattle calls, to see if I could pick up some acting work.

Lewis owned a ranch in the desert, which he said we could use for a little fun. We were also welcome to ride his quads. When I was suddenly surprised with a visit from my daughters, we took them, a couple of their friends and Lewis's 15 year-old son up to the ranch for the weekend.

The kids absolutely loved it, having great fun riding the quads and partaking in other enjoyable activities. At sundown, Billy suggested we go for a quick, romantic ride through the desert. Following him close behind, away we went. Billy knew the desert well, having been out here many times before. He would warn me when little hills would come up, advising that I step on the gas. A considerably bigger one appeared in my sight line, and I saw Billy as he steered around it. But I, myself, judged wrong.

Billy had stopped his quad, preparing to give me instructions, but it was too late. Being no quad expert, I had wrongly given it full gas. The last thing I saw was the look of horror on Billy's face as he screamed, "Noooo!"

Time both sped up, and stopped, at that moment. Smack in the middle of the steep hill, I flew backwards off the quad, only to have the 500 pound machine follow, bouncing off my chest and knocking the wind out of me.

Billy was hovering above me. Beside me, grazing my left side was a long, sharp piece of iron, sticking straight out of the ground like a sword. On my right side touching me were several old, beer bottles, the broken glass extending three to four inches upwards. This was truly a miracle! I was so exactly and perfectly placed, I had survived what likely would have been a gruesome death. Once again, the grim reaper passed me by.

I sat there for at least 15 minutes, trying to get my breath back. I felt weak, dizzy and without a doubt, "all shook up." And yet, I was otherwise unharmed. Billy had his arms around me, whimpering like a baby and feeling totally responsible for what had happened.

Wanting to get back to my kids, I pulled myself together; just enough to ride the quad slowly back to the house. We casually mentioned my mishap but made light of the incident. Later that evening while lying in bed, Billy was still extremely concerned for my well-being. He worried I might have suffered some internal damage, due to the weight of the machine pounding on me. Always the optimist, I assured him I was fine. Nonetheless, Billy barely slept, choosing instead to watch over me, "just in case." Looking back, I should have gone to the hospital, but unless there was obvious, physical damage, it wasn't really something that was commonplace. And, my immediate concern was for my children, as I didn't want them to be frightened and have our precious time together ruined.

The next day we left, with me very sore; very grateful and more than a little humbled.

There are guides and guardian angels that are always watching over us. I was very blessed on this day, knowing it was not my time to go.

When Megsy finished school, as I was still moving to Hawaii, she decided to go back home to Sacramento to work for her dad. Fortunately, we always kept in touch. Yet, one month had gone by, and Billy still hadn't made enough money for us to move. Both of us were spending most of our time lying around the poolside at Lewis's, and I was getting restless. I wasn't exactly sure when we were leaving, but I hoped it would be soon. Maybe this was good prep for my "chill out" life in Hawaii, but I wasn't thrilled with so much leisure time. Even when I moved, I still planned on designing fashions.

Lewis's son and I were chatting one night when it was mentioned that Billy had dated a girl for about two weeks, after we had split up. I had no reason to be bothered as I was the one who had filed for a divorce. The kid kept running off his mouth, offering further details, including something that DID bother me: Billy, whose biggest gift to me in all the years we were together must have cost $20, actually bought this girl a keyboard! What an expensive birthday gift (for him) – all for a two-week relationship? I hit the ceiling.

Our relationship and marriage was neither based, nor dependent, on money. But what royally pissed me off was not knowing what in the world Mr. Thrifty's motivation was, in spending so much money on someone he barely knew. Excuse me, but wasn't he, all the while, trying to get back together with ME?

I couldn't contain myself, and stomped into the other room to demand answers and to chew him out. The kid grinned as I walked past, looking like the cat that just swallowed the mouse. Needless to say, we got into a MAJOR fight. I told a dumbfounded Billy (who honestly couldn't figure out why I was so damn mad) I wasn't moving to Hawaii with him. In fact, I emphasized, I wouldn't be moving ANYWHERE with him. The more stupid he acted, the angrier I became until suddenly I blasted I was leaving immediately to find myself a little apartment back in Belmont Shore.

Billy couldn't listen to my out-of-control ranting anymore, and left to buy some beer and wine. He was going to get drunk – meaning I had to get out of there – and quick. If I didn't, I'd be in for some seriously, obnoxious behavior and, as he knew what I was planning, who knows where this would have led?

Minutes later, the phone rang. I picked it up, thinking it might be Megsy or Linda returning my calls.

"Hello?" I said.

I must have sounded really sad, as the voice on the other end of the phone responded, "Honey, what's wrong?" I explained I was leaving Billy, as we had gotten into it again.

"Awww honey, do you want to come up here to my place and talk about it?"

"Yes!" I answered emphatically.

Christian Brando's invitation couldn't have come at a better time.

# 30 CHRISTIAN BRANDO AND ME

In a matter of minutes, I was on my way to Christian's place, not wanting to run into Billy when he came home. I knew he wouldn't know where to find me, so this seemed to be a good choice. When I arrived, some of his "Down Boys" were playing pool, so he took me to his bedroom for privacy, and for a chat. We hugged and talked, with Christian being very sympathetic. He, too, was familiar with some of Billy's irritating ways so it didn't take convincing for him to know why I was this furious.

We had a slight attraction to one another – it was obvious to us both – but were aware of "the line" and up until this point, had never crossed it. Billy and Christian were like brothers, so everything in that area was "off limits." By this time, the Down Boys had left and we were totally alone. I dreaded the thought of going back to Lewis's, as I knew I would be met with Billy's drunken belligerence.

Christian sensed my apprehension, and asked if I wanted to stay the night. As there was only one bed in his small house, we talked openly about ensuring that nothing physical would happen between us. Christian thought Billy might literally try to kill him. Yet, while sitting on the living room floor, sipping the cocktail Christian had prepared for me, the topic of sex inevitably came up again. This led to a kiss. Christian wasn't comfortable. He knew Billy had a gun collection and might use it, if...

Yet, a short while later, both "nature" and "nurture" relocated us to the bedroom. Both fully clothed, we lay down on his bed, wrapped in one another's arms. The attraction between us sparked and arced, and without further thought, we made love. It was very exciting as Christian's passion was intense.

Right afterwards, reality slapped us in the face, with Christian insisting we both get dressed. Billy could drop by at any moment (as he often did) and the last thing he could see was us – not only having crossed the line, but sprinting far away from it! Christian's house was located on Wonderland Avenue, at the very top of the hill, and because it was so secluded it was never locked. I told him to lock all the doors, but the entrance from the outside to the kitchen was broken.

Not long after, I sensed round #2 was on its way, and we made love again. Then as before, I grabbed my clothes, but just as I was almost all dressed, we looked up and saw Billy standing in the doorway! We were completely numb; personally, I couldn't believe what I was witnessing.

Billy, drunk as I had predicted, muttered, "I'll be back."

Words tumbled out of my mouth, attempting to erase what he had seen. However, my pleas that nothing had happened were in complete contrast to evidence lying on the floor – proof that spoke louder than words.

Billy walked out.

The horror of our predicament left us shaking and terrified. We spoke about what to do; what to say; what NOT to do, and then it hit me: The safest thing would be to return to Lewis's and talk to Billy. Christian thought this might be too dangerous but I insisted, knowing that we couldn't live in fear indefinitely.

Thankfully, by the time I arrived back home, Billy was still there. I figured I would try to calm him down, but was met with hour after hour of pure hell. There was NO talking to him and as I pretended to sleep, Billy screamed at me, calling me all sorts of names in-between hurling cruel insults. Finally, liquor and exhaustion got the better of him, and he passed out on the couch in the wee hours of the morning.

With virtually no sleep at all, and yet needing to stick with my original plan, I called Megsy, recounting what had just happened the night before. Megsy told me to leave immediately and stay in her apartment in Long Beach. She had an extra month's rent paid up, so hurriedly, I gathered a few things before I left.

I called Christian to let him know I was safe, and that I was driving back to Long Beach. He too, was up all night with worry and fear, and now, felt more than ever Billy would return to his house to kill him. Christian asked if he could come with me to Megsy's and for the next month, we stayed together in her apartment.

Christian wanted to rent a place in Los Angeles, to act as a hideaway for us, but by this time I had already found a small apartment in Long Beach. Although he and I were together as a couple, he couldn't help but keep looking over his shoulder, in case Billy approached us, payback on his mind. The little coke that we did now and again also served to fuel Christian's paranoia. He would point to the big tree outside the bedroom window of my new apartment, swearing that Billy was perched on one of its branches. Although I was sworn to silence during these times and giggling, thought this to be ridiculous, his seriousness had me almost convinced that we were being stalked.

With most of my belongings left at Lewis's house, I called to ask whether Billy had tossed everything. Fortunately he had not, and in his kind way, Lewis suggested I come by whenever I wished to pick everything up. Not long after I met a moving company there, hoping not to run into Billy. I knew he would never physically hurt me but I didn't want a repeat of the drama that I had experienced the last time we were face-to-face.

As fate would have it, Billy was sitting on the sofa when I arrived, but he was calm; saddened. I could barely look at him as my things were loaded. With only a few words spoken, I left.

Christian's new apartment in Los Angeles was near one of his favorite restaurants, Musso and Franks. Although he still exhibited paranoia in relation to the "Billy situation," he really wanted to take me there. We dressed up to the hilt one night and went. Management and staff catered to us, and with Christian ordering much, more food than we would actually eat, dish after dish was brought to the table. I ate my share but Christian only sampled the plates, barely eating a full portion of food. I wanted to take the leftovers with us, but he wouldn't take anything home.

Christian and I shared many deep and personal talks. In what went beyond trust, he opened up to me. He revealed hippies kidnapped him when he was a young boy. He told me in detail about the horrible custody fight between his dad and his mom, actress Anna Kashfi, with his father finally being awarded custody. He learned his mom would put booze in his baby bottle, in order that he would fall asleep. He swore he saw his dad levitate, and believed he wasn't of this planet. There were many, more stories like these, and it became clear that Christian suffered from a very, traumatic childhood. My heart, connecting to him as a result of my own emotional predicaments, hurt for his suffering.

I was late! Amidst all the bonding time with Christian, I missed my period – in fact, I was three weeks late! I was NEVER late! I shared this news with Christian. Could it be true? Perhaps I was chosen to carry on the legend of the great Brando!

Christian became elated, his joy spilling onto me. He had been told it was unlikely he could father a child, due to a low sperm count. I was 42, not the optimal age to conceive. And yet...perhaps this was a miracle child. For the next week, I daydreamed about all the worlds my little Brando might experience. Would "he" inherit the talent and greatness of his grandfather? Would "she" have both her mother's charming dimples and father's intense gaze? The possibilities were endless!

The morning arrived for me to take a pregnancy test when suddenly, my period started. Teary-eyed, we knew it was not meant to be!

Throughout the course of our relationship, we took turns staying at either Christian's apartment or mine. Sometimes we went back to his house. Billy never did find us but of course, knew we were together, and the rumor was he never stopped looking for us.

One day, while at Christian's apartment, we had done some coke, and a temper I hadn't seen from him before was unleashed. Suddenly he started kicking his television set, breaking it into bits as he talked about his mother, and about abandonment. He turned to me, and while his Rottweiler glared at me face-to-face, threatened that the big, black dog would chew me up in a minute, if he gave the command. I had no idea where this sudden meanness was stemming from. He even invited one of his scruffy friends over. And then – Christian disappeared.

With his friend showing up shortly thereafter, I again started feeling uneasy, as the guy began to hit on me. I called for Christian, but he was nowhere to be found. Running through the apartment with his friend following, shocked, I stopped in my tracks: Christian was huddled in the empty bathtub. Fear crept along the entire length of my body, and, grabbing my purse, dashed out of his place towards my car, which was parked in a secure parking area.

Suddenly I realized I was trapped, as I didn't have the garage buzzer to exit the complex. Locking my doors, I sat on the horn, praying someone would show up and let me out. Someone did approach the driver's side door – Christian himself.

I refused to open the window and through the glass, saw him mouth the words, "I'm sorry, honey." Speaking louder, he pleaded with me to come back inside. I didn't budge, and while still blaring my car horn, with a forlorn expression on his face, he reluctantly buzzed me out.

By the time I had gotten home, 10 minutes of messages were flashing on my answering machine. They were all from Christian, telling me he would never hurt me; that he would deliver the moon, if he could. He apologized over and over, expressing his love for me and asking for forgiveness.

Although his demonstration of affection was very touching, I couldn't go back. And after about a year, this wild, exciting and tumultuous union between Christian and me ended. As friends however, we continued to remain in touch.

Christian reflected the same, intense complexities as his father. In fact, his passion reminded me of Marlon's famous movie, "A Streetcar Named Desire."

# 31 TRYING TO ESTABLISH NORMALITY AGAIN, SPENDING TIME WITH FRIENDS; AND I MET JON BON JOVI

I was getting used to my new apartment, while catching up with friends I hadn't seen in awhile. I was also enjoying some "alone" time, something I hadn't had much of, either.

Megsy flew me to Sacramento often, as we really missed one another. We also enjoyed attending several concerts, including seeing Elton John, Ricky Martin and the Rolling Stones. Once, we were even invited to the Stones after party, so life was filled with light and fun again. We took several trips to Tahoe together, she, being the very, best friend I could have ever wished for. Honestly, I don't know what I would have done without her in my life. Always so cool, always sweet and positive – keeping my spirits up, and absolutely beyond generous in every, single way – that's MY Megsy!

By no coincidence, Megsy and my son Stevie, (whom I gave birth to at age 16) were both born in the same year, both in practically the same location in northern California AND only one day apart. I only realized this a few years ago.

I even started designing again, albeit just a little. During the entire time I was with Christian, I didn't design one piece of clothing. All this helped to establish some much-needed normality in my life, while generating some revenue, as money was getting scarce.

Megsy was dating a British guy who worked for famous rock groups. As his work took him around the world, she traveled with him as often as possible. One night she asked if I wanted to see the Scorpions, as they were performing in Irvine. Her German friend, Oli (whom I had never met) would be meeting me there. It sounded like fun so I agreed.

Oli was responsible for managing the stage lighting during the performance. I wore my own custom, skin-tight black leather design that evening, and managed to go backstage before the show, courtesy of Oli.

Out of the corner of my eye, I saw Bon Jovi. I smiled at him, remembering that he was the one Megsy had a crush on. He sent a big smile my way, and shortly after, introduced himself simply as "Jon," something that I thought was cute as he was the REAL Bon Jovi! I didn't know at the time his actual name was in fact, Jon Bon Jovi. His name may as well be translated into A-D-O-R-A-B-L-E, as he most certainly was!

Just before show time, Oli had me sit with him in the lighting booth area. I looked around, spotting Jon sitting a little behind me, smiling at me once again. It was obvious he pointed me out to his manager, and his little display of flirting, as well as some conversation really made my night!

I had a lot of fun that evening, and Oli invited me for more of the same the following night, too.

I also met a new friend, a beautiful, young girl with long blond hair down to her bottom, who worked in a boutique on 2nd Street. Genevieve Chappell was about five years older than Tiff, and I knew this small "connection" to my girls made me want to help her, as she was in need of some assistance. We exchanged phone numbers and indeed, she called the next day.

Genevieve explained her roommates were treating her in an awful manner, and asked if I could pick her up, as she didn't own a car. I did, and she spent the night on my couch, after I cooked us a lovely dinner.

The following day, I drove her home to Seal Beach, meeting her family in the process. Her mother was younger than me and combined with her four, younger siblings, the entire family looked like Barbie Dolls. Genevieve felt responsible for her family, and seemed much older than her biological age. Occasionally we would go for dinner and hang out, with me taking the opportunity to bring little goodies for her siblings whenever I could.

I also hung out with a male friend of mine, John Burton, a painter who helped with tasks through the years. During the movies we attended together, or the happy hour drinks we shared, he would remind me he had a crush on me. I just smiled at his sweet confessions, telling him that friends are forever, but boyfriends are usually temporary.

I was feeling a little down one weekend and John invited me to go to Vegas with him and three friends. It was during the Super Bowl weekend, and on the spur of the moment, I said yes. We had great fun – and I was learning that spontaneous, "no strings attached" pleasure was good for the soul!

Marti Klarin was another great friend of mine who owned "Another Nail Place" in Huntington Beach. I met her years ago through Linda, and we traded services – her doing my nails and hair in exchange for being given some of my designs. She was extremely sweet and generous, rarely taking anything from me but insisting, nonetheless, on taking care of my beauty needs. I set up monthly appointments, and during my visits, entertained all her clients with my outrageous stories. Her salon felt like a home away from home. Honored, I gave her permission to use my photograph in an advertisement for her business.

Several times, Marti held events in her shop, just so I could show my fashions. Happily married, she still fell in love with Billy, wishing for "one night of sin" with him! At least we were forthright in laughing about this fantasy of hers!

I sent for my mom to come visit for a few days, and I enjoyed spoiling her in every way that I could. I took her to her favorite Italian and Mexican restaurants, went shopping together and mainly, shared a lot of catching up. I took her to meet Marti, and as she too, adored my "momsy," treated her to both nail and eyebrow "do-overs," two most important beauty upkeep rituals for my mom.

Afterwards, I took her to meet Linda, something that was long overdue, given our years of friendship. After meeting her, Linda shared that she understood me even more deeply.

Back at home, it was becoming obvious I no longer had a boyfriend. The owner of my apartment complex, who lived in a big house in front of the building, started constantly hitting on me. It made me very uncomfortable, and I kept an eye open for a new place to move. Fortunately, I ran into some old friends and learned they were renting out their small two-bedroom house in Belmont Shore. I jumped at the opportunity and moved one month later. Actually, this worked out better in the long run because maybe – just maybe – my girls could spend some nights with me. Like the tide, which was so much a part of my daily landscape, so was my missing them – some days more, some days a little less, but all days I felt the hurt.

# 32 CHRISTIAN SHOT HIS SISTER'S TAHITIAN BOYFRIEND

It was 1990. Not long after I moved into my new place, Christian Brando shot and killed his sister, Cheyenne's Tahitian boyfriend. I was stunned, but the sound of the phone ringing off the hook startled me back into the dreaded reality of what I had just heard on the news. Yes, Christian had a bad temper, but I never thought in my wildest dreams he would ever shoot anyone!

ABC News asked if they could interview me. I agreed but didn't know anything about the shooting, as Christian and I had broke up three months before, and rarely spoke at all. I did know what a troubled soul he was, as he shared many personal stories about his life with me.

The newscaster showed up in 30 minutes, noticing I had several photos of Christian and me hanging on the walls. I love documenting cherished life's moments on film and also had a huge display of friends and fashion photos. The interview concluded, and along with it, my life suddenly turned upside down.

Money had pretty much run out, as I didn't put much energy into designing anymore. I knew this apathy had much to do with the absence of my children, of not moving to Hawaii with Billy, and the entire Christian affair. These elements seemed to stunt my interests and dam my creative juices, but Megsy would pull me out of the blues, claiming parts of me were just "on strike" and not on a permanent hiatus!

I also put my beloved Mercedes for sale in the Auto Trader, as I really needed the cash. Luckily, I didn't need to follow through with this, as the sale of some photos and a short story to Tony Brenna for British tabloids helped to put some cash in my pocket. Although I was very thankful for this, I still didn't know where I was going or what in the world I would do

123

next.

Although I was no superstar, I also considered posing for Playboy, as I knew they shot photos of celebrities in good taste, for their stories. As I had been a love interest of Christian's and as he was now in the spotlight, I thought they might be interested in me.

I was desperate and judging by what Susie had earned for her layout, knew they paid well. This cash reimbursement could be considerably higher if one made "Playmate of the Year" status. I could only imagine what they paid for a discrete celebrity shoot!

Always one to embrace diverse and unique opportunities in life, I mailed a couple of fully dressed, yet sexy photos of myself as part of an introduction to who I was. As I had hoped, I was contacted immediately and the request was made for me to attend an in-person meeting.

I drove to the Playboy offices in Los Angeles and was introduced to one of the magazine publishers. After we talked, I was told they were not interested in this sort of scandalous story. She did ask if I would be interested in getting a few test shots taken of me. I refused, remembering that Susie was paid approximately $10,000 for hers.

Penthouse did more risqué photos, but I could put my foot down if they were interested, agreeing to just a little "exposure" as well as insisting on a shoot in good taste. I did contact them, sending the same photos and introduction. Bob Guccione's secretary called me back right away and said they were very interested. I was offered a hefty amount over the phone but turned it down, telling them I would sign for no less than an undisclosed amount (one I cannot reveal due to stipulations in my contract).

I was asking for a lot of money, and was told Guccione would have to consider my request. In less than one hour his secretary called me back, and we did a little more negotiating. Eventually we agreed on a final figure, one that would annihilate all my financial woes.

I was extremely proud of myself, as the amount offered was in itself a lot of money by anyone's standards. But I held out for more, and got it. Plus, I negotiated that my photos were to be shot in good taste.

The following day a photographer was sent to my house, as Christian was the hot topic on the presses. He took a few test shots to basically make sure I had a decent enough body at 42 years of age. This also served to alleviate any concerns I might have had. Alan, the photographer, made me feel incredibly comfortable and I adored him for his laid-back attitude.

He left to show Bob Guccione the photos and soon, we were a go! The contract was signed and arrangements were made to photograph me for Penthouse Magazine.

A few days prior to all this, I drove up to the Los Angeles County Jail and visited Christian. Although he had refused many other visitors, he was very happy to see me, putting his hand up on the glass for us to "touch." I couldn't help but feel sorry for him. One word of what he had been accused of was never uttered, but rather, I wanted to be there as his friend and to show my caring towards him. I will never forget the shock on Christian's face as a result of what had gone down, and he barely spoke one word.

I always try to reserve judgment of a situation, as we occupy this human form to learn lessons, as traumatic as these might be. This particular lesson of Christian's could very well have been the most difficult experience he would ever face.

# 33 MY PENTHOUSE WHIRWIND

Along with appearing in the magazine, I also signed a one-year contract promoting Penthouse, making appearances on several television shows and radio stations.

I realize this "chapter" of my life might be a bit controversial; however I have never made any excuses for myself as I act on free will. Every single choice we make in this life, and every event we experience guides us to exactly where we are now. In my case, I live with no regrets and love where – and who – I am.

I knew my children would never see me in this magazine. However, I was prepared to discuss the photos with the girls if it ever came up when they were older. I hoped they would understand.

On the day of the photo shoot, I met Alan in the valley, so we could drive together to the specified location. As it were, temperatures hovered around 100 degrees (and higher), not making the outdoor portions of the shoot any easier.

We arrived at a huge mansion in Beverly Hills, the owner opening his home to us for the day. I brought my own leather fashions and was thrilled to be able to wear them in my photos. Penthouse agreed wholeheartedly with my wardrobe choice, and felt that my Indian designs would appeal to Marlon, Christian's father.

I was dressed and in full makeup, preparing for the day. Suddenly the air-conditioning broke, and the entire shoot was a mess. Not only was I sweating profusely, as was the rest of the crew, but my hair was wet and sticky from the rising temperatures. At this point, I was almost tempted to reveal everything that the Good Lord gave me! In-between powdering me and placing phone calls to get someone out to immediately repair the air conditioner, I wasn't a happy camper. We didn't have the time to wait several hours and as such, did the best we could.

Under normal circumstances, young Playboy and Penthouse models generally shoot in many different locations for at least a six month period, taking thousands of photos to land those perfect few for their layouts. Problem was, we needed to hit the press while the Brando story was big news, and so we had a mere, two days to complete the shoot.

The following day we worked at a different location, outside on a ranch. In some of the photos, I wore my favorite, white Indian leather fringe mini dress. In others, I wore a pink fringe leather jacket, with a small, sheer pink wrap, while riding on a beautiful white horse. The day was another scorcher, but being outdoors made it more tolerable. I had never ridden on a horse bareback, but thankfully, the owner was nearby to act as a support.

Apparently I didn't follow directions well enough, and the horse almost galloped me over a cliff! Later, when I was told to stand next to the horse for additional photos, I felt a mouth nibble at the fringe around my cleavage. I was in love with this four-legged comedian, his "horsing around" providing a welcome laugh for us all.

I was very happy when both days of shooting were behind me. Working with Penthouse staff was fabulous as they were extremely professional and accommodating. Other than the intense heat, it was an enjoyable experience.

Next, I flew to New York to meet with Bob Guccione and the writer who would write my story. While there, I was asked if I would appear on Geraldo. I feel I did very well, answering his questions as honestly as I could.

When I returned to California, I appeared on several other television shows, including Inside Edition, as well as many others via satellite. I was interviewed on a number of radio shows, too. Appearances such as these were all mandated in my contract, as I wouldn't receive final monies owing to me unless I fulfilled them.

At one point I was asked to go to Santa Monica and stay overnight at the Loews Hotel. A press conference was being held the following day and I was to appear at it. The press hurled question after question at me, but I remained my cool and calm self. The questions were the same ones asked over and over, yet the answers were always the same: I knew nothing of the shooting!

Dane, my press manager was fabulous, staying by my side at all times. He even accompanied me on several of my appearances. After the press conference had finally winded down, we celebrated with an elaborate dinner.

Over dinner, Dane observed, "Shirley, I see you really enjoyed your mini bar in the room." I corrected him, saying that I actually didn't drink or eat anything at all from it. However, as it was fully stocked and I didn't want to waste all the goodies, I packed them in my luggage. He, along with everyone else found this to be hilarious, but I didn't understand what was so very funny. As I had never seen a mini bar in a hotel, this must have been the time when hotels just started adding these luxuries to their rooms. How generous of them, I thought.

In the nicest of ways, Dane informed me that all items in the mini bar were "for purchase," thus, there would be a bill generated for each and every item I so meticulously packed! In yet another "brush" with death, (I almost died from embarrassment,) I let him know I was going to put everything back immediately. He wouldn't hear of it, and I was graced with a bunch of treats to enjoy when I got home.

Once again, all my friends were extremely supportive of me, and were very excited to see my photos and read my story when the magazine eventually hit the newsstands. I actually didn't like the photos at all, but I had to deal with it. I also found myself autographing hundreds of copies for friends and other interested parties.

In line with how I have always lived my life, I told the truth about the passionate love affair Christian and I shared, as this tragic event – and its repercussions – happened a mere three months after we broke up. The media attempted to portray my actions as being potentially harmful to

Christian's defense, but this was ridiculous. How could I possibly hurt him as I wasn't there; nor did I know anything about it. The media also tried to claim I was still married to Billy during my relationship with Christian. Wrong. My story was nowhere near as scandalous as it was being portrayed. But media will always be media, and sensationalism sells.

In another testament to my character, before my actual interview and shoot, I wrote to Christian in jail, asking him what he thought of me being in Penthouse and of me recounting our time together. Having been friends for seven years, I thought this showed great respect and integrity on my part.

Needless to say, I greatly honor human life, period. What happened here was truly tragic.

In the end, the Penthouse piece was done. And Christian never responded.

## 34 CHRISTIAN BRANDO'S CIRCUS TRIAL

In a classic case of life imitating art, the film in which I played Christian's girlfriend and he, the killer, came to pass. Marlon blocked the Italian Twentieth Century Fox film from showing in the U.S. as originally intended, since his son was facing murder charges in real life. Publicity like this would have been detrimental, however the film did make the rounds all over Europe.

I was served with a subpoena by the District Attorney to appear at Christian's trial. I had no idea why, as I wasn't a witness to anything. Later I learned the reason: The DA was desperate for witnesses, as Cheyenne herself wasn't able to attend the trial, since she was in a mental institution in Tahiti. She wasn't stable and not long after, Cheyenne Brando hung herself.

Months before the shooting, I had met Cheyenne for the second time, this time as a young adult. She and her boyfriend, Dag, were visiting and dropped by Christian's house. Dag seemed very nice and laid back, typical Tahitian style. As they came only to pick up a helmet, our meeting was brief.

It was said that Dag had been physically abusing Cheyenne while she was pregnant with their child. Cheyenne told Christian and understandably, he got extremely angry. One night he went over to his dad's house and found Dag watching television. Christian walked over to confront him, a few argumentative words were exchanged, and then Christian fired the gun.

I took my friend, Genevieve, to court with me the first time, as I didn't want to go alone. I figured correctly that Billy and Christian's ex-girlfriend would be present, and I was definitely not winning any awards for being their favorite person in the room.

Paparazzi surrounded me, blinding me with flash after flash as they continuously snapped photos, even though the Penthouse issue I was featured in wasn't even published at the time of the trial. The press must have assumed I was somebody, for as soon as Christian's brother, Miko, saw me, he came up and hugged me.

Marlon attended each moment of the trial. His face registered pain, yet he looked at no one. This was not your typical court case; this had the feel of a circus.

One person who DID look at me, and in fact, couldn't take his eyes off me was Billy. He was hanging out with Christian's ex-girlfriend since we all knew each other, and had all been friends. Even though she and Christian had long since broken up as their relationship was very volatile, she couldn't stand me now.

The trial kept getting prolonged, yet I had to show up each time, not knowing whether or not the DA would want to talk to me. As things turned out, he never did.

I became friends with the big, wild-haired paparazzi who earned his fame as a result of his helicopter spying. We had lunch at the same table and, at one point, he took a portable phone out from his pocket. I had never seen a "cellular" phone before and he let me use it. I loved this little device and we ended up exchanging numbers.

A French friend of mine, Emmanuelle, accompanied me to court the next day. We arrived late and the seating on Christian's side of the courtroom was filled. We sat on the opposite side, with all of Dag's French

Tahitian family members. It felt so very sad; so senseless.

As Emmanuelle and I walked out of the courtroom, I saw Christian's ex-girlfriend scurrying to get near me. She was acting a bit whacko, but my friend assured me she would act as my protector, if need be.

Suddenly I heard her shout, "Wipe that powder off your face!" What a bizarre remark, I thought. Wondering if my makeup might have been smeared, I asked Emmanuelle if I needed to touch anything up. Laughing, she replied the comment wasn't about cosmetics, but "coke."

It didn't take Mr. Paparazzi long to call me, but it wasn't for the reason I was thinking. Instead, he asked me for photos of Christian. I sold him one, to the tune of five figures. He then asked me out, but I had no interest in dating him.

It was very painful seeing Billy at the trial, and worse, we never spoke a word to one another. Eventually, I wasn't required to attend in person and watched the proceedings on television, along with everyone else.

I recall an experience we had in Italy, which gave me the creeps. The producer took us to the actual cell of the killer. It left both Billy's and Christian's skin crawling, saying they could never survive such a claustrophobic confinement.

The trial concluded with Christian's conviction, and sentencing was set at 10 years in prison. I wondered if he would survive his incarceration. He did, and in the end, served only half of his time.

# 35 A MINI BREAKDOWN; SURPRISINGLY IT WASN'T MAJOR!

For now, my financial problems were over and with it, any interest in designing. I knew my talent would never disappear, but the interest just wasn't there. I started going out to nightclubs with my friend, Heidi that moved in next door, and even began to date a little.

On one such night I met a guy named Robert, who looked a lot like Yanni, the musician. Immediately, he wanted me to go to Mexico with him for the weekend. Both Linda and Megsy were concerned for my welfare, and insisted I take down his personal information as listed on his driver's license. Admittedly, he was a little rough around the edges.

With everything transcribed, we drove my Mercedes (rather than his Corvette) towards the Mexican border. It was a fun yet strange weekend, with us dancing the nights away in smoke-filled discos and eating at authentic local restaurants. At one point, Robert became jealous, accusing me of playing footsies with a young Mexican boy sitting across our table. I couldn't have reached his foot if he stuck it out and tried to trip me with it! Robert suddenly left the club, and shocked, I followed him in disbelief. Before that, at dinner, he purposely faced me towards the wall in order that I couldn't look at anyone else other than him. I don't know why I didn't take this as a more serious sign but I probably chose not to.

I returned home safely, albeit with a massive hangover, and as fast as he entered my life he disappeared for awhile, which was fine with me.

Not long after, I started seeing Bernie, a very, wealthy man from Beverly Hills whom I had met once at a party in Los Angeles. I wasn't particularly attracted to him but I thought I might be able to learn to love him. He was extremely kind and enjoyed taking me to the finest restaurants in Beverly Hills. Everyone seemed to know and greatly respect him. He insisted we go shopping and bought me high-end tailored suits, as these fashions were most "suited" to his lifestyle versus the suede and leathers I enjoyed wearing.

During Christmastime, he invited me to his family's home in Brentwood, an enormous mansion right out of the movies. His mother, another character off the big screen welcomed me graciously.

"I would show you the grounds, but it's too dark out there now."

Definitely "old" money, I thought.

Relatives from all over the world arrived at the mansion. With all the embraces and warm wishes, I should have fit right in. The only problem was my heart wasn't in it so I knew I didn't belong.

Bernie showed me just how much he liked me, by offering to move my mom here from Denver, in order that she be closer to me. Although he was attractive and likeable enough, what was MOST attractive about him was his potential ability to help get my daughters back into my life. I couldn't help think that if I was to become his "Missus," I would by default, be filthy rich and that would act as just the right ammunition to fight Klaus, once and for all.

In the end, I couldn't follow through with this plan. I wasn't in love with him and thus, ended the relationship.

I was a strong woman. No matter how much I fantasized, I could never allow a man I didn't love to act as a solution to my problems.

I received my final payment from Penthouse, which luckily, would carry me over for a few years. I splurged on a new southwestern bedroom set, but smartly saved most of it to live on. I took Genevieve to Hawaii for a few days, as I needed to get away, and enjoyed seeing her travel on an airplane – her first, time ever.

One day, after the region had a minor earthquake, I received a call from Billy. No matter what, he always worried about me. Honestly, it was great to hear his voice, and we both confessed we missed one another. Billy came over the very next day.

We barely spoke of Christian. He did complement me on my Penthouse photos but said he could never read the accompanying story. Together, we agreed to take things one day at a time, yet in a matter of a few weeks, I asked him to leave once again. He did, with regret.

We both agreed that as an "us," things weren't working well. There wasn't any fighting; it wasn't anything even specific. I myself just wasn't happy, as I was searching for a new and completely different journey. But as soul mates we remained very close, this giving us both comfort.

On Mother's Day, my mom came out for a visit. For years, she expressed a wish that all her children and grandchildren be together at the same time. So with some planning from siblings, we arranged to meet for brunch at a seaside restaurant in Long Beach. Temperatures were hot that day, and I wore a cute pink mini dress, albeit a little low cut, but mom gave her approval.

I'm not one to attach specific attributes to clothes. Either they look good, making the wearer happy and confident, or they don't. Looking back, perhaps my choice of attire wasn't the most appropriate for a Mother's Day celebration but I wore it because it made me feel happy and light. After all, this was supposed to be a joyous occasion!

What really lead to my excitement was that I learned my younger half sister was picking up Tiff and Mo, and would be bringing them to our brunch.

At some point through the years, unbeknown to me at the time, she had become best friends with Klaus's wife. I wasn't privy to this information as we were never close. Besides, she wasn't the focus that day: my kids and my mom were.

It had been quite a long time since I saw my children and I COULD NOT WAIT! Excited with anticipation, I planned on bringing them back to my house after brunch so I could show them where I lived, having the second bedroom they could use while staying over. Hopefully this would be the start of regular get-togethers once again and with those thoughts, my mom and I drove to the restaurant.

We arrived and immediately saw Tiff and Mo walking up. I smiled from ear to ear and went over to hug them. Tiff was seated next to me and I couldn't stop chatting with both my children, I had missed them so much. My mother was seated on my other side, and our "reunion" was going wonderfully well.

Also present were my other half siblings and their children. With me being remembered as my mother's favorite child, along with judgments on the "wild" life I lived, jealousy and contempt reared their ugly heads. We may as well have been sitting on opposite sides of the ocean for all the closeness I felt both towards and from them. At various points over the years I did try and reach out, but our communications were short-lived. Eventually I wrote them all off. Family isn't just comprised of blood relatives, and in my case, my family included all those who loved me unconditionally.

*"People are not disturbed by things, but the view they take of things." ~ Philosopher Epictetus (AD55-135)*

*"If you look closely, you will find that by far the greater part of any unhappiness in you is created NOT by the situations, but by what your mind is saying about them. It's created by the self talk in your head. How to end it? Meet situations and people without judgment. Give your fullest attention to the present "moment" without mentally labeling it. This is a new state of consciousness that frees your mind from its old conditioning. This new consciousness will give rise to a new world." ~ Eckhart Tolle*

Some guy who likely consumed a little too much alcohol was practically going crazy over me. Smiling with a wide, goofy grin, he asked if I would please take a photo with him and his family. I'm not a conceited type and figured it wouldn't hurt. Besides, it was just one moment and thought if I complied, he'd quiet down. I got up and went to stand next to him when suddenly, he pulled me onto his lap as the photo was taken. I smiled politely and went back to my table, amidst a row of strange looks from my so-called "family" members, with of course, the exception of my mom.

As my focus and attention were on my children, I barely noticed that brunch was winding down. I told Tiff and Mo that before I drove them home, I wanted to stop at my house so they could see the new place. Plus, I had also bought Mo's birthday present (a stereo), which I wanted to give to her, as she celebrated a May birthday. Acting responsibly, I added that this short, side trip wouldn't take long and that they would be back home in time for celebrations with their stepmom.

In a move I didn't see coming, my half sister stood up and rudely interjected, "Here Tiffany, take this quarter, because you had better call your MOM and get her permission."

In a flash of anger, I snarled, "You must be crazy! Don't you DARE interfere!"

Right then and there, she made the biggest mistake of her life. Where did she get off on calling the girls' stepmom, "MOTHER," right in front of their own, REAL mother? I should have sensed where her comments originated, in that, a complete inability to connect me as the girls' mother, due to her not knowing me at all, but there was no forgiveness in this moment. This May day, in what should have been nurturing; beautiful, started to unravel at a pace that even had me unnerved.

I stunned her to silence, my chest literally hurting at her revelation that "I" was the "OTHER MOTHER!" The only thing that prevented me from really lashing out at her was my children, who were becoming very uncomfortable. In a small voice, Tiff said they better go back with them. Mo just got up and left. I said goodbye to my eldest and with these words still echoing loudly in my ears, ran out of the restaurant. My feet felt like lead as I made my way to the car ahead of my tears, which threatened to drown me as they came flooding out.

I waited in the car sobbing uncontrollably, as my mom showed up a few minutes later. The two of us drove home, my poor momsy being subjected to me screaming, crying and even cursing. For hours on end this behavior continued and from that moment, I was NOT okay.

Several years later, my half sister mailed me a book on "Forgiveness." At the time I just threw it in the garbage, never opening it. She died young, in her 40's, within one month of being diagnosed with cancer. Right before she passed, while in the hospital, she asked to see me. I went for my mother's sake and all was forgiven.

Forgiveness does not imply bad behavior is acceptable, or okay. Forgiveness allows YOU to let go of your anger, resentment or fear.

A few months later while getting ready to visit Megsy, I noticed the roof in my bedroom was leaking. Rainwater was dripping steadily onto my bed. I called the landlord and he informed me there was nothing he could do. Needless to say, my weekend was ruined as I was forced to stay behind, emptying buckets of rainwater. Even a few months later, despite my multiple requests, there was no attempt to fix the roof.

Ever since Mother's Day, everything started to go downhill for me. I wasn't the same upbeat Shirley, with everything making me sad and reminding me of things I could not change. Robert, the guy I went to Mexico with for the weekend, dropped by every so often. He was fun, unpredictable and someone I looked upon to have fun in the moment, versus any sort of long-term relationship.

There are times in life when you feel as if everything you touch turns to sadness. It's hard to realize in these moments that you might be suffering from clinical depression. I now know this is what I went through. When I spent my final Penthouse payment, I feared my life was likely over. I thought to myself, once the money was gone, there would be no reason to live. I never thought much about the future but I did sense that my desire for living was absent, and I would simply cease to exist. What happened was a true testament to Spirit: I DID survive. Whether I would just get by, or be embraced by a miracle, either was fine.

My landlords, who I thought were friends, were making no effort to improve my quality of life. I felt I had to move again, although it wouldn't be easy without having a current job as a reference. I was still good friends with Scott, the lawyer who handled my divorce from Klaus, and knowing he owned several apartments, I gave him a call. Luckily he had one available that I could rent. It wasn't in the nice, beach town neighborhoods I was used to, but the rent was low so I decided to accept his offer. It was during this move I severed my ties with fashion designing, selling my industrial sewing machine, supplies and other equipment connected to the business.

Genevieve came over to help me prepare for my move. Suddenly I stopped packing, as my breathing was fast and out of control. Terrified, I altered between gasping for a solid breath of air, and crying uncontrollably. I was smack in the middle of a full-fledged panic attack, but again, didn't know this at the time. She sat me down, instructing me to close my eyes and take deep breaths, and I attempted to calm down while she finished packing for me.

Suddenly, Robert showed up at the door. He approached us both, bluntly stating he's "taking over and would be moving in with me." In what felt like a dreamscape, I agreed. Why not, I thought, everything was already so out of control and besides, the tranquilizer pill he so conveniently palmed and gave to me made me agreeable to almost anything. At least I was feeling calmer; saner.

We lived together for a total of three months. I came home one day to find him completely moved out and gone. I had gotten used to him but wasn't saddened to see him go. Rather, I was shocked, like being awoken out of a deep sleep, only to be plunged into another reality. A lot about him never made sense to me, and later, I learned he took many wealthy women for their money, eventually landing in prison. Fortunately, I was not one of these ladies.

Alone again, I decided to call Billy. His friend, Dave told me Billy was in Hawaii, but he promised to give him the message. As he was likely staying with Uncle Bob, I telephoned him there. Billy was really happy to hear from me, and told me he was coming home in a few days.

I wasn't aware at the time, but Billy's wealthy aunt had passed away, leaving him a handsome chunk of money. For the very first time, he was in the midst of renting his own little apartment in the peninsula, in Long Beach. Finally after all these years, Billy was now in the position to "save me." This couldn't have come at a better time, as I was out of work, had no income and was almost entirely broke again.

# 36 BILLY HAD SAVED AND RESCUED ME

Billy returned from Hawaii a few days later. He came over, moved me out of my apartment and settled me into his. He had landed a few parts in movies, including a role in the Sharon Stone blockbuster, "Basic Instinct." He was feeling better than ever about life, with one of his dreams – to take care of me – seemingly on its way to manifesting.

He never acknowledged or accepted our divorce, always continuing to refer to me as his wife. Recent movie gigs qualified him membership into SAG, or the Screen Actor's Guild. He added me onto his health insurance as his spouse, this being important to him, as he wanted me to get a check up and complete any dental work that needed doing.

Billy seemed to be floating somewhere around cloud nine, or higher! First, he had me back in Belmont Shore and second, he felt I actually needed him, maybe for the first time. I loved Billy so much, but it seemed our relationship was one part "positive" and two parts "damaged." There was simply too much baggage in our pasts that had worn me down to the point where I didn't want to be married to him. Not again.

I was very honest, telling Billy that while I was content for now and appreciated his help, the situation was only temporary. I literally did variations of nothing, while Billy pampered me, cooked for me and made me feel like a princess – all because that's the way my Billy was.

At times, I flat out told him that I really wasn't very happy. He responded that it didn't matter, because HE was! Many times I viewed Billy as a big, overgrown, baby boy.

One day on my way home from visiting Linda, I drove through Huntington Beach. For no reason at all, I decided to stop at a liquor store to buy gum. It was very strange, since I never chewed gum and secondly, a liquor store? I couldn't help but overhear a guy tell the clerk how he was a local Blackjack dealer. Never shy about approaching a stranger, I asked him where and how, as gambling is illegal in California. He explained he worked for a "Games" company that specialized in events for office parties and holiday entertainment. Thus, it wasn't technically gambling.

This sounded very interesting, given my background as a 21 dealer in Tahoe. He said that if I were interested, he would give me the telephone number to call. Thanking him, I couldn't wait to get home so I could do just that.

Once again there are no coincidences in life. Who knows why I suddenly stopped at that liquor store, *and at that moment* to buy gum? My guides, forever watching over me, must have saw this as an opportunity and placed me on this path at precisely this time.

I was so excited to tell Billy what I learned. He thought it sounded a little dangerous, as I would be driving home late at night. Nonetheless, I contacted the company and they put me to work immediately. The pay certainly wasn't great, although I was allowed to put a tip jar on the table. This helped a little. Honestly, just the fact I was actually doing something again made me feel much better about myself.

Billy never wanted, nor expected a penny from me. Yet I reminded him that once I saved up enough money, I would be moving out to get my own apartment. He never said much but I noticed that same look on his face – the one he would always show me when he was hurt, or feeling dejected.

I met many people while working at this job, and immediately became friends with a girl named Debby. Clearly several names in my life have popped up, over and over!

As a struggling actress whose money was scarce, she told me about another better paying gig, dealing 21. She provided the contact information for Bill, a guy located in Huntington Beach who owned this business. He owned a total of eight Blackjack tables, all placed in various nightclubs from Los Angeles to Orange County. Dealers who worked for him rotated amongst the different clubs.

This sounded like a fantastic opportunity so I contacted him immediately, and he hired me. I paid myself nightly via a percentage of monies I took in for him. I charged customers between $10 and $20 for chips to play, also paying the nightclub their percentage from these funds as well. It was all fine as it was for entertainment purposes only. I was assigned to work in his regular nightclubs, strip clubs and country western clubs. I couldn't claim boredom from staying in one place too long, and besides, I never worked in a strip club before!

Most of the girls were really sweet and I became good friends with a girl from Sweden that danced slow and sultry – and only to Elvis songs! When she married a cute, young American guy, I was her maid of honor. Her family came from Sweden, including her father, who was a doctor. Sworn to secrecy, when asked if I worked with her, I said yes; that we were both waitresses. Shortly after that, she quit dancing and we lost touch.

It's almost hard to believe, given my state of depression just a short while ago, but I was actually starting to feel happy again. I had even saved enough money to move out from under Billy's protective wing. With hope in my heart and the prospect of better times ahead, I rented a U-Haul to move my belongings. If it weren't for Billy feeling so melancholy, I would have been even more excited. Billy helped me move into a beautiful condo across the beach in Huntington Beach. One thing we both knew: He would always be there whenever I needed him.

# 37 MOVING TO BEAUTIFUL LAGUNA BEACH AND BUYING MY OWN BLACKJACK TABLE

It was 1993 – six months since I moved into the condo and all was going well – or so I thought. One day out of the blue, the owner's son called me. Apparently he had just divorced and wanted to move in, giving me very little time to find a new place. I was so disappointed. I loved the place and now I would have to move – again!

While I was living here, I ordered my own 21 table. I wanted to run a little 21 company, and planned on hiring girls to work for me. I sent the money I had saved for the table to a P.O. Box in Nevada. And then when I never received the table, realized it was a scam. I had worked so hard to save up funds – for this? How could anyone with even a sliver of a conscience steal someone's money, I wondered. I wasn't about to give up easily though, and threatened the guy whose ad I had initially responded to, that my father was the Chief of Police in Los Angeles. But professional thieves, aside from being cruel and dishonest, are also savvy when it comes to avoiding being caught. Eventually I gave up, as it wasn't worth the stress any longer.

My mom felt awful for me. Using practically all her savings, she insisted I purchase another table from a local seller, which I did. Later, I tried paying her back, but she would never accept the money. I met a DJ that told me he was starting a new gig working inside The Red Lion, a nightclub in Costa Mesa. He said he would put in a good word for me, and with luck, I could get in there and work my own table.

I met with the manager, and explained how my business worked, including offering them a percentage. He declined my percentage but welcomed me nonetheless, giving me a spot in their club. I was ecstatic and tipped the DJ $20 nightly for helping me get in.

I was to start immediately, as there was a Fireman's convention in town and they were expecting a huge crowd. My very first night paid for half the table, and I knew from the get-go I would love this job. I even wore some of my hot suede and leather designs again, which helped draw people to come and play at my table.

One evening I met a tall, good-looking high school coach. We met for coffee a few times and then made plans to spend a holiday weekend together. It didn't take me long to discover that I didn't like him as much as I thought, and didn't want to continue the weekend in his company. As I had to move ASAP, I figured I'd look for rentals, scouring the Orange County paper. I found a large single in Laguna Beach at an unbelievably low rental price, and promptly asked him to leave in order that I could go take a look at the place. I called right away and a nice-sounding woman answered, telling me that it just became available.

I drove up to Laguna Beach, locating her beautiful, wooded home at the very top of a hill on RICO Road – no coincidence there! A friendly face greeted me at the door, and I was invited in. The lady, Christina, told me the rental was downstairs, and came complete with a separate entrance.

A hidden treasure was bestowed upon me, absolutely taking my breath away. There was a private, wooded back yard, peeking out at the ocean, with the apartment itself one, huge room – more than enough space for a bed and couch. White, plush carpet covered the floors, with Spanish tile placed throughout the large kitchen and entrance. Plantation shutters, also white, adorned the windows. Perhaps most breathtaking, aside from the high ceilings which I loved was the large, open stone fireplace that burned natural wood. Soaking in all the beauty and warmth of the place, and yes – the bathroom and closet areas were huge – I couldn't say "YES PLEASE" fast enough!

She shared with me that normally, she uses rental agencies to screen applicants but for the first time, she decided to rent out the space herself. Christina and I hit it off immediately, especially after she shared she was going to rent the apartment to me out of sheer intuition. A wealthy, newly divorced lady, she simply took comfort in having someone decent and kind living below her. I didn't even have to complete the standard rental forms; she only asked for a check in the amount of one month's rent. With a promise that I would collect her mail while she was on vacation, I moved in almost immediately.

Again, I have Spirit to thank. Should my date had not been as disappointing as he was, I would have never had the opportunity to peruse the newspaper that day, and would never have found such a gem. It was literally THE most beautiful place I had ever rented, for basically pennies.

Once again, Billy helped me move, including moving my new Blackjack table to the nightclub. He absolutely loved my new pad and was genuinely happy for me. He stayed over the first night before driving back to Los Angeles the next day, where he was now living, in the guest house behind a lady's main property.

His landlord had offered to help him sell his scripts. I know almost nothing would have made him happier than a chance for Billy to be recognized as the competent writer that he was.

# 38 THE MOST WONDERFUL REUNION WITH MY DAUGHTERS

Mentally, I was in such a happier place now. Tiff was graduating from high school and through my mom, heard that she wanted to get in touch with me, but didn't have my current telephone number. I didn't need to hear another word, as I was so happy to hear this!

Calling immediately, I spoke with both Tiff and Mo and our conversation flowed as if no time had passed at all. The joy of hearing their voices again was indescribable, and we set a time to get together the following day. In just a few hours, we would be together once again, and I KNEW this was the new beginning my mom, Megsy, Linda and Billy had been reassuring me of all these years!

I picked the girls up at their place in Pedro, walking through the gate towards the back of their house. First, I saw Tiff as she walked out, smiling. She looked exactly the same; always beautiful. I threw my arms around her, radiating with pure joy, my eyes welling up with "happy tears."

I then spotted a girl right behind her with long, dark blond hair. Thinking it was one of her friends, I threw her a quick smile. While fussing over her, moments later, Tiff looked at me, a glint in her eyes as she asked, "Aren't you going to say hi to Mo?"

Mo? I didn't even recognize my own daughter! Calling out her name, I ran over to her, hugging her profusely and apologizing for my major faux pas. She looked so pretty, yet so completely different! I was used to Mo being a tomboy of sorts, but she just smiled in her shy way, happy to see me too, and we all laughed at what had just happened.

Our first stop was to a shoe store in Palos Verdes, as Tiff couldn't wait to introduce me to her high school boyfriend that worked there. I recognized the importance of this as my daughters once again, in this very special way, connected to me in sharing private and important details of their lives.

Next, we went to Belmont Shore, where we spent their "growing up" years. Hungry, we enjoyed Mexican food at Panama Joes on 2nd Street. A celebration was definitely in order so we drank virgin strawberry margaritas. Sharing stories with much laughter in-between brought me to my happiest moment IN YEARS. Nothing could have made this day more beautiful than spending time with my beautiful daughters!

Later, we drove through the old neighborhood, visiting the Claremont house in which they grew up. We drove past their schools, taking time to reminisce about old teachers, neighbors and friends. We even knocked on the door of an old neighbor who lived on Pomona Street. She had been very fond of us and remembered the girls well from when Tiff was just 1+1/2 and Mo, a newborn. What a kick, taking this stroll down memory lane.

Tiff told me she received a scholarship and would be attending Dickinson College, in Pennsylvania. Mo would have to wait one more year, before attending San Diego State College. I was beyond proud of both my girls, delighted at Mo's relative close proximity and looking forward to spending more time together.

They adored my place in Laguna Beach and stayed overnight with me. I felt as if the three of us were best friends, versus "just" mother and daughters as we enjoyed our very first sleepover in years.

From that moment on as I knew we would, we stayed in touch constantly, calling and writing one another often. Tiff came home to visit each Christmas, spending much of the holiday season with their REAL MOTHER – me.

Mo and I started to hang out on a regular basis, going to movies, shopping and with her taking me on several hikes.

In a strange and magical way, it felt as if there had never been any separation between us at all. My life was completely and totally back on track now, and I knew I would NEVER suffer from any sort of absence from my children again.

In fact, LOVE never dies at all.

*"Love has no separation. Although our bodies may be separated at times, we are still Spirit and we are always together; we are all ONE." ~ Shirley Anni Njos*

# 39 BILLY'S FATAL MOTORCYCLE ACCIDENT

Sometimes our most profound moments occur in the nothingness of silence. For it is within this "nothingness" that all is possible; that everything exists; and time has no relevance at all.

It was January 1996 and Christian Brando was given an early release from prison. Laura, my good friend from the movie in Italy, was living in Los Angeles again. I drove up to see her often, going out for dinner and reminiscing about all the wonderful memories we had made, and shared. She gave Christian my telephone number, as he wanted to call but didn't know where to reach me. When he called, I told him Billy and I had completely made up. It would be wonderful if they too, could be friends, I added. I also shared this with Billy, asking if he would consider being friends with Christian again. He hesitated momentarily, and answered he probably would, but that he wouldn't make any special effort.

Typical, stubborn Taurus's, both of them! I set up a meeting so they could spend some "face time" together. They both showed up at the designated space, a poolroom, and sure enough, became friends again. It was a little awkward at first, but I was delighted they took the first step.

Billy and I talked often, and once in a while he came to visit me in Laguna. He was such an incredibly nurturing soul towards me that one day in the fall, he reminded me to take the flu shot, as I had suffered terribly from influenza three years in a row. He said he was going to put $20 cash in the mail to cover the cost of the injection. I could have told him no, that I could pay for it myself; but it made Billy happy to do little things for me.

Warmly, I thanked him. Sentiments like these were what truly kept Billy in his own, special place in my heart. Occasionally, I mailed him sweet little cards to let him know how much he meant to me, and always would.

A couple of weeks later, it occurred to me that I never received Billy's envelope. I found this strange, as, being a man of his word, Billy wouldn't have forgotten to send the note and money. I brushed it off, thinking that perhaps Billy had landed a gig and got busy.

My all-time favorite photo of Billy, such a gentle soul.

Just then the phone rang. It was Violet, Billy's mom. She said she was staying in Billy's tiny back house in Los Angeles and as she saw a card from me, looked for my number in his address book and decided to call. I always dated my cards so she knew Billy and I were still in touch.

There was a moment of silence – suddenly the air went wrong; in fact, in a matter of seconds, everything felt wrong.

"Yes?" I said, more of a question than a response.

"I called because surely you know about Billy's motorcycle accident."

Motorcycle accident? I flashed back to 1981 when Bill Bates had been hit and killed by a drunk driver while riding his motorcycle.

"WHAT accident?" I interrupted. "How serious is it? I didn't know anything about an accident!"

Her words cut through the prickling thickness of the air. She responded that Billy's accident was quite serious; that's why she was staying at his place, so she could be close enough to visit him.

Each word pounded louder in my head than the last, my heart picking up the deafening rhythm as tears formed in my eyes. I couldn't write down the information fast enough, wanting to leave immediately and drive to the hospital in Los Angeles where Billy had been admitted. It was late and the drive was long, so I resolved to leave early the following morning.

My eyes were focused on the ceiling all throughout that night. I tried to avoid looking around the room for fear that MY BILLY might make his presence known as Bill Bates did all those years back. I shut out the internal chatter, refusing to accept anything other than that Billy WOULD recover, and before long would be out of the hospital.

I learned that during the day on October 16, 1996, Billy was riding his bike through Laurel Canyon. I speculated he was probably just running an errand, which he would typically do on his motorcycle. Oh God! A thought flashed through my mind that maybe he was on his way to the bank for my $20! Traffic came to a screeching halt and Billy hit the brakes, yet crashed into a large truck in front of him. He was thrown completely off his bike, and although Billy was wearing a helmet, it was ripped from his head. He was taken immediately to the ICU in the emergency room.

Violet almost didn't call me that day, but I am beyond grateful that she did. Billy didn't have a phone in his back house, and I would have never called him in the main house, out of respect for his landlord. Nor would I have driven up to Los Angeles. By the time I would have found out, it might have already been too late – something I could have never reconciled. His mother's telephone call was no coincidence. I was able to make my peace as a result of it.

The next day I arrived at the hospital, not having a clue as to what condition Billy was in. His mother wasn't overly descriptive, and even if she had told me the full extent of his injuries, I wouldn't have been able to comprehend this until I saw for myself.

When I first saw Billy I started to shake from head to toe, feeling the stirrings of a panic attack creeping in. Keeping calm and even smiling at him was a Herculean feat; I myself was amazed I could even pull this off. I guess this is what my love for him brought out in me.

Billy had a halo on his head, with screws going directly into his forehead. He couldn't speak at all, and had a tracheotomy in his neck. Needles went in him everywhere I looked. I had never seen anything like this in my entire life!

I spoke softly to him, speaking as if his injuries weren't serious at all.

Medical staff told me otherwise, as if I needed any confirmation. I was told he was a total quadriplegic.

It took every ounce of strength in me to not break down completely and sob my eyes out right in front of him. What I really wanted to do was to crawl into his bed and just HOLD HIM FOREVER.

Billy looked at me then, mouthing sounds that I struggled to translate into words. Word by word, I finally read his lips. He told me that his wallet was stashed up in the hospital ceiling lights, and he wanted me to climb up and get it out for him. Adamantly, he kept repeating this request, over and over. Believing him momentarily and feeling utterly confused, I stopped, sadly realizing his brain was also not working properly.

I ran to the bathroom and like water pouring from a faucet, so did my tears. I couldn't stop crying but thankfully, was able to hold back the screams, which threatened to rise from my chest. With my eyes swollen and red, I returned to Billy's ICU room. Nurses told me not to stay too long. So, embracing Billy very gently and kissing him on the mouth ever so lightly, I told him I would be back tomorrow.

The robot that became me drove home, with my "real" self beyond numb and feeling sadder than words or emotions could ever describe. Every day, with the exception of the weekends I had to work, I drove up early in the morning to visit Billy. And every afternoon when I made the long drive home back to Laguna Beach (around 3:00 p.m. in order that I avoid the rush hour), a small part of me was left behind with him.

I sat with him, reminiscing about all our amazing times together. I gently massaged him for hours, although I knew he could not feel my touch. Other times I just stayed quietly at his bedside while he was sleeping, so he could see me when he opened his eyes.

I learned that I needed to help keep his mind working, and so I tested him on simple things like what country he lived in, or asking what his date of birth was. I couldn't imagine not going every single day that I wasn't at work, for I knew just how much Billy needed me now. That, and the love I felt for him was the purest form; a love that never dies.

Arriving home in the evenings, I was absolutely exhausted and drained – mentally, physically and emotionally. But Violet asked that I give her full reports on my daily visits, so I always called her as soon as I got in.

Billy's mom was elderly and couldn't make a lot of trips to visit her son. Eventually, she returned to her home in San Louis Obispo. She remained so hopeful when I would fill her in on the day's events, holding on to any progress at all, and most of all, loved that I was there caring for her son in every, possible way that I could. She loved hearing when Billy's little finger twitched one day, or that he was more aware on another day. And naturally, I too, never gave up hope, praying for Billy to have a full recovery.

All the staff got to know me very well, and when the nuns came into his room, they called me an angel; this making me blush. Billy was hospitalized for 1+1/2 years in total, and during this time, was transferred to two different hospitals.

I must have been in complete denial, for over that time period, I witnessed the slow deterioration of Billy's physical body. Despite having had two major surgeries, my prayers and hopes were just not being answered.

Violet felt she was too old to make any decisions regarding Billy's care, so she put his sister in charge of all his medical decisions. Billy and his sister were never very close as adults, and it was times like these I wished I were still legally his wife so I could have been put in charge of all this. I knew without a doubt what Billy would have wanted, and his wishes were the ONLY best decisions, as far as I was concerned.

Around this time, I learned what caused Billy to become a quadriplegic. During the first operation, a doctor left an operating tool in his back. The tool slashed around, causing him to suffer from complete paralysis.

Billy's sister attempted to stop me from visiting Billy, because when she saw me, she was reminded of my fling with Christian. This was absolutely not the time or place for such thoughts, as all our focus needed to be on Billy – and on loving and caring for him. One day she screamed at me right outside the door of Billy's hospital room, yet again, about my relationship with Christian. I just stood there silently, tears welling in my eyes, as I thought of my Billy, lying just a few feet away from me. Outwardly, I could do "silent" very well, but I couldn't believe her misplaced priorities, and how her judgment of me had made her act so toxic. Even her boyfriend tried to calm her down, looking at me with apologetic eyes.

Billy made it crystal clear he wanted me there. Many, many times he mouthed that he wanted everyone out of his room except for me, longing for only the intimacy of "us." And as I knew Billy so well, I would do all the "translation" for the doctors and staff. I knew exactly how his mind worked and thus, reading his lips became easier for me in time, in fact, I became very good at it.

Thankfully, the staff ignored her demands of not allowing me to visit. Everyone working in the hospital sided with me, knowing how much Billy wanted and needed me there. Even Violet told her to let it go. Sometimes, staff went so far as to hide me until she left, as she eventually made her request legal, in an attempt to forbid my visits. But the "caring" sister that she was didn't actually visit often, so this was less of a problem and more of an inconvenience, the few times she was around.

Not long after Billy's accident, lots of friends visited him. Once I ran into Elvira (Cassandra). It was nice to see her again, and that she continued to care deeply for Billy. Intense prayer groups were held for him too, but nothing was working. Nothing.

During one particular visit, Billy looked at me very intensely and mouthed, "Bang! Bang! Bang!" It broke my heart, as I knew exactly what he meant. He wanted me to shoot him so he could just die and end his suffering.

By now, he had developed huge, oozing bedsores, his entire bottom and back completely covered with open, raw welts. This in itself was shocking and I wondered if Billy would die from the obvious trauma to such a large area of his body. It was a horribly painful procedure to clean and change his dressings, as evidenced by the expression on Billy's face. During these times, I would hold him on his side, gazing directly into his eyes, telling him over and over that I loved him.

One thing I learned was not to be intimidated or afraid to ask questions, no matter what they were. I made EVERTHING my business. In the case of Billy's bedsores, I was informed these were common for a patient that was bedridden. I learned later that it's not necessarily common at all, at least, not the type Billy was suffering from. Since I had no legal say, I asked Violet to let her daughter know.

Once, a sweet, soft-spoken nurse told me in a hushed voice, "Take him out of here," and that he would just die here if I didn't. Alarmed and confused, I didn't know what I could do, as my hands were (legally) tied. The nurse claimed she would be fired if anyone learned of what she had told me.

One day amongst the many, depressing days I spent in attempts to keep Billy's spirits up and filled with hope, Billy once mouthed for me to telephone his friend, Lewis. I was to demand that Lewis bring his big crane with the long ladder, which they used in their large, tree trimming jobs – and to bring it NOW! He was extremely insistent, wanting to get out of the hospital that moment. Billy knew Lewis was the go-to person to rescue him via extraction out of the hospital window. After several attempts to change the conversation, I finally called Lewis at Billy's constant insistence, feeling the urgency and priority of this very moment.

Lewis answered the telephone, to my dismay. I repeated what Billy asked of me: to come and pick him up immediately, as he wanted to leave the hospital. I requested that he bring the big crane with the ladder, with Billy glaring at me all the while, ensuring that I conveyed his every word perfectly.

I prayed Lewis would "get it;" that this indeed was a false alarm. Unfortunately, in less than 30 minutes he showed up, dropping everything to come to Billy's assistance! I was shocked and crushed. Lewis had thought Billy made an instantaneous and miraculous recovery! Confused, Lewis looked at me, then Billy, then back to me. Finally he caught on, witnessing Billy's impossible pleas for himself. He saved the day by reassuring Billy he would see what could be done, as he requested.

I walked Lewis out of the room, apologizing profusely, telling him I had hoped he would have understood this as false, and that I had done this purely for Billy. He understood, and realized I didn't know what else to do. In retrospect, I could have faked dialing, but it didn't occur to me at the time.

My main mission, aside from watching over and protecting Billy, was to give him inspiration to fight for his life. I told him that I would indeed, marry him again, but he needed to walk down the aisle to meet me at whatever altar we designated, whether be under the stars or at a place of worship. And I meant every word! I even thought about marrying him while he was still in the hospital. This would have given me full power over his medical decisions, but I was deterred from going through with this, as I knew it would stir up trouble with Billy's sister. And that was the last thing either of us needed. I just wanted to do anything and everything to make Billy happy and give him a reason to live!

If ever my love for Billy was doubted, my commitment to him during the worst days and hours of his life unequivocally proved otherwise. I loved him more than I ever thought humanly possible, and was literally prepared to make a deal with God, Spirit, or whomever else would listen and had the power to reverse Billy's horrific predicament.

Four months into Billy's hospitalization, I decorated his wall with little things he would like. I made him a very special Indian poster, laminating it so he could stare at it during the long days of his hospitalization. I wrote only inspiring words on it, always being mindful never to do anything that would alarm him.

Billy saw us in this way.

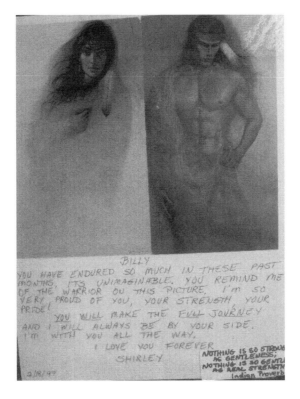

BILLY
YOU HAVE ENDURED SO MUCH IN THESE PAST
MONTHS, ITS UNIMAGINABLE. YOU REMIND ME
OF THE WARRIOR ON THIS PICTURE. I'm SO
VERY PROUD OF YOU, YOUR STRENGTH YOUR
PRIDE!
     YOU WILL MAKE THE FULL JOURNEY
AND I WILL ALWAYS BE BY YOUR SIDE.
I'm WITH YOU ALL THE WAY.
          I LOVE YOU FOREVER
               SHIRLEY        NOTHING IS SO STRONG
                             AS GENTLENESS,
2/8/47                       NOTHING IS SO GENTLE
                             AS REAL STRENGTH
                             Indian Proverb

It got to a point that recovery or no recovery, I resolved to marry him again, and dedicate my life to taking care of him. I never told Billy this, as I doubt he was even aware of the seriousness of his medical condition. He wouldn't have wanted to hear this – and God only knows how much faster he would have deteriorated, knowing he would never walk again.

Billy had now been in the hospital for nearly 18 months. Visits from rehabilitation nurses gave me hope. For a full hour, Billy was hoisted out of bed via a "crane" and placed into an electric wheelchair. This grand production exhausted him – I could see the pain in his eyes but knew he was fighting as hard as he possibly could. Perhaps even more so, knowing that I stood close by, encouraging him each time.

While Tiff was visiting from college, I told her about Billy's condition. I asked her if she wanted to ride up and visit him with me, and she agreed. During the drive up, I tried preparing her while she asked a lot of questions, looking sadder with every one of my responses.

Billy was terribly gaunt, appearing frailer each day. He was barely recognizable, and yet, as we both walked into his room, I put on my happy face, never ever letting him know how sick and fragile he really looked. Smiling, I said, "Hi Billy. Look who came with me to see you today." He stared at his visitor for a second, and then slowly mouthed "T-i-f-f-a-n-y." I couldn't believe he immediately knew who she was, given his medical condition and that he had never seen her all grown up. We both fought back tears and were touched beyond belief at the realization that Billy's heart was truly still "with us," despite his dire condition.

Shortly thereafter, Billy was transferred to what looked like a tiny hospital, except with much, less medical equipment. I learned this was a hospice center. Not being familiar with such a place, I thought it felt more like a rest or rehabilitation center than a medical facility. There was no large, front desk as other hospitals had, and instead, it was very quiet.

On one hand, I was confused: Wasn't Billy supposed to be in a therapy program, in order that he works towards getting better? On the other hand, this small, quaint facility provided me with peace – much, more so than the impersonal quality of the larger hospital. Besides, I knew Billy would like this environment much better as well.

In this calm, perhaps almost too calm environment, Billy lay in yet another strange bed. He looked half dead now, and I wondered how or rather, if, he could possibly rebound here. A male nurse (or a hospice volunteer) came in to stroke his feet while I was visiting. His extremely kind and empathetic demeanor added to the calming vibe of the place.

It was getting close to 3:00 p.m., the time I normally left for home. And as I had always done, I told Billy I better leave before rush-hour traffic hits. Surprisingly, he slowly mouthed the words: "Please-just-stay-a-little-longer."

He had never asked this of me before.

Throwing my sweater onto the chair, I responded, "Of course I will." With a warm smile that I hoped, radiated every ounce of love I felt for him, I told him I had all the time in the world for my Billy!

I sat back down, cupping one of his hands with both of mine. Slowly, his breathing slowed to a barely audible level as he fell back asleep.

When I was sure he was sound asleep, feeling our souls mingle into complete and utter oneness, I kissed him gently and tiptoed out of his room. Smiling, I told the staff I'd be back tomorrow.

Early the next morning, the telephone rang. In my half-dream state, I dreamt Violet was on the line, telling me of Billy's accident. Sun streamed through my bedroom window. Where was Billy going, so early in the morning, I wondered?

Just then I bolted awake and grabbed the phone. I was informed that Billy had passed away that very night.

I felt as if I had just been surgically "hollowed out," feeling completely empty and in a total state of nothingness. One emotion only – pure relief – made its way into my heart, as Billy was finally taken out of all his suffering. And on March 7, 1998, the once-breathtaking physical form that Billy occupied, was no more.

Spirit lets us know when our time in this realm is nearing completion; and when our transition into the light is coming near. Today, I am absolutely aware that Billy knew he wasn't going to make it through the night. That's why he asked me to stay a little longer on this day – because he was readying to surrender to Spirit.

Both of my "Bills'" – both Taurus's – died as a result of motorcycle accidents.

About a year after Billy died, his mother, Violet, received a one million dollar malpractice settlement for her son's death. His sister had sued the hospital.

## THESE WERE MY OWN SENTIMENTS AS WELL AS HIS MOTHER'S

"In tears I saw you sinking,
I watched you fade away,
My heart was fully broken,
You fought so hard to stay.
But when I saw you sleeping,
So peaceful free from pain,
I would not wish you back again,
To suffer that again.
A million times I hurt for you,
A million times I cried,
If love could have saved you,
You never would have died.
If I could have but just one wish,
One dream that could come true,
I'd pray to God with all my heart,
For yesterday and you."

May 2, 1946 – March 7, 1998

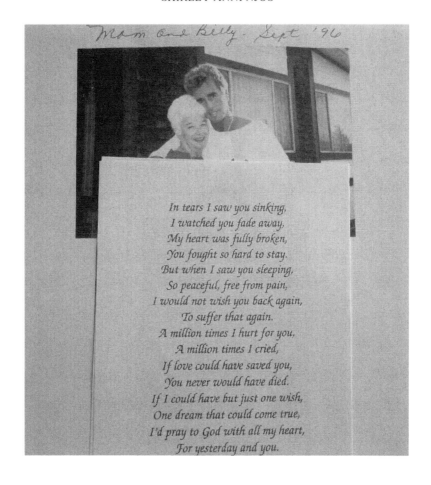

*Mom and Billy - Sept '96*

In tears I saw you sinking,
I watched you fade away,
My heart was fully broken,
You fought so hard to stay.
But when I saw you sleeping,
So peaceful, free from pain,
I would not wish you back again,
To suffer that again.
A million times I hurt for you,
A million times I cried,
If love could have saved you,
You never would have died.
If I could have but just one wish,
One dream that could come true,
I'd pray to God with all my heart,
For yesterday and you.

# 40 BILLY'S CELEBRATION OF LIFE

A big gathering in Marina Del Ray marked Billy's service and his Celebration of Life, all organized by his sister. As Billy firmly wished, he was cremated, with his ashes to be spread in Hawaii – this private cremation to take place on a boat in Hawaii at a later date. I'm so thankful his sister honored Billy's wishes, as his mother wanted Billy to be buried next to her, already having paid for a chosen plot and headstone.

After Billy's passing, telling me "we all belong together," Violet also gifted me with a crypt, about 30 feet directly back from theirs. It's located at Pacific View Memorial Park, in Newport Beach. The spot is beautiful, three feet away from where the great John Wayne is interred. Although hers was a most loving gesture, I will never use it. I believe in cremation for myself, and don't want my ashes to be placed in a burial-type plot.

In Billy's absence, it was a very difficult day for me. Megsy dropped everything to fly out to be here with me, as well as to pay her respects to Billy. Together, we left for Beverly Hills where his service was being held. I sat next to Billy's mom on one side; and Megsy, on my other side. Marti, my lovely friend showed up, too. On the opposite side to where I was sitting, I saw my sweet friend, Laura. I also spotted Pee Wee Herman (Paul), sitting a few rows behind me. The church was entirely full, but I didn't look around any further; I wanted to focus on Billy's memory and essence.

There were two huge, beautiful poster-size photos of Billy beside the preacher. As hard as I tried holding back tears, I could not.

After the service, I greeted a few friends. Megsy and I then left for her hotel, where we got ready for Billy's Celebration of Life, scheduled to take place later that day.

It was late afternoon when we arrived at a beautiful location by the water in Marina Del Ray. Walking inside, I wasn't feeling nearly as sad as I did while in the church. I saw Billy's gorgeous photos displayed

159

EVERYWHERE and quite literally, my breath was taken away. All were tastefully mounted on thick cardboard, and all were much larger-than-life.

Suddenly I felt a strong presence – Billy's.

Several people showed up, many of whom I had never met. Some of his high school friends introduced themselves to me, and it was here where I witnessed a truly amazing gathering of love. Billy's mom, although sitting at a table with older relatives, made sure to acknowledge me. Once again, Elvira and Pee Wee Herman attended, along with some other show business people.

There was a microphone for anyone who wished to get up and speak. As much as I would have liked to, I didn't think I could hold myself together long enough to do so. Besides, I'm a terrible public speaker. Pee Wee did get up, sharing a speech that was both heartfelt and funny. He made us all laugh and as the ice was already broken, I decided to speak after all. I introduced myself, and then spoke very briefly, telling everyone of our strong connection and our love. When my tears couldn't be held at bay any longer, I sat down.

As I was leaving the microphone, Pee Wee ran up to hug me, and then quietly shared something funny about Billy to me, which only I could hear. His gesture of kindness transformed my tears to laughter, as we both remembered this sentiment all too well. My mood was lightened once again. Elvira, who was sitting with her husband across from me, brought along a photo album full of pictures she had saved of Billy. She handed the album to me to look at, and to pass around and share. Most of the photos contained were of them performing together in Las Vegas.

The one person who was visibly absent was Christian. I knew he had moved away and I deliberately did not tell him about Billy's Celebration of Life, as I knew he shied away from all public gatherings. If he had known about it and had considered attending, I knew Christian would ask me about it at some point. It might have been a blessing in disguise: God knows how Billy's sister would have reacted if she had seen him there. Things worked out for the best in this regard.

I actually found myself laughing quite a bit, especially as Laura was sitting next to me. We reminisced about some very funny times we shared with Billy, during our time together in Italy. I knew he would have wanted me to be happy, because he knew EXACTLY how very much I loved him. After all, it was called a CELEBRATION of life!

Overall the entire day served as a perfect tribute to Billy. Thankfully, his sister remained cordial, saying nothing to me at his service or celebration. I thought at various times during the celebration how much he would have loved it. There were moments when I almost expected him to walk through the door, apologizing for being late. How much I had wished that he be there in person, to witness the outpouring of love for him.

However, this was not to be, as the Billy I loved, in human form, was gone.

As the celebrations winded down and I prepared to leave, another strange "wave" came over me. I felt as if Billy's presence stood beside me, leaving here with me, too. At the time, I just brushed it off as wishful thinking.

In the following months after Billy's passing, I grieved him deeply, many times screaming at the top of my lungs as songs came on the radio which reminded me of him, while driving home after work, late at night. Again, I would feel his presence in the car next to me, so very STRONG.

Today, I KNOW that Billy was there – that's why his presence was so strong around me. It's also why, during certain moments, I was able to smell his own natural and wonderful scent.

When we have returned to our Spirit form, we attend our own funerals and celebrations, wishing for all our loved ones not to grieve but rather, to remember us in joyous memory. We are all still very much alive, albeit "living" in a different dimension; on a different level of consciousness. This realm of Spirit is a place filled with pure love.

# 41 TIFFANY GRADUATES FROM COLLEGE; MO LEAVES FOR NEW YORK

Three months later, Tiffany was getting ready to graduate from college. We discussed her graduation ceremony, and where she would live and work. The best part of all this was that I was helping her make some big decisions, which I loved.

I had only $500 saved, and being practical, asked if she would rather that I attend her graduating ceremony or send her the much-needed cash, in order that she start out with a little money. I couldn't afford to do both, so we agreed that I would send her the cash, as every penny counted now, and she was for the first time, going out in the big, wide world!

Still living in Pennsylvania, her very first job immediately after graduation was working as a nanny for a divorced father with a couple of children. As she felt lonely most of the time, we tried, via daily conversations, to come up with other possibilities. Soon she received a good job working at Enterprise Car Rental, which at least provided her with a free car. Not long after she was hired, a position in California came up. She applied for a transfer and was accepted.

How wonderful it felt, having Tiffany back home again. As soon as she returned, she came right over. She was so happy, being around her friends and family once again. There was even a guy she liked from work, named Alan.

Tiffany didn't have a lot of work clothes, and as I still owned some beautiful suits that Bernie had bought me, we decided to indulge in a fashion show. Tiff was smaller than me, but was able to wear my suits, and looked gorgeous in them! I gave her as much as I could, including some shoes and hosiery. I was so incredibly pleased I was able to help her out in this way.

Mo attended San Diego State College, and while still in school, was

162

offered a job in New York as a soccer coach, at a young girl's summer camp. She loved New York and after two years of college, decided to take a break and move there permanently. It was a city she felt strongly connected to; where she knew she belonged.

We spent many great weekends together while she was attending college, hiking on several wonderful trails in Laguna Beach. Although I was happy for Mo, I was truly sorry to see her leave.

Based on some of the fun letters Mo wrote to me, it sounded as if she was having the time of her life. She had a real gift of words – her writing and descriptions literally coming to life as I read through her letters, and I thought she demonstrated some serious talent.

Although I lost my hiking partner with Mo in New York, I continued to hike on the trails alone. I also kept busy with work and even went on a few cattle calls, now and then. I had never taken any serious acting lessons, except when Genevieve and I attended some classes up in Los Angeles.

My actress friend, Debby called me one day, asking if I wanted to go with her on an audition, playing 21 dealers in a casino for a couple of movies. The first film was a Steven Segal and Kris Kristofferson movie called "Fire Down Below." The other film starred Patrick Swayze, and was called "Letters from a Killer."

We both landed the extra parts and had fun on the film sets. Steven Segal looked exactly like he does in films, larger than life, with his double the spitting image of him. I absolutely adored and loved Kris Kristofferson, and was even able to talk with him off set, being invited to dine at his table during the lunch break. One of the producers took a Polaroid photo, while he squeezed me and I hugged him. He was unbelievably kind, offering to autograph the side of the photograph, writing, "Thanks Shirley, Love, Kris Kristofferson."

Patrick Swayze was simply a doll. After filming through the entire night, he still made the time to chat with me and take a photo, too. I have nothing but the nicest things to say about this gentle and wonderful man.

Not long after Billy crossed over, I received a call from Christian. He told me he was pretty saddened about what had happened to Billy. He himself was living a very secluded and lonely life in Kalama, Washington.

He owned a home there, telling me that after he was released from prison, he was too scared to go anywhere in Los Angeles, for fear of being recognized. He was also concerned that the cops would pick on him, stop him for no reason and harass him.

We talked for quite some time that night. I had empathy for him, as I usually did. Christian asked if I would come for a visit. The thought of seeing Christian, in a strange way, made me feel closer to Billy again. He made all the travel arrangements, and one week later I left for Kalama.

## 42 I VISITED CHRISTIAN AFTER HIS RELEASE
## FROM PRISON

Kalama was a very small town near the Washington-Oregon border, thus I flew into the Portland airport. As I got off the plane, Christian was right there to greet me. It was great to see him again. He looked really good, a far cry from when I saw him last, which was at the beginning of his prison sentence over five years ago. I figured perhaps Washington and all its beautiful, natural surroundings had been great for his health and soul.

I was never one to live in fear, and I certainly didn't fear him at all. I chose to see Christian in only one way: as an old friend that I loved and genuinely cared about. He needed me now and I would be there for him.

We both shared fantastic memories together of some of the most exciting places in the world. I was forever grateful to him, and being born a "Brando" he had afforded me the luxury of helping me experience some of my greatest dreams.

Hugging one another and talking nonstop, we walked towards his truck. I never thought of bringing up anything about the shooting or his time in prison, unless of course, he chose to discuss it.

He was anxious to show me around Portland, as I had never been there before. We drove through the downtown districts and as it was evening, all the lanterns were lit. It was a beautiful city.

As we crossed over into Washington State, he drove off the main road to a little cabin in the woods that sold cigars. There were a few small seats for people who chose to just sit and smoke. And that's exactly what we did – I even tried a few puffs myself.

Momentarily, we looked into each other's eyes, and locking our gaze, suddenly it was as if every, single wonderful memory we ever had together came flooding back to us both – at the exact, same time. We smiled broadly at one another, then Christian finished his cigar and we left, in search of pizza. Finding a great pizzeria, we ordered one and then went to his house.

His house was old and small, but it was cozy, boasting a huge backyard with lots of trees and greenery. A large lake was also on the property. In the living room above the fireplace, some framed family photos of Marlon, his dad, were on display, with one particular cool photo displaying Marlon's arm around Christian.

After showing me around the house, we just relaxed, with him offering me some wine with our pizza. Christian however, wasn't allowed to drink. He shared he was still on probation, and every morning, he was required to go to the pharmacy and drink something which would make him very sick if he touched alcohol or did drugs. He was really tempted that night to find out exactly what would happen if he had a drink, but I suggested he better not, as I didn't want him to get sick. In fact, I was fine with a non-alcoholic beverage myself,

I asked why he picked Kalama in which to live. Christian told me his dad had bought him the house some time ago, and in truth, he was glad to get out of Los Angeles. I also learned his Godmother lived in the area, and that we could stop by later so I could meet her.

Wanting to get the Penthouse thing out of the way, but not wanting to make a big deal out of it, all I said to Christian was that I was nearly broke when I did Penthouse. I explained that doing the magazine basically saved my life. "That's okay, honey," he responded, hugging me. When Christian was sweet, he was THE sweetest and kindest person. One couldn't help but love him.

We talked about a lot of things, including once again, his father. This time, it was mostly about financial dealings that were in the works, which he would benefit from. At the time, I wondered why he was telling me about his detailed financial inheritances.

Eventually as I knew he would, he asked a little about Billy's final days. I was in the process of filling him in when the telephone rang. It was his brother Miko. When I saw that the conversation was going to take a little while, I checked out the backyard. Temperatures were colder here than back in California and soon, I came back inside, only to be greeted with a pillow thrown my way. I laughed, and then wrestled Christian. No one was going to throw a pillow at me and not expect some retaliation!

The following day he took me on a little tour of his town. He lived just down the street from the shops, but aside from a few antique stores, the town looke_ _ost deserted. We went inside the tiny pharmacy and Christian _ _ne pharmacist present, joked around. He was a sweet and funny_ who laughed when I asked if I could drink the poison in place of ( _tended to take a sip and we all started to laugh.

After, we_ _ive around Washington. Christian pointed out all the log m_ _cally the only industry in the area. After doing more_ _ed at a shopping center to check out some music. Chr_ _e Mode and asked me to listen to some of their songs _ Next was a visit to a collectible store, with him falling in_ _lar, fancy set of knives. Finally, we went to the grocery stor_ _nted to make something special for me that night.

He was really enjoyir_ picking out everything that looked good and riding on the shopp_ _ing very playful once again with me. I loved seeing him this happy_ _ree, as he really did suffer from having mostly had a rough life. On_ _t have guessed though, with him being the son of the most famous actor in the world.

He picked out some pasta, along with a variety of fresh seafood and Parmesan cheese. I was informed he was making me his "specialty." My job was to choose what we would enjoy for dessert and whatever else I wanted. Like a couple of kids, I threw some fun items in the cart for us to indulge in later.

The minute we got back to his place, he started cooking up a storm, cracking me up the more playful he became. The one bottle of wine that he bought for me, he insisted on opening, in order to celebrate.

In the end, his mixed pasta seafood dinner turned out delicious; absolutely fabulous!

We were having so much fun that I decided to enjoy just a small glass of wine. Christian popped the cork, and being the little daredevil that he was, poured himself a glass too. Ready to pay the consequences, he took a few sips, but stopped when I asked him to.

The next morning, indeed he didn't feel well, but fortunately this lasted only a short while and we were able to enjoy the day with one another.

Christian was a great welder and it was also a passion of his. Understandably, he was excited when he received a telephone call to come in for an interview for a welding job he had applied for. I sat in a small waiting room while he was being interviewed. He emerged, smiling, telling me the job looked very promising. And with Christian feeling hopeful and happy, I too felt as if things may finally turn around for him, making me happy too.

Over the next few days, Christian kept dropping hints that he would love for me to stay longer, and possibly even move there with him in the near future. I could see why as it could be quite lonely and boring, living there all alone in this tiny town.

However, my life was back home in California. Everything was going great for me now, and although a small part of me wanted to stay there with him, I wasn't prepared to pick up and move again. What I really did want was to leave a little of my "light" behind for Christian. I wanted him to be able to draw upon this for strength, as he embarked on his journey to rebuild his life.

After several days of fun and intimacy, it was time to go home. Christian said he would call me, and also gave me his mailing address. Teary-eyed, we both said goodbye, promising to keep in touch by phone and mail. I told him I'd love to visit again sometime soon. Eventually, he returned to Los Angeles, but this was the last time I ever saw Christian Brando.

# 43 I JUST HAVE TO TALK ABOUT AGE

I cannot embark on writing my life story, without a chapter on "AGE." In most ways, age hasn't really mattered to me, but in some ways, it has.

"Age" and "time" are purely human measurements. There is no such thing on the other side as time. And, as we are all Spirits, we are completely ageless. This is how I have chosen to view – and live – life.

I have lived my life primary as an "ageless" being, believing myself to be young in spirit but an old soul. Maybe however, it's the other way around!

We are all given gifts in this life, and I have been given plenty, including the gift of a more youthful appearance. It's just a statement of fact that ever since I turned 40 years "old," I have actually looked about 15-20 years younger than my human age.

It goes much deeper than that pesky number. Age isn't just "skin deep," so to speak. Rather, it's more about our Spirit's attitude, and there you have it – my secret as an ageless being!

Fortunately, I have never feared growing old, and at the same time, could never really imagine it either, since living in the present or in the "now" has been my primary way of being. I'm actually laughing, as I still cannot imagine I just turned 65 human years at the time of this writing!

And for the record, I've never had a facelift or injected Botox into my face or body – nor do I have any plans to. Never? I would be foolish to commit to such permanence; however, let's just say that I cannot envision this, at least, not how I feel or look "today!" My own, personal preference is for a more natural look, and I believe looking natural and healthy is sexier than any procedure could provide.

Having said this, I do believe in the saying, "To each their own." In other words, if someone does something for his or her self that makes him or her feel happy, then I say, "Power to them!"

I have sported bangs as long as I can remember and think it

automatically contributes to a more youthful appearance to one's face. Mine cover my high forehead – that's why I plan to keep them. I've used Dove soap most of my life, including on my face, and enjoy applying a good facial scrub/cleanser as well. Finally, sunscreen is an absolute must and Neutrogena, a more natural product, is my daily preference.

I've largely reduced the amount of makeup I wear, but still love wearing a little foundation, blush and lipstick when in public. Then I'm good to go! I've been asked what my favorite cosmetic companies are, so: My primary choice in foundation is Lancôme, the blush I love is by Laura Mercier, and last but not least I can't live without Smashbox's "Latte Matte" lipstick. Sometimes, I splurge on Burberry's new matte colors, too. And that about does it for cosmetics!

Linda always used to compliment me on my beautiful skin, as early as in my 20's, something I've been very fortunate to be adorned with. I only recently learned I was actually lucky to have such skin, for to me, skin was just that – skin – a covering, or a shell. I now look at skin in a more unique way, in that; skin provides a face and an expression for Spirit.

Fortunately, my outward-facing expression of Spirit has held up beautifully over the years, and I do consider this a wonderful gift. Let's "face" it, everyone enjoys looking his or her best, but one should never forget that true beauty comes from the inside.

This photo taken on my 64th birthday outside on a beautiful sunset and ocean waves.

I'll share a couple of funny "age" stories:

One year, Linda hosted a Christmas party. At the time, I was in my late 40's, and several friends whom I hadn't seen in many years attended. One lady, Barbara, couldn't believe I had changed so little, saying to me, "Shirley you look EXACTLY the same as when I met you 20 years ago!" She took a deep breath, and in a voice which was a little, too loud, asked: "What have you DONE? Did you make a deal with the devil?" Barbara's sarcastic humor was hilarious, and we couldn't stop laughing! But to clarify: No, I didn't make any deals with anyone!

Another time while visiting my mom in Colorado, we decided to go gambling at Black Hawk. Remember, as I live in California, I wear shorts, no matter rain, snow or sunshine. It was snowing that night, and out I went in shorts and a warm jacket, my hair in a long braid. I'm sure my cheeks (facial that is) were rosy from the cold weather outside.

As soon as we entered the casino, security stopped me at the entrance, asking to see my I.D.! I squealed, "Yes!" It just happened to be my 56th birthday and I was indeed beaming from head to toe that night!

There are other stories too, several of these involving men, as my youthful appearance has naturally attracted much, younger men throughout my entire life. By the way, this was just fine by me, since young is my preference! Seriously, I believe most younger men are not as controlling, or as set in their ways. At a very young age I was negatively influenced by my mother's choice of husband and there was no way I ever wanted to be involved with another stomach-turning relationship again, whether it be directly or indirectly.

I don't have a true "type" that I gravitate to, per se, although I'd call myself a "face girl." Rather I just sense a special connection, lots of chemistry and BINGO! And to share, Christian was 10 years younger than me while Billy was one year older.

Working in nightclubs for several years while in my late 40's and early 50's attracted lots of very young men, as young as in their 20's.

Amongst the interesting "younger" men in my life:

There was a 24 year-old man from Persia who was the spitting image of Elvis. I used to tell him he looked just like Elvis, since he really wasn't trying to be an impersonator at all. He simply looked like him – A LOT. This guy wouldn't stop asking me out, but as tempting as it was, I declined.

I actually consider myself extremely fortunate that I've never had any problems with being asked out, for the most part. Usually, I would politely smile and decline, claiming I had a boyfriend, or that I was married (which in fact, I was most of the time).

One night there was a wedding party at the hotel where I worked. Some of the guests came into the nightclub. A young guy with shoulder-length dark hair kept asking me out, as I declined. Smiling, he bought me a drink and sat it down in front of me. With this type of job, I was able to enjoy a couple of sweet martinis while socializing and dealing 21.

Anyway, it was late, and while finishing my cocktail, I suddenly felt very ill. I left my 21 table and barely made it to the ladies room, where I started vomiting, nonstop. Then without warning, I collapsed on the couch inside the restroom.

I could barely speak as my speech quickly became slurred. In the distance, I could hear a couple of girls washing their hands, and with great effort, I muttered, "Help! Get security!"

All the security guys were my buddies, and entering the ladies restroom, they found me lying listless. Fortunately I remembered – and was also able to communicate – Linda's telephone number.

The next thing I knew, Linda and her husband, Dave were standing over me, ready to drive me home. The strange guy with the long hair was standing next to them. I heard him tell Linda and Dave to go home, offering them $20 for their trouble! He told them he would drive me home. As the GREAT friend Linda was, there was no way in hell that she would leave me with a strange guy, or anyone for that matter.

Although I'm sure she didn't appreciate waking up in the middle of the night, and at that moment, assuming I merely had too much to drink, yet she was still my best friend and would do anything for me – along with a scolding, later!

On the drive home, my mouth had difficulty forming words but my brain was thinking pretty clearly. I was slurring words to her, to the effect that, "The weird guy slipped a date rape drug in my drink."

"Uh huh," she responded, her life so "normal" as compared to mine.

Not only did I attract younger men, but younger girls also wanted to be best friends with me. Several cocktail waitresses in their 20's would ask me to go to bars and hang out with them. There were two that needed roommates and asked if I wanted to move in with them.

I couldn't feel OLD if I tried!

Several young girls had serious "crushes" on me, and although I support all gay rights, was born totally heterosexual. I do truly love all my female friends but in a spiritual way only.

I never lie about my age, but I don't necessarily volunteer this information either, not until NOW! I have received the most stunned looks when I "confess" how old I am, making me feel like I just did something wrong! C'mon, aside from perhaps some teenagers, who lies about being older than they really are?

My younger appearance has actually worked as a disadvantage at times, when I didn't get the due respect I deserved and was treated like a kid. (Not complaining!)

At other times, people were relieved to learn I'm as old as I am, learning that the mother of my two daughters – me – is indeed, a real "grown up!"

Another time, a gorgeous, young guy came into the club – a tall, blond, blue-eyed sort with full lips and wild, golden locks. I hadn't seen a more strikingly handsome guy since Billy. We flirted and talked, and as he opened his mouth to speak, I detected the cutest Australian accent. I couldn't resist him, later learning "him" was named Darren and he asked me out on a date.

He took me to Splash, one of the finer restaurants on the water in Laguna Beach. Soon, I discovered Darren knew full well what to do with his mouth, earning him the title of "best kisser." Darren was also the most intelligent man I had ever met, making me feel pretty smart as well. He was different, mature, incredibly sweet and playful. In fact, I absolutely adored him.

He was much younger than me, and I started to realize there could be no future for us because of our 18-year (or so) age difference. We would talk about family, and he had even met Mo. He knew that I was older than him but never knew by how much. Being the gentleman that he was, he never asked either.

While Darren and I took barefoot walks in the sand, he shared he would like lots of children someday. That was something I could no longer provide him with, given my age. We dated for several months, and although it was difficult, slowly I had to let him go. I'm not sure if he ever understood why. I know if I had been younger in years, we could have possibly been together for the long haul.

I also tried dating a psychiatrist who was only six years younger than me, not feeling this to be an age difference at all. He came to see me often and was very persistent, writing beautiful poetry about me and having them printed professionally. I'm one that loves verbal expression so I finally decided I would give the relationship a try. I wasn't physically attracted to him though.

He lived in Hermosa Beach and we went out a couple of times. I thought he was a little odd, but nice. His parents were nudists in a nudist colony, but (fortunately) when we met them, they were dressed.

Mo was staying with me for a week, and while she was here, I seriously contemplated whether or not I wanted to continue dating this guy. He insisted on meeting her though, and the three of us went to dinner and a movie. It was when we exited the theater, that I saw him nudge my daughter out of the way so he could walk closer to me. I had seen enough, and that was the last time I ever went out with him again.

Then there was charismatic 29 year-old Marc, from La Jolla, who came to The Red Lion because he was in town for a convention. He told me he doesn't go to nightclubs and nor does he drink, but he noticed me and decided to play a little at my 21 table.

Marc was 17 years younger than me, and whenever I looked into his face I couldn't help but smile. He had the sweetest, boyish expression, with large, green eyes and the best smile with teeth as white as snow.

He was funny and charming, yet shy. He looked as if he could have been a beautiful Chippendale dancer, yet he owned his own exotic salt-water fish aquarium business.

He told me he would be in town for two days, and that he'd love to have lunch the following day, before driving back to San Diego. I said I'd love to, and that marked the beginning of a long on and off relationship lasting several years.

Telling Marc my age didn't matter to him whatsoever, and he wasn't sure if he ever wanted any children. Our relationship was extremely sweet and very, very loving, but some things left me feeling puzzled at times.

Marc came from a wealthy Jewish family and his mother seemed to baby him in the letters she wrote. His father, whom I met during a trip we took to Northern California, by Marc's own admission was crazy, and needed to take regular medication. At the time, I didn't really know anything about mental illness and thought he was classifying his father in more of a generalized way (i.e., a wild and crazy guy), versus a literal one.

Marc bought me a beautiful diamond ring and asked me to marry him, proposing on one knee during sunset on a hill overlooking all of San Diego. I was really overjoyed!

However, something was wrong. When I spent time with him, I recall seeing pills in his medicine cabinet. It didn't occur to me to read the labels and ask what they were for. Once an ex-wife called, mentioning something about his condition, but I had no idea what she was talking about and really didn't want to ask.

On one occasion, he told me he had seen some very scary and strange things in the middle of the night that made him run out of his home, barely dressed. I figured it was a bad nightmare. Rarely analyzing things, I knew we were all unique in our own ways, and that's what made life so very beautiful.

The last time I drove down to La Jolla, I called him on my cell several times to let him know I was on my way. He didn't answer his phone. Thankfully, he was there when I arrived, and I learned he was sleeping so soundly he didn't hear the phone ring. It was truly hard to comprehend, as I called so many times, wanting to make sure he would be there to answer the door when I showed up.

Later that day, Marc was again very tired and took a short nap. I tested him to see "just" how soundly he would actually sleep, calling his home number from my cell. After several rings he jumped up to answer it, only to find out it was I, checking out his claim that he was truly a deep sleeper. We fought about it afterwards as he thought it was an awful thing for me to have done. Our day was ruined and when I said goodbye I meant it: I would not be back.

I adored Marc and may have in fact, returned, but fate had something, and someone else in store for me.

I realize now having experience and knowledge in bipolar disorder, that sleeping very soundly for days at a time is perfectly normal for people suffering from this condition. I regret what I did to him.

What I didn't regret is meeting the great guy rollerblading on the bike path near my home. And now I could give him a chance – after all, he was only nine years younger than me!

# 44 MEETING MR, KELLY, THE QUARTERBACK

The day I had subconsciously been dreading had arrived. After five fantastic years, I had to move from my beautiful place in Laguna Beach. Christine's daughter was moving in and tearing out the walls, as part of some planned renovations. Christine cried when she told me, saying she just couldn't prolong it any longer. Graciously, she allowed me to take my time, in order that I could find another special place to live, and grow. I had been so happy here and wished it could have lasted forever. As such, Christine refused to accept any more rent money from me during the 1+1/2 months it took to find another residence.

As rentals were scarce and much too expensive, it really wasn't possible to stay in Laguna Beach. After looking in several other beach areas, I ended up finding a place back in Belmont Shore, complete with a bike path and ocean view. This had actually been my last choice, as it happened to be very near to where Billy and I lived. Mentally, I didn't want to move back there, because it held too many memories of Billy, but it was the only reasonable choice, for now.

I began riding my beach cruiser bike again, and also learned how to rollerblade. I spent most of my time outside, meeting many healthy "outdoorsy" types.

My red, beach cruiser bike was the biggest and last gift Billy bought for me. It meant a lot so I held onto it, even though I could never ride it in the hills of Laguna.

I also began running on the sand backwards for an hour each morning. I had never been this athletic in my life, but I was in better shape now than ever – and it felt fabulous!

Violet, Billy's mother, and I had become very close once again. She mailed me many of Billy's personal belongings, including a treasured silver moon chain that he always wore.

She insisted on me going to a Swedish Massage School, offering to pay for it. On a couple of occasions, she had noticed how long and lovingly I massaged Billy, while he was in the hospital. She assumed it was another one of my callings.

I went to school and enjoyed it more than I ever thought I would, graduating with an A+ average and receiving my official certification. Returning to Long Beach had been a much, happier experience than I could have ever anticipated!

By no coincidence, The Red Lion was also closing their nightclub, leaving me the responsibility of finding a new location for my 21 table. A good friend of mine suggested I contact a "happening" club, Cohiba, in Long Beach. I knew John, the owner, from years back and after talking to him and George, the manager, they gave me the okay. I moved my table in and it became the best location for my little business yet. I loved working there, even better than The Red Lion!

One weekend in April, the Grand Prix was in town and the place was overcrowded with people. While I was enjoying making some serious dough, an attractive guy sat at my table and started dropping several $100 bills in my tip jar. Other guys started to approach him, asking for his autograph. In fact, this guy was surrounded with what appeared to be a fan base, and being mini-mobbed, I figured he must be a famous race car driver. Finally, I said to him, "I don't mean to insult you. I can see how popular you are, but who are you?"

He told me his name was Jim Kelly, and I still didn't know who that was, so I smiled and asked him again. He told me he played football.

Lots of guys surrounding him were chuckling and mouthing to me just how famous he was, but since I wasn't into football, it didn't mean a thing to me. Jim Famous was getting more attention by the minute and seemed to be simply adored!

Jim sat at my table for quite some time playing 21, but he wasn't concentrating on the game at all. He was hitting every single hand and busting, clearly, much more interested in me.

I liked him, as he was funny and had a great personality. Throughout the evening, we talked and laughed a lot. I mentioned that I was also a massage therapist, telling him he could win one as a grand prize, if he just stopped busting. He didn't care about winning a massage, but he did book one on the spot for the following day. He told me he would need a massage after the race, since he was one of the celebrity drivers.

The next morning I awoke with a cold. In massage school we were taught to never spread germs to our clients. I called his hotel and left a message that I was sorry, but I had to cancel his massage. I did manage to go to work that night.

Jim returned to the club that very night and asked why I was working, as he thought I was sick. I told him I had a small cold but wasn't sick enough to not work my table. And with a bunch of guys and girls vying for Jim's attention, he stood by my table, looking rather hurt. For whatever reason, his focus was all on me, despite a gorgeous young, dark-haired girl trying to get him to notice her.

It's not that I didn't find him attractive, I did! However, I had just gone out on a first date with someone else, not that he asked me out, anyway.

Jim was polite and took a photo with the girl, yet instantly returned to my table, smiling at me the entire time. The crowds were crushing once again, and as I closed my table, security came over to escort me to my car safely, as they always did. I gave Jim one, last smile and headed out.

Sometime later, I found out that Jim was the quarterback that took his team to the Super Bowl four times but never won. He was also "happily" married!

## 45 HANGING OUT WITH "THE" JOHNNY DEPP

Finally, I started believing that my return was a real blessing. Having moved around all my life, as difficult as it was at times, I still wouldn't trade it for living and growing up in just one place. These diverse experiences have been "real world" eye openers, making me foster a true appreciation for life.

I was on a new and different journey now, and part of my shedding included no longer pursuing part-time acting jobs. Yet, there was always a lot of filming going on in Long Beach, since the area is very spread out and serves as a great "stand in" for a number of locations.

It was July 2000 when I found a note in my mailbox: Filming was going to commence right next door to me for a movie called "Blow." I didn't know any more details other than what was on the note. But as it sounded pretty cool, I was anxious to see who was starring in the film.

It was a little peculiar I thought, as the house next door was tiny and didn't look particularly special. But there are no coincidences, and soon, the area in which I lived was transformed into a 1960's hippie neighborhood. Old Chevys and Fords were parked on the street, with the street itself blocked off and only those who lived there allowed in. When the film crews showed up, my excitement started to build!

I made friends with the cameraman and crew, and one of them spilled the beans: This was a Johnny Depp film! Hearing this, I got really excited, hoping to see him on the set. Just because he was the male lead didn't necessarily mean he would be in this location, in these shots, but I was optimistic.

On the first day of filming I immediately spotted my friend Paul, "Pee Wee Herman!" I couldn't believe my eyes. I hadn't seen Paul since Billy's memorial two years ago, and I thought to myself, this was THE strangest coincidence. From all the locations in the world, Billy's good friend Paul would be right here in Long Beach, and smack next door to me. Funny thing, Billy often invited Paul to visit us in our laid-back community, but being the busy actor that he was, he never made it out.

I know that Billy, in Spirit, made this happen. It was another way he was reminding me of his presence; that he would always be with me.

Paul was getting his makeup put on when suddenly, he looked over and saw me too. I had been watching him, waiting for a good time to say hello, but didn't want to disturb the makeup artist's work. As soon as our eyes met, he jumped up from the chair and ran over, hugging me in disbelief.

Paul first asked if I lived around here, and I smiled, pointing to the duplex next door. I am sure we both thought how very strange that was. He told me that he had "just" made a new dedication to Billy in his movie, "Pee Wee Herman's Big Adventure," and that he was really happy to see me and be able to share this in person. With a promise to talk more later, he hurried back to finish make up and commence filming.

Still feeling high from seeing Paul, I turned to walk away, only to spot Johnny Depp, a mere few feet away from where I was standing! I couldn't take my eyes off of him – no wonder! He was busy talking to what I assumed was the director, and just as I was planning my strategy to get closer to meet him, he was rushed into the little house to start filming. By now a few more neighbors had gathered and the energy in the air was building!

Someone was sitting on the wall of my dwelling, getting "aged" by the makeup department. As I walked by, he smiled at me, his eyes following my every move. A neighbor I was friendly with (Debby) whispered to me, "Oh, Ray Liotta likes you!"

Wow, I had no idea it was him! Looking over and smiling, I couldn't believe so many famous stars were right here in front of my home, on this movie set, all on the same day!

Eventually, Johnny came out of the house as everyone took a break. This was the moment I chose to make myself known – to Johnny, that is! Calmly I walked up, and smiling sweetly I said, "Hi Johnny, I'm Shirley, and we have someone in common!"

Johnny smiled back, and as he looked at me a little curiously, I told him I was a friend of Marlon Brando. Johnny admired Marlon, and starred in several films with him. We talked for over 15 minutes, with him also sharing how much he enjoyed being a daddy to his lovely new daughter, Lily Rose. Afterwards, I politely asked him if he had time to take a photograph with me.

"Of course," he said. Promptly I called Debby over to take one of us.

Johnny couldn't have been more wonderful and gracious, and I ended up getting several photos with him. His spiritual essence was aglow, so much so that I felt it, and enjoyed basking in it. He was truly a very special and gentle soul that was ever so easy on the eyes. That day, feeling as if we were old friends, I became a huge Johnny Depp fan and friend.

Paul was only on set for day one of the three-day location shoot. After we said goodbye, I never saw him again. He always sent Billy a Christmas card, and now, he continued to send me one each year, along with a special handwritten note.

Johnny was on set all three days. Although he was very busy with filming, he always took the time to socialize with local admirers.

I asked some of the crew if they would like a Swedish massage on their breaks, telling them I was a licensed massage therapist. A couple of cameramen were very grateful for someone to ease their tense muscles, so I was able to drum up some business. Thinking how much I'd like to assist with relieving tension for Johnny, I asked his agent, whom I spoke with a fair bit, if Johnny would like a massage as well. After all, I WAS licensed!

Unfortunately this didn't come to pass. Heck, what was I thinking? Johnny's a big star and anyone could have taken advantage of him, trumping molestation charges up at a later date. All I was thinking however, was, darn it, I wouldn't charge Johnny a thing! I would have done it for FREE!

# 46 MEETING MY HUBBY, AND I PROMISE IT IS THE LAST ONE!

My weekend job at Cohiba's was more pleasure and less work. I have always believed that when you love what you do, it's no longer "work" at all!

Although I carried this attitude with pride, Linda still worried about me a lot, wondering how much longer I could fulfill the late nights at my age. She wished I would just find myself another husband, and both our worries would be over! I never gave this too much thought, and honestly I probably turned down a lot of prospects over the years. I hated the very formality of dating, feeling it to be very awkward and "staged." In addition, I had also been in an on again, off again relationship with young Marc for several years now. Once we were engaged; now we had broken up, again.

The rare times in my life when I was actually alone, I was happy and content. I enjoyed my alone time and never indulged in worry about the future. At the same time however, I was always open to meeting someone wonderful. That's the beauty of living in the "now" – all things are possible, and people and circumstances flow in and out of one's life at the times they are most needed.

Of course, if I were actually going to meet a new husband, given my aversion to dating, this guy would literally have to fall through my roof. Or, land on my doorstep (or in my kitchen, or living room) or in some other magical and mysterious way!

One night while at work, George, the manager told me he needed to talk. I sensed the urgency in his voice and was concerned about the vibe I was feeling.

George looked sad as I approached him. With obvious regret, and clearly not wanting to hurt me, he told me I had to close my table. The city inspectors had come by, and considered what I was doing, "gambling."

For a moment I thought he was kidding, because over the three years I worked there, we shared many jokes. Unfortunately, this was not the case. As part of my business and rapport with people, I bought small prizes for people to win when they cashed in enough chips. This made it more fun to play, and also why the city considered what I was doing gambling.

With a heavy heart, I closed my table, storing it downstairs in their basement until I knew what I was going to do. I was also served court papers, and was completely confused how to handle this.

Megsy's dad offered to come down from Sacramento to represent me free of charge, which was a huge relief, as I knew I would be in the best of hands. However, the owner called me, and concerned about the very real possibility of his place being closed down, insisted that I use his attorney – which I did. Gratefully, I never had to appear in court, and in about a month's time, all was settled.

I wish I could have said the same about my personal life, as once again, I had no idea where I would go or what I would do. My fingers were starting to cause me pain, cramping up when giving massages. My small clientele, mainly comprised of clients who won a massage as a grand prize for winning a zillion chips at my table were becoming more difficult to service.

There didn't seem to be any way to work at this full-time so with some of the money I saved up, I booked a trip to visit my mother in Colorado. Fortunately, I maintained my healthful activities of running, skating and biking on a daily basis, so aside from the pain in my fingers (an occupational hazard), I was in great shape.

"Worrying" was never much a part of my vocabulary, learning long ago that so many things one worries about never come to pass. I best handled things "in the moment," too occupied with doing what needed to get done to even have time to worry about any future issues.

Several guys would skate or ride their bikes next to me, in attempts at striking up conversation, but I just wasn't interested. However, one particular guy did stand out, and he alone, got my attention. I had noticed him before and one day he stopped me, telling me I should never walk my skates in the sand. When I asked him why, he said it was bad for the wheel bearings and would ultimately ruin my skates. He took that opportunity to look at my skates, telling me they were on too loosely.

"Would you like me to adjust them for you?" he asked politely.

With manners like these, how could I refuse? I was quite impressed now – I really liked this guy!

Introducing himself as Eric Njos, I couldn't help but marvel at his lovely, dark shoulder-length hair. Although I wasn't able to get a good look at his eyes because of the dark blue shades he was wearing, it was obvious he was very good looking.

I asked what kind of name "Njos" was, and spelling it out for me, he told me it was Norwegian. I was surprised as given his dark tan, he looked more Italian. And with that, I hardly let him get a word in edgewise, telling him while we skated, what had just happened regarding my work. This man not only listened to each word I was saying, but was extremely patient as well. An hour later, telling him how nice it was to talk his head off and that I appreciated his good listening skills, I went home, saying that maybe I'd see him later!

Just then, he removed his dark shades, and I found myself gazing into THE kindest and most beautiful green eyes I had ever seen. They actually had a glow to them; a "holy" glow. I couldn't stop staring at him, as his eyes – truly the window to his soul – absolutely warmed my heart. I had a sudden feeling of "familiarity" and comfort that I couldn't explain.

He said he would like to take me to lunch sometime at his favorite place in Seal Beach, adding we could either bike or skate to it. Eric also shared with me he was an engineer for the railroad, and was only in town about half the time, as he was always on call. His runs were to Yermo, California and Yuma, Arizona, requiring him to stay overnight on trips. How fascinating I thought, as I had never known anyone who had this kind of job, driving big cargo trains. As he was getting ready to leave for another work shift, our lunch would have to wait until he was back in town.

I gave him my phone number, letting him know I was leaving myself for Colorado for a few days. Sadly, I hadn't heard from him before I left. Yet, I was pretty sure about one thing: we both really liked each other – a lot.

When I arrived in Colorado, my mom and her friend were waiting for me at the airport. Upon arriving back to her apartment, I told my mom everything that was going on. Many times in the past she tried to get me to move to Colorado, suggesting that I move in with her and allow HER to look after ME! It always made me laugh, for as much as I loved my mom, I knew I'd go crazy if I did! However, as gambling was legal here, I could deal 21 at the nearby casino in Black Hawk.

That night we went to the little main town of Evergreen, taking a shortcut by climbing over the back of her steep hill. I always enjoyed going to the local and very popular cowboy bar, which boasted the greatest entertainment. In fact, people came from all over, driving the 40 minute trek from Denver, just to hang out at the venue, The Little Bear. The place was always crowded and very "happening!"

A good-looking cowboy approached us and asked me to dance. While we did, he tried to talk to me, but the music was so loud I couldn't hear a thing. Afterwards, I introduced him to my mom, and he asked her if he could take me next door for a few minutes to talk. He assured her it would not be for long, and smiling, my mom waved us on.

We sat down next door and he told me he owned his own home and business, had two big dogs, a truck and a Porsche – all which was starting to sound like a proposition! I told him I was considering moving here, and he responded by saying he would love to see me if I did.

About 15 minutes into the conversation, I wanted to get back to mom as she was already left alone too long. He took my number down, telling me he would call, which he did.

It was a fun trip as always, but soon it was time to return home. With lots on my mind, I arrived back to find a message from Eric on my answering machine. I was immediately uplifted to hear that he had called, since I had thought about him while I was away.

The following day, September 11, 2001, I had just walked in my front door from an early morning skate, when I noticed that I had an enormous amount of messages on my answering machine. All my friends called, because they knew my daughter Mo lived in New York and wanted to make sure she was okay.

Not knowing what this was about, I raced to the television to turn on the news, and to my horror, learned of the attacks that had just took place there, as well as other parts of the U.S.

Fear instantly flooded my body. I immediately attempted to call Mo yet couldn't get through, as all lines were busy. Tiff arrived at my house, and we snuggled up to one another, glued to the TV. I tried calling Mo over and over, and finally several hours later, managed to reach her. I was beyond thankful she was okay. Tiff left to go back to work, and while very relieved about Mo, we were both shaking at what had happened.

When Eric arrived in Yermo, he called me as soon as he heard, remembering I had a daughter in New York. What a memory, I thought; and what kindness he demonstrated towards my family and me.

Eric got back two days later, and I met him on the bike path. I told him I had a great time in Colorado and that I may move there in the near future. He asked if I still wanted to go to lunch.

"Of course!" I responded, thinking to myself, "Du'h, why wouldn't I?"

We rode our bikes to Walt's Wharf. Eric's good friend, Renee, worked there and we were introduced. She was entertaining, funny and sweet, and we became instant friends, exchanging phone numbers.

Over lunch, I learned that Eric had been in a five-year relationship just over a year ago, but they broke up because he hadn't married her. I thoroughly enjoyed talking and laughing with this man and his friend. So much so, that both Eric and I got a little buzzed. I felt as if we had known one another forever, in a very positive way. Finally, we got back on our bikes and made it safely back home.

Our date didn't end there. Eric asked me over to his home later that day, as his friend and neighbor (Bill; yes!) was cooking a fresh salmon meal for dinner, and he wanted me to attend.

Eric's high-rise beach apartment was a 10-minute drive from my place, and as soon as I got there, Bill greeted me with a sweet, specialty martini. We sat outside on the balcony, overlooking the ocean while enjoying delicious, gourmet salmon. Everything was right out of a romantic movie, with the exception that the image was starting to get a little fuzzy: The martinis hit Shirley, the lightweight!

I whispered to Eric that everything was starting to spin and that I felt a little sick. I asked if I could lie down and thanking Bill, we left and walked over to his apartment. Starting to sweat in my warm sweater, Eric, looking straight into my eyes in the kindest and gentlest way, helped me take off the knitted garment.

"It's okay, you're my girlfriend," he said sweetly, and cuddling, we both fell asleep.

I awoke to find myself smiling, and thankfully, in the absence of a hangover. In fact, I was feeling just plain old warm and fuzzy. I wasn't sure if the room was lit with sunlight, or by the radiance from Eric's smile.

We went back to my place, he bringing a few things along including his rollerblades. We spent the entire day together, until work called him.

From this day on, we were inseparable. As Tom Hanks said in Forrest Gump, "We were like two peas in a pod!"

# 47 MEETING SOME OF THE FAMILY

It was so very clear to us that we belonged together, and it wasn't long before Eric told me he wanted to marry me. From the moment we met, he stayed at my place every night, so we started to move his things into my small apartment. Eric sold much of his stuff and literally worked miracles with his belongings, even hanging our bikes from the ceiling to make it all fit.

Thanksgiving was just around the corner, and Eric's parents called to let him know they were coming for a visit. Having moved in with me, he was ready to give his notice, but as his parents would need a place to stay for the week they were in town, he decided to pay another month's rent. When his parents arrived, Eric was on a train on his way home, so I told him I would call them.

Skating on the bike path, I looked up at Eric's large apartment building, and saw two people on the balcony of the sixth floor. As I assumed it must be his parents, I stopped and waved, shouting in my loudest voice, "Hi Ray and Dolores, I'm Shirley!" Would you believe they actually saw and heard me from six floors up and 100 feet away!

Afterwards, I called Eric's apartment and invited his parents over for coffee and homemade scones. Although I offered to pick them up, they chose to walk 40 minutes over to my place. After a more formal introduction, they visited with me for about an hour.

As the next day was Thanksgiving, I told them we would gather here as I was cooking the best turkey dinner ever! It had actually been quite a few years since I cooked a turkey but I was confident that I hadn't lost my touch. I knew what a great cook I was!

On Thanksgiving morning, Eric and I got busy in the kitchen, getting ready for our little feast. His parents showed up at around 12:00 noon, and with a combination of great cooking and sincere intention, everything

NO COINCIDENCES ONLY MIRACLES

turned out perfect. Eric's dad commented on how tasty my gravy was, but he needn't have said another word, as I pride myself on my gravy recipe.

Eric's younger sister Joni flew in for a few days right after Thanksgiving. I think she liked me, although I felt as if I was still under "probation," as our relationship was so new and no one really knew me. She did share that Eric had called her, excited that he finally met me (beyond the "Hi" that we once exchanged), as he would watch me skate from his apartment! Joni was on a roll, and went on to say that her brother referred to me as "Raquel Welch" before learning my name.

Eric's secrets were out: He had actually tried to time our introduction in such a way that he would be in the position to talk to me when I skated by. I couldn't stop laughing, loving that we could share sentiments about her adorable brother!

I liked Joni right away, but I knew it would take a little time for her to get to know and trust me, naturally feeling protective over her big brother. Fortunately, it didn't take long, and we became very close.

Once Eric's family left, next was for Eric to meet Tiff. As she was living relatively close in Redondo Beach, we made plans to meet her and her fiancée by the Long Beach pier, at La Palapa, a great tropical restaurant on the beach. I had met Alan before and liked him; now I was hoping Tiff would like Eric.

We walked to the restaurant and saw them on the bike path, walking towards us. We all hugged while making our introductions and then went inside, sitting at the exotic bar while waiting for our table.

I have always had THE best time when getting together with Tiff. Both our energy is high and we always spend a fantastic time catching up on anything and everything.

Everyone was getting along really well, with all of us laughing and talking a hundred miles a minute. When Eric excused himself for a moment, Tiff looked at me with enthusiasm, saying, "Mom I just love him!" Alan shot her a look that translated to: "Say what?"

Tiff wasn't one to express her feelings so quickly, so her admission made me extremely happy.

# 48 TIFFANY'S WEDDING AND "BOTH OF MINE!"

A couple of months after Eric and I met, Tiffany called me with a change of wedding plans. She told me she and Alan were now getting married in the Bahamas on January 11, 2002, inviting Eric and me to join them there.

I was thrilled, and we met for dinner to discuss their final wedding plans. At this time, we also shared our plans to get married, saying we didn't yet have a date formalized. Tiff was absolutely thrilled to hear this, suggesting we should get married at the same time we were in the Bahamas for theirs! I was really moved by Tiff's sweet idea, but would never be one to rain on her parade, reminding her that this was their special day. She kept insisting that she wouldn't mind at all. We smiled, and that was the end of the discussion.

I had to get my passport in a hurry, as my German one had expired. I liked my German citizenship, but it was always a hassle getting it renewed. Having been a permanent resident of the U.S., I knew that I was likely eligible to receive my American citizenship. After a lot of research and completing a pile of paperwork, along with help from my mother, I finally received my American passport.

Eric and I flew to the Bahamas, enjoying our very first trip together. Tiff and Alan were staying at the Sandals resort, an all-inclusive hotel. We were invited to spend her wedding day there, enjoying unlimited food and drink all day.

Mo also flew in, arriving from New York, and it was fantastic to see her again. She hadn't made any room reservations in advance, and asked if she could stay with Eric and me. What a great idea, I thought, as it would provide them with an excellent opportunity to get to know one another.

On our way downstairs to get some things from the snack shop, we ran into Klaus. He grinned at us in his strange, unreadable way. I hadn't seen

Klaus in many years, and felt that on Tiffany's special day it was a time to celebrate and be cordial. More friends and family arrived, but it remained a small and intimate affair.

On Tiff's wedding day, I helped her fasten the buttons of her beautiful, long white dress. She looked breathtakingly stunning. As we were walking through the pool area towards the beach, while holding the back of her dress and not paying attention to the ground, I stumbled, coming within an inch of falling into the pool.

Little did I know this was a warning sign of things to come.

After the ceremony, Klaus stood up to deliver his speech. It was in absolutely poor taste; insulting to me and totally unforgiveable. I ran from the building, crying uncontrollably. Why in the world would he want to provoke me NOW, I asked myself.

*To WIN.*

And in his eyes – he had!

Eric and Mo followed close behind, attempting to console me. Mo tried to apologize for her father, stating he merely had zero social skills. What was most upsetting to me was that this caused drama where none should have existed. Tiffany deserved her wedding day to be perfect. As her father, Klaus's priority should have been to ensure that it was.

I can overlook a lot; I can forgive much; I can even skim over that which I know to be wrong, but this was just too hard-hitting, and came completely out of left field. Justifiably, I'm extremely sensitive when it comes to my children, especially after the pain I was put through over the years.

Eric and I decided not to go back inside, as I was still suffering from intermittent outbursts of tears, but as difficult as it was I did try to make the best of the remainder of the day. Eric suggested we all go on a short boat ride to one of the other, little islands and with Mo, we went. This "time out" on the water definitely helped calm my inner and outer turmoil.

On the following day, nothing much was said of the previous night's incident. Fortunately, as the resort was huge and filled with hundreds of tourists, we didn't run into Klaus again. The beach and its turquoise water continued to act as a perfect remedy, both calming and fun. The evening saw us playing a little 21 with both my daughters, and later, we took Mo out for a fresh, lobster dinner.

Two days later, Eric and I quietly decided to get married. I had a feeling, so much so that I brought a copy of my divorce papers with me.

We took a local bus downtown, arriving at the tiny courthouse. A couple of hours later, our turn came up to say, "I do." It was simple, quick and yet the most memorable January 14 I would ever spend! We couldn't get our marriage certificate that day, as I didn't have the paperwork required (they needed original copies of my divorce decree.) Although this put a damper on the day, it wasn't the worst thing that was about to happen.

On the bus ride back, we started to notice we were the only passengers on the bus, with the exception of a local man standing up front, next to the driver. The driver himself looked a little frightening, blasting the music extra loud, while driving dangerously erratic through neighborhoods that one would never want to drive through, much less walk in.

Eric threw me a sideways glance, and I met his gaze, sensing we both were sharing the same concerns. This was no regular route and I started to feel some very strange vibes coming from the energy of place, so to speak. Rather than picking up passengers, one guy would run in and out of houses, returning to the bus, and then the cycle would start all over again. To make matters even more concerning, the driver kept glaring at us through his rear-view mirror.

Eric and I would have exited the bus, but were concerned we might be truly jumping in harms way. Thankfully, after about 45 minutes of what should have been a 15-minute ride back to the resort, relief overwhelmed us as we saw we were back in the main town, where regular tourists milled everywhere. Our thoughts? That was one hell of a ride on the "Rasta" bus!

We returned safely back to the hotel, and the first person we spotted was Mo, basking in the sun. Smiling, we shared the news with her that we had just got married! Laughing, she jumped up to hug us, congratulating us both. Tiff had already left for her honeymoon to Paradise Island, so we called her later to relay our joyous news. Excited, she was looking forward to getting together with us at a later date for another celebration – ours!

After several days of dining, gambling, sun bathing and weddings, it was finally time to go home. We arrived at the airport and only 20 minutes into our flight, the pilot announced he was turning back! No one was told why and we were put up in a hotel, our departure put off until the next day. Strange!

Arriving back home to Long Beach, we decided with the slow Bahamas system, it might take years before we ever received our marriage certificate. So, four days later in Long Beach, we decided to get married again. On January 18, 2002, exactly one day before my birthday, I married my husband, Eric Njos for the second time in one week!

In the end, the only preacher we could find was in a chapel in the bad part of town. Although having preferred a beach ceremony, we were simply happy to have found someone to marry us on this chosen day.

We arrived to the chapel, dressed casually in shorts. The preacher was a real character, asking us if we had brought along a witness. Smiling, I looked at the forum, built out of cheap particleboard, and at the fake plastic flowers, too bright in their synthetic colors.

"Hold on, I'll be right back," said the preacher, running outside. A minute later he returned, with one very, drunken man as our witness! I don't know how Eric and I held back laughter throughout the short "ceremony," especially as the intoxicated man, slouched on the bench, started yelling out several funny compliments during our exchange. After we had said our vows, I turned to the preacher, telling him although our service was casual, this marriage would be one that would last forever.

To our delight, he said he "gets feelings" when he marries people and knew from the get-go that ours would last. Eric tipped the preacher, went over to the bench and tipped our drunken witness then together, we left to celebrate our second wedding!

Shortly after, a genuine marriage certificate arrived in our mailbox.

THE MORAL OF THE STORY: You don't need a fancy wedding to live Happily Ever After!

After re-living several memories and experiences I shared with all my husbands (as well as a few boyfriends, included for good measure), it is with pure joy to be writing about the ONE man who, moving forward, will be the ONLY man in this personal "capacity" now. We have had an incredible journey ourselves in the 11 years we have been together – one of great mutual love and respect. Knowing me as one who enjoys staying in the present moment, as one of my favorite authors, Eckhart Tolle expresses so well, visiting the past (as I have done while writing my autobiography) is not the same as "living" in the past. As an author myself, I both live – and write – from THIS MOMENT in time. In the case of Eric's "chapter" in my life, it's a pleasure and honor to describe his place in my life and heart, as the one chosen to "walk us both home."

# 49 I RECEIVED ONE OF THE WORST PHONE CALLS IN MY LIFE

I loved being married to this incredibly kind and very understanding man. He wined and dined me whenever he was at home. As well, we enjoyed eating out, especially sushi and Saki. We continued to skate constantly, and I even attempted snowboarding on several occasions! To this day we remain very active, jogging, biking and walking together. In short, we simply have the best time enjoying one another, and life.

Eric was the first man to "NOT" push any of my red buttons – something I had resigned myself as being nearly impossible. As such, we communicate and resolve any differences in the absence of screaming and fighting. The number of times I have even slightly raised my voice I can count on my hand – not too bad over the course of 11 years!

The funny thing, being so connected to Spirit, is that I wasn't even looking when I found this near "perfect man," and much later in life, I might add. He came with no baggage and amazingly, has only been married once – well twice in fact – both times to me! The fact that he never judged me on my number of marriages is in itself, admirable. Eric never needed any proof, but I have, day by day, proven to him that when you trust and follow your heart and intuition, one can never go wrong.

His parents were so happy to learn we had gotten married, that they threw us a big celebration at their home near Seattle, inviting more relatives than I could even count. I had met Joni, his younger sister and now, it was wonderful meeting Diana, his older sister. I immediately fell in love with his 92 year-old grandmother, feeling as though she had always been my grandma, too. There were cousins, aunts, uncles and friends, with everyone being truly beautiful human beings. I had never been around such a large and welcoming family in my entire life.

Eric's parents' home is built on several acres of beautiful land, so there was plenty of room for everyone. After indulging in much-too-much scrumptious food, his dad made a huge open-fire outdoors, and we continued to stay up late, laughing, drinking and getting acquainted with one another. After a truly enjoyable three-day stay, it was time to go home.

One day while Eric was on his morning beach run, he saw a "For Rent" sign, right on the bay in the Peninsula. We were feeling a little crowded in the small apartment, so we followed up with viewing the property. Feeling it was perfect for us both, we rented it. Eric owned a kayak and this was an ideal location for it. As the opportunity presented, I learned to kayak, too.

During this time I learned that Mo came "out" as being gay, which wasn't a total surprise to me. As long as she was happy, I was happy too. Needless to say, I love both my children unconditionally.

Having lived here only eight months, we were told that the building had been sold and would soon be torn down, forcing all tenants to have to move out. We wanted to live in a quieter place anyway, so we moved to what I refer to as the "Stepford Wives" city – Irvine, CA. Here, we rented a beautiful one-bedroom apartment, complete with its own gym and swimming pool. We marveled on how well the building and grounds were kept, and all was very quiet.

One day in 2003, having lived here for a couple of months, I received a telephone call late in the afternoon. On the other end of the phone, a young girl's voice introduced herself as my Mo's roommate. She went on to say that my daughter was taken to St. Vincent's Psychiatric Hospital in Manhattan.

Her words were so unexpected and came so fast I barely had time to react. In a state of disbelief, I heard myself ask what was going on.

She continued to tell me that the previous night during a small party they threw, Mo started acting strangely. She pounded on the couch, saying over and over, "Define yourself," frightening her and their guests. There were no drugs involved, she reassured me.

"How dare you take this kind of action!" a voice screamed inside my head, but I continued to listen.

On the way to the hospital, she revealed that Mo attempted to kill herself by throwing herself out of the moving cab.

At this point I had heard enough, and I thanked her for giving me this information. The ONLY THING on my mind was rescuing my daughter. It was a blessing Eric was home and not on a run. Breathless, I filled him in on everything I had just been told. The idea that all had been a mistake seeped into both our minds, and I made immediate flight arrangements to catch the first flight to New York – with an extra ticket for Mo, to bring her home. I then called the hospital, and as her mother, asked to speak with anyone who could help. I was connected to Mo's social worker, and disappointingly, was given very little information. I let her know I was flying out the next day and would arrive there soon.

I told Eric I could handle this myself, and that he should stay home and go to work when he got the call. I then telephoned Tiff to bring her up to speed. Tiff offered to go with me, but I insisted as I had with Eric that I would be fine going alone. Tiff helped me arrange hotel reservations and I started feeling calmer, believing that all would be well.

I arrived into New York early the next day, and in the freezing cold, caught a cab directly to the hospital. I arrived to a very crowded waiting room and tried to wait patiently as hospital staff worked through a bewildering amount of red tape, in order that I be reunited with my daughter.

Finally after four agonizing hours of waiting, the social worker came down to greet me, apologizing for the long wait. We rode up in a padded elevator, on our way to Mo. She escorted me into a private room, and seconds later, Mo came in wearing pink hospital scrubs. The shock, stress and fatigue had finally taken its toll on me, and fighting back tears, I stood up to hug her.

I noticed that Mo looked somewhat confused, dazed and very fragile. With the social worker out of the room and giving us the privacy we needed, I told her in a whispered and rushed voice that everything would be fine and I was in no way going to leave her there.

"In fact," I said, pulling out the plane ticket I had purchased, "Here is your ticket to come home with me." I continued offering reassurances that she needn't worry about a thing.

For a moment, she seemed happy when she saw the ticket, but then, after a few minutes, she asked if I would like to see her room. Although this was generally forbidden, we crossed the hall and curious, I took a quick peek. It was bare, with only two tiny beds, but was informed her roommate was a loud talker, a snorer and someone who smoked. We continued to the main visiting area, with me constantly reassuring her that when we were done visiting, I would talk to her social worker and make all the necessary arrangements for her release.

Slowly, she started speaking more, which made me feel better. But quite suddenly, her sentences didn't make sense. I now know this is referred to as "word salad." The more she talked, the more she asked, "Do you know what I mean mom?" Constantly.

I was speechless. It started to occur to me that something *was* actually wrong, and I began to cry openly in front of her.

Just then the social worker came back into the room, informing us that visiting time was over. Mo returned to her room, and after saying goodbye, I followed the social worker into her office.

She was a very nice, young lady and although she tried explaining some things to me, I was left feeling totally confused. She ended by telling me that a proper diagnosis usually takes quite some time, even years, but it appeared that my daughter may be schizophrenic and bipolar. Although I asked a lot of questions, I honestly had no idea what this meant. From the little I was told, it didn't sound good at all.

Wishing now I hadn't been so hasty in telling Eric and Tiff to stay home, I went back to my hotel and called them, filling them in on what I had learned. I spoke with Tiff for almost an hour, and we both shared in our shock and sadness. Eric and I were on the phone for hours, him comforting me until I passed out from sheer exhaustion.

Indescribably upset, the next morning I went to visit Mo again. She acted as if nothing was wrong. Suddenly, she informed me she would be staying in New York and would soon be released. Speechless once again, after our visit I summoned the social worker and was told that it might take a long while before Mo was released. With a promise we would stay in touch on a daily basis, I took Mo's plane ticket and handed it to the social worker, for her to use when she felt ready.

I flew back alone, dazed and utterly bewildered, with a different sense of sadness I had rarely, if ever, experienced, deep in the pit of my soul. What lie ahead for my child, or for me, I wondered. Looking out the window, watching the miles between Mo and myself become greater and greater, I resolved to learn all about the illnesses that my daughter was suspected of suffering from.

## 50 MO MOVED IN WITH US, UNTIL...

My life was changed once again, forever now, and I had no idea of the tumultuous times that lie ahead. I was on the phone daily, speaking with doctors, the social worker, and most of all, my Mo. I needed to show her that she would never have to go through any of this alone, and that I would always stay right by her side.

Every day was different when I talked to Mo, and with it, very difficult to hear the sadness and frustration in her voice. Being totally confined at such a young age of only 24 years old, her soul was beckoning for freedom. The medication she was given made her extremely lethargic a lot of the time, and I was told it could take some time to determine an exact dose, as each patient was different.

I hoped and prayed this was all just some kind of huge mistake, but as my consciousness drifted toward Spirit, I knew enough to leave things up to faith.

About three months later, Mo was ready for release. As I wanted her to come back to California to live with us, I had to sign papers, basically ensuring she would continue regular doctor visits, and most important, stay on her medication. Mo sounded pretty good but I could tell that she had been through a lot. I was just so very excited to see her, and help take care of her. I KNEW my love would cure her!

If only things were that simple.

We picked Mo up at the airport. and it was wonderful seeing her again! I had already chosen the clinic in Irvine where I would take her for continued after care, and by now, had learned a little more about mental illness. I still had a lot to learn, this becoming painfully clear as the days went on.

When we arrived back home late that afternoon, Mo told me she wanted to take a walk alone and explore our neighborhood. A couple of hours went by, and Mo still had not returned. I was getting ready to call the police, as darkness was beginning to fall, but Eric wanted to go out and look for her before I did. I waited at home, just in case Mo showed up. Not long after, Eric returned with Mo – and boy was I relieved!

Dripping wet, Mo told me she had completely gotten lost which was understandable, as so many of the hundreds of apartments in the area looked similar. She said she stopped a guy to use his cell phone to call, but after three attempts of getting wrong numbers each time, she gave up. Since she was already so tired, she decided to go rest and lie in a swimming pool, not knowing what else she could possibly do.

By no coincidence, the pool just happened to be the pool in our large apartment complex, out of so many others in the neighborhood. I knew at that moment she was being watched over by the divine. All this – and on the very first day she arrived!

I took her to the clinic regularly and was thankful for her cooperation, since she didn't like taking medication, telling me she knew she didn't need it. I insisted though, following doctor's orders. We converted our living room into her bedroom, and it was crowded once again. We didn't mind though, as she needed us now and rest was very important for her.

Eventually, Mo became bored, not doing much with her life. I thought perhaps she was ready to work at a carefree job, unlike the bartending gigs she held in some of New York's top nightclubs. Suggesting she apply to one of my favorite stores, Trader Joes, as many cool kids would surround her, she put in her application. To our delight, they called her back immediately, offering her a part-time job. I was so thrilled that I gave her my car in order that she be able to drive to work.

Certain days were extremely difficult for her mentally, but she continued to work and even made a couple of new friends. I loved that Mo was finally "back," and living a relatively normal life.

Nine months after we moved to Irvine, we were informed that as our lease was up, rent would be raised $200. We found this ridiculous, and after talking amongst each other, I felt that moving to Long Beach was the best idea. It had a large, gay community that would be great for Mo. She too was excited about this, and not long after, we found a nice apartment back in Belmont Shore. I also found a new clinic downtown to take her to.

I mistakenly thought Mo could easily transfer to a Trader Joe's in Long Beach, but they weren't doing transfers for someone with such a short length of employment, nor were they currently hiring. Mo did enjoy going to some of the gay bars, and would ride my bike there as I didn't want her driving the car, in case she had a drink. She wasn't supposed to drink while on her medication, so I told her to please be careful, while realizing she also needed some kind of social activity again.

As time went on, Mo would lie on the couch, and sleep most days. She still wasn't working, and we were all becoming frustrated at this. In addition, she wanted to move out and live on her own. Finally, she got a job at the Fish House in downtown Long Beach. In celebration, Eric and I dined at the restaurant, asking to be seated in her section. She was a great and extremely efficient server and as we were both very impressed, Eric left her a big tip.

Not long after as she was making good money, Mo decided to rent her own apartment. We helped her furnish the small single and dropped by often to visit.

One day, out of the blue, she said she was leaving and moving to Italy. And with very little warning, she was simply gone.

# 51 TIFF AND I MADE THE TRIP TO NEW YORK, TO VISIT MO IN THE HOSPITAL

Naturally feeling worried but yet, completely helpless at the same time, I eventually heard from Mo. She was back in New York, having flown in from Milan, Italy. She shared she didn't even know how she made it back to the United States.

She was struggling to hold down any job now, as working completely overwhelmed her in every way. She also confided in me that she could hear voices. Even her new living arrangement, sharing a space with a roommate, was quite problematic.

The next few years saw Mo in and out of different psychiatric hospitals, her having stayed as long as a year and a half in one such facility. During each hospitalization I became involved, as Mo always gave the various social workers my telephone number. It was exceedingly difficult but I had pledged to Mo that she would never feel alone. As such, I was there to do whatever it took; most of all, to show her how very much I loved her.

As far as I am aware, her father called Tiff on a few occasions, asking for an update on Mo. Once while she was living with us, he came over to talk with her, trying to make some semblance of her life. It didn't go beyond that.

Several times I received collect calls from her, and on one occurrence, she was homeless in the streets of New York. This had happened after living with us again, albeit for only ONE DAY, a mere 24 hours after we bought her a ticket for California.

I was grateful Mo at least knew to call me. Before she left, I had pleaded with her, warning her that she had absolutely no place to go, yet she wouldn't listen as she argued that she did. By law she was an adult, so I had no way of stopping her.

I was very tempted to book her a hotel for the night, but I also had lessons to learn; namely, what it meant by demonstrating "tough love." When she called in this predicament, I asked her to wait by the phone booth while I looked online for homeless shelters, and found her one for the night. Another time, she found shelter at the airport, where at least it was warm and safe.

Again, a pattern emerged, with Eric and I having her come back to live with us on many, more occasions. Sometimes her stays here lasted several months; yet other times, mere hours, but no matter where she was, I was determined to save her and make her well again with my love and care.

Yet as much as I attempted to drench Mo in love, her coming out to California – then back peddling and leaving again – was driving us all crazy! We would buy her tickets to fly back and stay with us, then no sooner had she arrived, she would want to leave the very, next day. With those sentiments came a strong determination, so there was just no stopping her.

I did apply tough love to Mo's situation, or else I would have had a breakdown myself (which in fact, I did, temporarily). Her excuse for leaving was the same each time: She was leaving to be with a girl that she loved in New York. This was some roller coaster ride, and I needed to get off! The very last time she tried this, I told her she absolutely HAD to stay, at least until the end of the week, as I had made an appointment for her to go to the Supplemental Security Income (SSI) office, in order that she could receive disability payments. This time, to my relief she agreed, as she wanted some money of her own. I went with her on her appointment, ensuring she had all the information needed to qualify for disability payments. Finally, she would have a little money; this helping us too as up until now, we were largely supporting her as she was no longer able to hold down a job.

In January 2005, Mo had been in the Manhattan Psychiatric Center for just over a year, and Tiff and I decided to fly to New York to visit her. Right before we left, I received a call that Mo was being released. Now the three of us could enjoy some fun together, with Mo experiencing freedom for the first time in many months.

Mo asked Tiff to bring her the snowboard she loved so much, and so across the country, Tiff lugged the huge piece of sports equipment. Something else Mo could now do was use her cell phone (This was prohibited while she was a resident at the hospital.) I called her on her phone when we landed, asking that she meet us at the hotel we were staying at.

When the hospital discharged her, they also gave her an apartment in which to live, as well as regulated medical care. The program, "PATHWAYS HOUSING" is something I will be forever grateful for. I cannot say enough positive things about them, as they saved not only her life, but mine as well. Mo is doing as well as she is today, as a result of

Pathways Housing, with her doctor and I staying in direct contact.

Mo traveled by subway to greet us at the W Hotel in Manhattan. What a heck of a reunion it was! Money was absolutely no object during the trip and did we ever live it up, drinking champagne and dining out in the finest restaurants of Mo's choice. Each night we went out, with Mo showing us around the city, taking us to clubs she used to work at and introducing us to some of her old friends. What wonderful therapy this was, for my heart!

Tiff was incredibly generous, insisting on paying for almost everything, as it was my birthday "month." Spending time with my two daughters was the BEST gift I could have ever asked for!

The three of us enjoyed extra special bonding time during this trip, including engaging in deep conversation about the time we were separated, while they lived with their father and stepmother. I learned it was no "Leave it to Beaver" family as I had imagined. In fact, their lives during this time resembled nothing I had believed it to be, being far from perfect.

We didn't want our happiness to be marred by going back in time, so the rest of our together time was spent in moments of love and celebration.

Mo needed things for her apartment, and as we also wanted to see where she lived, we took her shopping to Bed Bath & Beyond. The three of us, along with the snowboard and all her purchases, ended up at her place after a long cab ride. When we arrived there, her roommate seemed frightened to see so many people come in. Smiling, we told her "we are family" and that everything was okay. We didn't stay long as we wanted to get back to the hotel and go out again that night.

We finally experienced the "pulse" of the city, opting to take a subway back to the hotel, versus a cab. That night, while having a blast at an amazing restaurant, I completely lost my voice! Without so much as being able to whisper, Tiff called Eric for me, as we all laughed about my "misfortune." But "fortunately," Mo thought to bring back bitters from the bar several times, in an attempt to restore my voice. It didn't – not really – as between the nonstop talking and ingesting spicy hot sauce, it simply disappeared! The next morning, everyone had the benefit of the "full me" again, my voice completely restored.

Reminiscent of the sleepovers I enjoyed with my daughters when they were little, the three of us all shared one deluxe room. Tiff and I shared a huge plush bed, and Mo had the other, all of us able to sleep in luxury while sharing many memorable moments.

After three fun-filled days, it was time to return home. We were both very sad to leave our Mo alone in New York. We left very early to catch our flight, and Mo was barely awake when we both kissed her goodbye.

She called me later, telling me that she had awoken several hours later and realizing we were gone, became very sad.

"Where's my mom and sister?" was all she could think of.

I too shared the same thoughts during the long flight home. This trip was extremely special and memorable for me, remaining vividly in my heart. To this day, I will never forget how the three of us painted the town red!

# 52 ERIC FULFILLED MY DREAM, TAKING ME
## HOME TO FRANKFURT, GERMANY

We both felt a vacation was long overdue for the two of us. As I've always dreamt of returning to Germany to revisit the place I was born and raised, Eric made arrangements for us to travel there.

A short while ago, I had purchased a computer at a garage sale but aside from searching the Internet and performing other small tasks, I didn't know how else to use it. To me, it was a foreign device best suited to scholarly types and "smart" people.

Unfortunately, from when I was very young, my mother told me I was dumb. Although I'm sure she had long forgotten this, it was one of those things that stuck with me throughout my life. I knew I had more than my share of common sense, however when it came to anything intellectual or "bookish" I switched to auto pilot, assuming I wasn't up to the task and thus, blocking out many more capabilities. I'm not complaining though – my life as an artist is what I feel my soul enjoys the most. It's where I belong.

What did entice me to learn more about computers was something called "eBay." I had great things to sell that I no longer wanted or needed, including some of my own fashion designs. By listing these items on the website, I thought I might get decent money and enjoy the bidding wars that might ensue!

Tiff and Linda showed me how to list my goods and were very helpful in the beginning. I caught on extremely quickly, selling much more than I had ever planned. In addition to lightening my load, eBay helped bring in extra income, too.

Eric also found practical uses for a computer, finding it handy to manage his workload. Plus, he enjoyed planning trips – such as the one we were about to embark on.

I could hardly maintain my excitement, as soon, I would actually get to see my hometown again, which held so many memories for me.

While in Frankfurt, I was also going to try to find Willy Simon, my first cousin and only family remaining there. Thoughts of seeing him again brought tears to my eyes, as he was like a brother to me and I really loved him. To me, this trip represented the BEST TRIP, period, with no one other than Eric making this dream come true!

At long last, we arrived in Frankfurt, with April boasting great weather. We made a quick stop to our hotel, as I was too anxious to hang around for even a minute, wanting to find my building and street upon which I grew up. I hoped it would still be there, after all these years.

Eric, having researched our trip thoroughly knew which direction to take, telling me it was nearby. In all my excitement, I insisted on taking a cab – yet in less time than it took me to blink, there it was! We laughed at the brief cab ride and now understood why the driver gave us a funny look when we gave him the address.

If footage existed of this very moment, it would probably show me jumping out of a moving vehicle! I was here! I hardly recognized my building, or the surroundings, as the area had modernized with the addition of fresh paint and the absence of bombed buildings (a part of the landscape upon which I grew up). Emotions overwhelmed me as I went immediately to the wall of my building, extending my hands to touch the exterior. The moment my fingers felt the cool brick, tears streamed down my face.

It was still my building. My home!

I hoped Eric would hurry and pay the cab driver so I could get inside. The building was locked but not one to be deterred, I pushed every single buzzer! A young couple on the third floor leaning out their window saw me, asking who I was. As I recalled enough German, I was able to shout out that I had just traveled from the United States and I used to live in this building as a child. I asked if it would be possible for them to buzz me in so I could see again where I grew up. Smiling, they responded, "Sure" in English, and I heard the front door unlock.

Fresh tears threatened to fall as I became all choked up. As I commit these experiences to paper, I find it difficult to translate into words the EXACT feelings I felt, other than I was "HOME." Immediately, I saw the steep staircase that lead to the very top of the room where I used to live. Even Eric marveled at how steep it was, as we made our way up the long, wooden stairs.

Once at the top, I saw the door to the room I lived in, and paused to take a deep breath. The only toilet in the hall, located directly behind me still had the long "flush" chain attached. Clotheslines still hung in the hall, with laundry from the tenants drying on them. Everything I saw was so familiar, as if it were only yesterday when I helped MEINE MUTTI (my

208

mom) secure our clothes onto the line.

My heart racing, I took another deep breath and braced myself as I knocked on the door. A man opened it, and with Eric standing just behind me, I introduced myself, talking fast while hoping he would understand my nine year-old German vocabulary.

My knees felt weaker with each sentence I spoke, as I explained as best as I could that I was born here, and lived RIGHT HERE in his room from 1948 until 1957. I asked the question which I prayed I would hear a yes to: "Could I PLEASE take a quick look inside?"

I think what most shocked him was when I said "1948," and in a question, he repeated the date. Still trembling as my emotions were literally just beneath my skin the entire time, I nodded yes.

"The room is totally bare," he said. "I'm in the middle of painting it." As he spoke, I was brought back to the present moment and smelled the fresh paint, waffling through the crack.

And with that, he opened the door. I saw the tiniest little room, the entire space being a bit smaller than my kitchen in Long Beach. I spotted the part of the ceiling that angled down, and the one little window I remembered so well. A memory flashed into my mind, of me being on a leash outside that window, in order that I get some fresh air.

I also remembered the "angel hair" that hung from it, one Christmas. As angels had "just" dropped off a present, while flying away, they left a little of their hair behind – or so my mother told me. At the very moment my mother told me this, the tiny window banged shut, making this one of my fondest childhood memories. To this day I don't know how my mother managed to pull this off, or maybe real angels exist after all. (In Germany, angels bring gifts on December 24, while Santa Claus brings fruit and cookies earlier in the month, on the 6th.)

I couldn't help but marvel at how absolutely tiny the room was. I remembered it as being small, but not THIS small! As a child, it felt larger, just like the memories that had begun to make themselves so very real.

I talked a little more with the man as he expressed an interest in my journey, and then not long after, I thanked him and we left. Although I could have stayed there all day, I sensed that Eric wanted to do more exploring.

I took one long, last, teary-eyed look, and went back down the staircase – the one I remembered being carried down, kicking and screaming, into the cellar. I told Eric we couldn't leave until I saw the cellar again.

Walking back to behind the stairway, I spotted the little door that opened to the entrance of the cellar. Eric entered first, and I followed; so thankful to have him with me, especially in this moment.

It all looked so very familiar. The cellar was dark but not as dark as I had remembered, and the entrance had also been painted white. I saw the coal again and a locked cage, including some things tenants had stored there. It too was quite an emotional experience yet very healing, as it also wasn't quite as monstrous-looking as I had remembered it from my childhood. Everything had been modernized, taking into consideration that I was seeing it all again, 50 years later.

Eric suggested we try to find my school. From memory, I remembered which direction to take, and we began to walk. Not 10 minutes later, I spotted my school, gated and locked.

What was most interesting to me was seeing the little kindergarten section, just off to the right. I had spent a lot of fun time here after school, in this area called the "Hort." Here, mom was given leftover hot soup for us once in a while, it being a huge treat. It was also where they let me burn flower pictures into wooden hangers, to give as a gift for my mom on Christmas. It too looked exactly the way I remembered it, with the windows still decorated with children's art.

Walking down memory lane felt amazing and surreal, as these were the times I thought about a lot. The memories ingrained from this period of my life are ones neither my friends nor my children could relate to.

It has become apparent that much of my German upbringing has stayed with me throughout my entire life; so much so, that I don't think it's even possible to lose one's roots. Every single day I remain appreciative for all that I have been given. In my "present" life, I want for not, having most of what I want and need. This is in stark comparison to the struggles I faced as a child. Because of this, I have always remained humbled, never taking anything for granted.

We continued on, me being extremely happy to be able to share all this with my husband and silently wishing my mother had been well enough to make this trip with us.

Seeing many of the sights as an adult made it feel like I was seeing them for the first time. I think I remembered the big Eschersheimer tower, which was on my street "Eschersheimerlandstrasse," and appeared to be located right in the middle of Frankfurt. We stopped and ate lunch here.

Finally, Eric and I thought we better head back to the hotel and rest up a bit, before we got ready for dinner. This was literally our first day in Frankfurt Am Main, and in all my excitement, I never felt jet lagged at all!

Eric and I thoroughly enjoyed our first three days in Frankfurt, walking everywhere and taking in the sights while enjoying the delicious, authentic German food that I love.

Eric got a real kick out of my German-speaking skills, and I enjoyed translating for him as every day my vocabulary grew. One never forgets their language first spoken, and although it may get stagnant when not used on a daily basis, it remains inside our memory bank, waiting for a full return when triggered! The German people were very friendly, really enjoying my story as to what brought me here. One day, I told Eric, if and when the opportunity arose, I could see myself living here again on a permanent basis. Grinning, Eric warmed my heart when he said that maybe we could retire here someday.

We visited a building that offered panoramic views overlooking Frankfurt, and took a photo that was published in our local newspaper in

Long Beach.

Locating Willy was still very much on my mind, and looking in the phone book, I made several calls in attempts to find my cousin. There were many listings with the name "Willy Simon" and yet, although I thought I came close I had no luck. One man did say, he wished it were he!

A week before we were scheduled to return home, we rented a car. Eric drove on the Autobahn as if he were German, barreling down the road at around 100 miles per hour (over 160 kilometers, using their metric system of measurement), on our way to the Black Forest.

We loved Baden Baden and chose to have lunch there. We stayed in bed and breakfast type accommodations, meeting the nicest people on our travels. We spent days driving through the Black Forest. Beautiful and large, we hiked, walked and took in the sights, including visiting beautiful and famous castles. We stopped in Heidelberg on our way back, and loved it! Tiff was even an exchange student here, while in college.

While we noticed "exits" to concentration camps, we decided to save this for another visit.

We visited the "Struwwelpeter" museum that I really wanted to see. This was a scary children's fairytale that I grew up with, but as all the children did – I loved it! I bought several souvenirs, including Struwwelpeter watches, which I gave to each of my daughters, in hopes they would become valuable one day.

Our entire trip was simply fantastic. I give Eric a lot of credit for doing the amazing job he did, mapping all our points of interest. After several days of seeing much more of Germany than I ever had while living here, it was time to return to our hotel in Frankfurt for our last three days.

We walked around my old neighborhood one final time, taking a last bittersweet look at my building. In German, I said goodbye for now – "AUF WIEDERSEHEN."

Sadly, we also said goodbye to our friends at the hotel, local shops and restaurants, as we prepared to head back home to America, with a promise to return again.

# 53 IMPORTANT LITTLE FAMILY MOMENTS

Shortly after returning from Germany, it was time for a change. I decided to go blonde in 2005 since I was getting more grey hairs than I could pull.

Believe me, I LOVED my jet black hair, but felt going lighter in color at this "age and stage" would give me a more youthful appearance. So, I had traded my long tresses for "short and spiky," making it much easier to transition into such a dramatic change. Surprisingly, my daughters and friends loved it and Eric simply liked whatever I did to myself. I think the look suited me well, and as my hair gradually grew out, I loved it even more.

Menopause had crept up on me some time ago; there was no more denying this. I didn't intentionally try to hide it, but I was just oblivious in a way, except for riding the waves of hot flashes, so to speak. And there were many. Thankfully, I never experienced the mood swings and certainly felt blessed in their absence; however it was obvious from my physical changes (including some weight gain, which I had never suffered from before) that my hormones were out of whack, something my mother had brought to my attention.

Eric and I felt that it would be a nice gesture for his parents and my mom to meet. We arranged a trip to Lake Tahoe, choosing to stay at Megsy's cabin. I called my mom and once she learned we were having a family get together with my in-laws, she became really excited.

My mother arrived first, and I made sure, as always, that I was right there as she got off the plane. I asked security for special permission to meet mom where I did, as she was elderly. The first thing out of my mom's mouth was "Ta-daaa!" This was her favorite expression and she used it often. She was so happy to see me and really liked my blonde hair, but then immediately asked for Eric, as he was standing behind me and out of her

214

sight line.

We enjoyed a light lunch and then went back to pick up Ray and Dolores, Eric's parents. Everyone was chatting now and we were all in a good mood, happy that everyone had met. At the cabin, we made coffee then later, popped the cork off a bottle of champagne. "TA-DAAA," mom exclaimed, the moment the cork flew out of the bottle. This was not surprising, as champagne was another favorite of hers.

My mom loved Dolores the moment the two met. She said they would have been best friends, if they had lived closer together. It was cute and heartwarming. Both of Eric's parents were getting a real kick out of my very lively and chatty mom. I caught myself holding my breath a couple of times once the champagne started flowing, hoping she wouldn't embarrass me, as she did at times, purely unintentionally.

Our plan was to visit the casino later in the day for some gambling fun. My mom must have been born with a horseshoe, as she never lost a single time while playing the slot machines. She would show off by winning once again! Ray, curious what her secret was, asked my mom how he too could win at the slots. My mom basically told him that she had a "vibe" and a feel for the winning machines. Who was going to argue with that?

Eric's parents stayed in a nearby hotel, while my mom stayed in the cabin with us, loving every moment of it.

We also took a long and lovely drive through the lake, so everyone could admire the beauty of the Tahoe area. We stopped at a scenic spot to enjoy the surroundings and take some pictures.

We came across a large, wet puddle, and with mom's ballerina slippers, she had no chance of crossing it. Eric offered to give her a piggyback ride – something my mother adored. From then on, whenever I called her, it was all she talked about. Over and over she'd remind me how much she loved the piggyback ride Eric gave her, since no one had ever shown her such courtesy as he had.

At one point while we were lingering around the lake, Mo called, telling me she wasn't feeling well again and wanted to come back to California and live with us. After listening for a while, I told her I would call her back as soon as we returned home.

We all shared an enjoyable few days of socializing and gambling. When it was time for everyone to head back home, both mothers cried while saying goodbye to us at the airport, asking how soon they would be able to see us again. We were so happy everyone finally had a chance to meet, and planned on doing something similar again soon.

Returning home, Mo came back to stay with us, and Tiff made arrangements for all of us to get together in Beverly Hills at the famous Koi Restaurant. It was a triple celebration, for Mother's Day, Mo's birthday and for Eric's too.

Tiff arrived first to the restaurant, with us arriving shortly after. I immediately noticed the atmosphere, as it was extremely beautiful. The restaurant was known for its celebrities as well as fabulous food, and Tiff told us not to be surprised if we saw some famous people that night.

She ordered a family style dinner and we were brought a little bit of everything. Filling up on the best varieties of food, we took this splendid opportunity to celebrate one another. Tiff gifted Mo with a little guardian angel necklace, which she had special ordered for her. This display of emotion from sister to sister touched me deeply.

For people born in Europe, it's customary to receive a little gold guardian angel necklace at the time of one's birth. Both Tiff and Mo received one, being of European nationality. Somewhere along the way, Mo lost hers, and knowing this, Tiff thought it would be a kind and meaningful gesture to replace it for her. Given how far away she lived, we both felt relieved that she would have a little angel to gently grace her shoulders. Mo put the necklace on right away, loving it and thanking Tiff.

There was no celebrity spotting that night, but Mo enjoyed flirting with a table full of pretty girls next to us.

I was grateful for this wonderful and memorable family night, one we were all able to enjoy. It is something I will always remember. With Mo living in New York most of the time and Tiff relocating to Colorado and now Portland, enjoying a successful career in the pharmaceutical industry for several years, it wasn't often we could all get together as we did.

# 54 MO WENT MISSING!

It was 2006 and Mo moved back to New York after a short while living with us. I enjoyed calling her on a regular basis, looking very forward to our conversations. As we both share the same sense of humor, we laugh together much of the time, this being very healing for us both.

Mo opened up to me, sharing many personal thoughts on a variety of topics. Most significant, she felt she should have been born male; with her "male" Spirit trapped in a female body, not unlike Chaz Bono's identity awareness, and eventual resolution. These feelings aren't "human choices," but rather simply a part of who we are, and how we relate to the world around us.

We are all created unique, with a "one size fits all" philosophy impossible and ridiculous, if not dangerous to implement. Not everyone is born heterosexual; not everyone is gay. Our individuality allows for opportunities to embrace another's diversity, and isn't something which should be scrutinized. What matters is that we are all "ONE," regardless of sexual orientation or anything else for that matter.

I continue to call Mo, "her," until or if such times as she asks me not to.

While still in Spirit, some choose exceptionally difficult lives, sacrificing themselves to teach humanity about unconditional love. Many such souls exist on an advanced plane, residing in higher dimensions before incarnating into the physical.

One day I picked up the phone to call Mo, but couldn't get a hold of her. Sometimes she slept for a few days in a row, as there were times when she needed more sleep. Sooner or later though, I always reached her.

Not this time.

I tried every day, several times a day, but still I received no answer. I knew if she had been hospitalized again, someone would call me right away, however there was no effort to reach out.

Week two came and went, and still no word from Mo. I was getting very concerned and Eric, seeing how distressed I was, suggested we call the police to assist us in helping to locate her.

I called several precincts in the New York Police Department, and although they checked inside her apartment on a daily basis, she was never there. They reassured me they would put a call out and continue to search for her, using the description I had provided. Meanwhile Pathways Housing continued a search of their own.

I too decided to do some sleuthing, calling every single hospital in the New York vicinity. It was very difficult to get information about potential psychiatric patients, but as her mother, I pleaded with them to release any information they might have on Mo. To my dismay, no department – not even the emergency or regular intake – had any record of her ever being admitted.

Unable to bear the brunt of Mo's disappearance any longer, I finally called Tiff. I had protected her from worrying as long as I could, thinking that Mo would show up soon. However given the length of time, I felt she needed to know what was going on. Tiff tried to stay calm for me, and being on the same wavelength, she offered to do something I couldn't: call the morgues local to Mo's general neighborhood.

Barely able to breathe, I hung up, and Tiff called every one of them.

Nothing.

More time had passed and I became unable to sleep at night. Eric, a friend of his and me considered flying to New York to help find her, but we knew it would be like looking for a needle in a haystack.

I suddenly remembered the name of her favorite gay bar, Henrietta's, and called. The girl on the other end of the phone said she hadn't seen her for a long time. I asked if she would hang a "MISSING" poster in their establishment and help me distribute as many copies as possible. Thankfully, she said she would be happy to help me, and via Express Post, I sent a batch to her the next day.

Pathways Housing also continued their search and checked her apartment daily, yet there was still no sign of her having returned there.

I cannot imagine a worse nightmare than not knowing what happened to one's child – MY CHILD! The more time that passed, the more I feared bad news. I cried constantly and didn't sleep more than short bursts at any given time, feeling completely tortured and not knowing how long I could survive this.

Eric and I both felt helpless, because we did everything reasonably possible we could think of doing. Although Eric tried to cheer me up, suggesting we buy the wedding band we had been meaning to purchase, I declined. Nothing interested me.

About a week later, I sat, robotic and unfocused in the car as Eric drove to the exquisite jewelers, Dave Schneider's. I tried to appear happy as we made our selection, picking out a beautiful platinum band with diamonds, to match my engagement ring.

While Eric was making his payment, the clerk said to me, "I would like to give you one of our little stuffed teddy bears." I thought it was strange, but forcing yet another fake smile, I thanked her.

I was handed the cutest and softest teddy bear imaginable, complete with white "angel wings." The little bear gave me chills, and suddenly, I knew that Mo was okay and would be found.

I was filled with great hope and slowly felt an authentic smile cross my lips.

Divinity had touched me once again, reaffirming that there are no coincidences in this lifetime.

On the drive home, I kept telling Eric over and over, how strange it was that I was given this bear with angel wings. He agreed, happy to see me smile, and almost back to my usual self again. Truth be told, I was "almost" more excited about the bear than the diamonds!

Less than 24 hours later, on the following day, I came home to a flashing message on my answering machine. It was a hospital, out of the usual region, informing me that MY MO was a patient there!

I cannot even begin to describe how happy I was to hear that Mo was alive and safe, yet I wondered why it took so long for anyone to contact me.

I immediately called Mo in the hospital and told her how very worried I had been about her. She didn't realize how much time had passed, being totally oblivious to the fact.

All she said was that she was happy I called.

Again I felt it might be time for her to come live with us, once she gets released. As fate would have it, we found a beautiful large, two bedroom and two bathroom apartment, right on the ocean in the Peninsula. We rented it immediately.

I believed all things would work out for the best, as we now had a place with ample room for Mo.

I say these next words with conviction: I feel Eric is a saint, as he has literally been "my ROCK." I truly have no idea how I could have ever handled many of the extremely difficult events in my life, which started less than one year after we were married. These circumstances could have split many couples up, but it only brought us even closer together.

I believe I have been given an "Earth Angel" of my very own.

UPDATE: Several weeks since I wrote this chapter, I decided to make a copy of the first page. I wanted it handy when I called Mo to read a paragraph to her, asking for her permission to talk about her gender. The Angel Bear sits on a vanity in the same room. Just as I was making my copy, the Angel Bear suddenly fell to the floor, yet I was nowhere near it! No California earthquake hit, either! Smiling, I knew Spirit was playfully reminding me I was never alone.

# 55 LEARNING ALL ABOUT MENTAL ILLNESS AT "NAMI"

October 2006 saw us moved in and loving our new spacious apartment, especially enjoying its mesmerizing ocean view and sounds. I told Mo that it would be nice to have her live with us again. The hospital was ready to release her, but only on the condition that she would come immediately here and also, that she continue her aftercare. We all agreed.

When it was time to purchase her ticket, Mo informed me she had lost her DMV ID, and with the strict airline rules, was unable to fly out because of it.

Eric suggested that she take a Greyhound bus instead. I was a little concerned, given the long length of the trip (three days) and wasn't sure if she would be up to it. Our choices were limited though so Mo agreed, eager to get out of the hospital once again.

The hospital took great care in her release, even assigning a male companion to drive her, and wait for her until she had safely boarded the bus. But as the driver and Mo arrived at the Greyhound bus terminal, Mo stepped out of the vehicle – and bolted!

I was under the impression she was securely on the bus, and on her way to California when I received a call from her social worker. Honestly, I couldn't believe this had happened YET AGAIN, and now, all I could do was wait and see where she would show up. I focused on remaining calm, and a short while later Mo did call collect from a telephone booth, stating she had run away. I told her she had better get back to the hospital, as she now had nowhere to go and no belongings, since they were still in possession of them.

As these words spilled from my mouth I thought to myself, "When will this ever end?" All this confusion I felt from not knowing, nor understanding what was going on in her mind, left me feeling really drained most of the time. I lived every moment worrying about Mo and I realized it had consumed much of my entire life.

Thankfully, she returned to the hospital later that day, and I was told they would add her to the list for apartment availability, something which was scarce in New York. I was very relieved to hear this, and although the process could take a year or more, at least she was safe for now.

I learned that an injectable drug called "Risperdal" administered every two weeks was working better for Mo than only the oral medication she was taking. The injections stabilized her, likely keeping her out of hospitals while the oral meds relied on total compliance on the part of the patient taking them. Mo didn't always agree with this, but I am proud to say she made her own choice and has been taking the injections. As her mother, I feel the quality of our visits and the depth of our communication has improved, while Mo continues to live on her own and for several years, has had no hospital admissions. Someday we will find a cure – perhaps with stem cell research holding a vital key – but for now, we struggle with the barbaric stigma and handling of mental illness.

A short while later, while walking past the television, I caught the tail end of a commercial about a charity walk happening in Huntington Beach, held by "NAMI," the National Alliance on Mental Illness. Later we looked online and through their website, learned the organization was committed to supporting and assisting the mentally ill. We signed up for the walk.

I asked Linda and Dave if they wanted to do the walk with us, since they lived in Huntington Beach. Linda's heart had always gone out to Mo, and as she herself had been clinically depressed for a couple of years, I thought it might be a good thing for her to participate and connect with this organization. Although Dave wouldn't be able to walk that long due to a leg injury, Linda let me know she would try to make it.

I was becoming concerned about Linda. In all the years I had known her, she had kept me grounded. And yet, for the past few years she was emailing or calling me every day, sharing how awful she felt inside. Although she was seeing a doctor and had tried several medications, nothing helped and in fact, she was convinced they only made matters worse.

In retrospect, I wish there was more that I could have done for her, other than to listen and offer support as a best friend. At the time, I thought Linda's inner malaise was only temporary, something that would eventually resolve on its own. In contrast, Mo's illness had no cure; and could only be treated symptomatically.

The day of the walk finally arrived, and Eric and I drove to Huntington Beach to participate. We couldn't believe how many people were in attendance of this huge event. I became very excited and felt I had stumbled upon something extremely helpful. I listened to the various speeches on mental illness and gathered all kinds of brochures and resources. Hungry for information, I picked the brains of several people there and learned that everyone I spoke with either had a loved one who suffered from mental illness, suffered themselves or were simply passionate about learning more about this "silent illness."

One mother I spoke with had a son the same age as Mo. She advised me to sign up for the "Family-to-Family" nationwide program, in order that I learn everything I need to know about how to handle this, as well as meet other families in similar situations. Finally, I felt that real help was on the way!

The moment I got home I found the Family-to-Family brochure, completed my portion and mailed it immediately. A month later I reccived a phone call, telling me a new three-month class was beginning in Huntington Beach. Without hesitation, I confirmed my participation. Eric also wanted to attend, but with his irregular work hours, it was impossible to determine whether he would be home during these specific nights.

For one night a week for three months I attended. I cannot stress enough just how much valuable information I gathered. First and foremost, I learned a brand new and much better way to communicate with Mo, and also confirmed what I knew deep-down: I must start to take better care of myself. In fact, this was the best thing I could ever do for the both of us.

Knowledge equals power, and I felt extremely empowered with this array of helpful information. I was amazed at how much there was to learn on the various conditions of mental illness, and how exactly the brain functioned in these circumstances. About 50 people attended the class, with many of them sharing either similar stories or experiences even more intense than mine. I learned also that New York healthcare was one of the best in the country for the mentally ill. For the first time ever, I felt that Mo was living in the right "state" after all.

At the end of the course, I had amassed a huge folder filled with tons of helpful material, and would always have a reference to turn to. Each year that we are able, we attend the NAMI walk and will be forever grateful to them.

I hope that I live to witness the day when mental illness no longer suffers from the stigma that it does now.

Honestly, I believe that much of the horror that takes place in the world is a result of mental illness. Rather than turning the dial to "hate" when condemning people who cause suffering to others, we need to approach this and these circumstances with education, research and love. It is nothing to fear.

This is much more common than we care to admit; almost everyone knows someone that has been touched by mental illness.

And yes, learning about mental illness and supporting our ongoing knowledge and treatment of it has become my biggest PASSION in this lifetime!

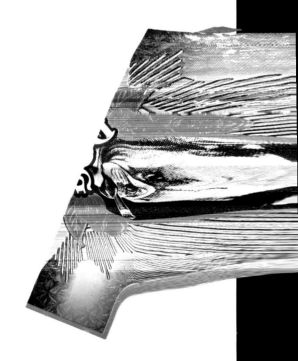

# 56 MY LINDA...TAKES HER OWN LIFE

Linda had been my longest and best friend in life for nearly 35 years, and it was rare that a single day would go by that we didn't have some kind of contact with one another. She had practically lived my whole life with me, from the very first day we met back at Charley Brown's while in our 20's. She was so much more to me than a friend – I've never even had a sister that I loved and felt this close to. She was, simply, a huge part of me, and a part of my life, each and every day.

Linda always did what she felt was the right thing to do; oftentimes sacrificing herself and her needs in the process – a definite "people pleaser."

Eric met and liked her, and we both enjoyed getting together with her and her husband Dave, whenever time permitted. Linda's humor was so funny and sarcastic, bordering on the "sick" that I never experienced a dull day in my life! I am absolutely sure that my own life experiences entertained her as well.

For the past few years, having computer access and email, we mostly communicated this way versus the regular telephone calls we had become accustomed to. She emailed me daily, telling me about all the frustrations she was experiencing. She shared that she had visited several doctors, filling a variety of new prescriptions; none of which seemed to work well. In fact, she said, it seemed she was getting more deeply depressed with each passing day, but still, was able to hide it well.

She could never understand why, since she had a good family life, and grandchildren that she loved and spoiled. She and Dave went on regular vacations, living a wonderful and much better life, than most.

Linda confessed that she was ashamed about what was going on "inside her," unable to share this intensity and depth of despair with others. Thankfully, she was comfortable telling me almost anything; knowing about

Mo's struggles I'm sure helped her open up. Also, judgment was never in my vocabulary, for the most part.

She discontinued most of her psychiatric medications, with the exception of Xanax, which sometimes helped calm her down. Linda gave me daily reports on the amount she was taking, the quantity varying from a half a pill up to three pills. She never took them all at once and was thrilled when she needed less, as reducing the amount of meds was becoming a compulsion for her.

This formed part of our normal daily communication, and although I felt bad, didn't give it that much thought. I just knew it would pass one day, or eventually, she would find a medication that worked well for her on a consistent basis. I felt the less we dwelled on it, the better, but I always took care to listen with love and concern.

In April 2007, Eric and I decided to take another little Tahoe trip. While sitting in the casino coffee shop, enjoying eggs with all the trimmings, minus the meat, (something we never indulge in at home due to the high cholesterol content in eggs) I received a call on my cell phone.

The screen indicated the caller was Linda, and as it was highly unusual that she would ever call while I was on vacation, I picked up the phone immediately.

"Hi Linda what's up?" I asked.

[Unrecognizable response.]

"Linda? Are you ok?"

"You're not going to like what you hear," her voice slurred on the other end of the phone.

Tears started to form while I struggled to understand this "foreign" voice. Slightly more coherent, Linda told me she was calling from the hospital, and that she had tried to kill herself.

I fell silent – and completely numb. The only sound I made was gasping back tears, which were now streaming down my face so fast they actually fell onto my plate.

She continued to tell me that while Dave was out playing golf, she took an enormous amount of Xanax in an attempt to end her life. He came home to find her unconscious, and called 9-1-1. Linda was promptly taken to the hospital and her stomach was pumped.

Shocked; saddened; dumbfounded – heavy emotions ran through my mind yet each one left me feeling more hollow than the last. I was trying to stay calm but when I started to weep openly, Linda began comforting ME as she has done her whole life. Eric put his arm around me not knowing yet what happened.

In a quiet voice of sorrow, I told her we would leave Tahoe that day, but as we drove up, I wouldn't be able to see her until tomorrow. Linda said she didn't feel like seeing anyone, and that she would be okay.

I told her I loved her, and we hung up.

Any words I might have had left choked in my throat; I couldn't speak at all, nor could I finish my breakfast. I just needed to leave. Totally bewildered, we went back to the cabin, undecided as to what exactly we should do next. I had no interest in gambling or doing much of anything else, but as the drive home was long (seven hours), we decided to sleep on it.

First thing in the morning my cell phone rang again. I was certain it was Linda but the number was one I didn't know.

"Hello," I answered.

A stranger, identifying herself as a friend of my mother's told me she and my mom were heading to the mall when suddenly, my mom suffered a stroke. She too was in the hospital!

I started to feel as if I was caught in the middle of a nightmare. How could this all be happening at once?

Eric and I immediately packed up and drove home. I had learned my mom's friend had accurately identified the symptoms of a stroke, her husband having one himself a year before. Thankfully, my mom had only suffered a light stroke and she was expected to make a full recovery. This bit of good news shook me out of the Twilight Zone, and I couldn't wait to call my mom.

In a short while I got my mom on the phone. After telling me not to worry and that she was "just fine now," relief started to seep into me. Living close by, Tiff visited my mom in the hospital immediately, and I was even more relieved as she said how good my momsy looked. I also reminded myself that Linda had SURVIVED – something she was likely happy for, too!

As soon as we arrived back to Long Beach, I called Linda again because I HAD to see her, and now. Yet once again, she told me she "looked terrible" and wanted no visitors. I didn't care what she looked like, but reluctantly, I respected her decision.

My mom was now back home, acting like her health scare was no big deal, and I believed her. She said she felt perfectly fine, so I didn't jump on the next plane to see her.

Linda also returned home from the hospital the following day, and we started emailing right away.

~

Emails from Linda – May 2007

May 1, 11:13 a.m.

Linda: My general doctor I went to this morning, and he has put me on another medication. He is going to call the psychiatrist I want to see (I have an appointment with him on May 14) and see if he can get me in sooner. I have an appointment with a psychiatrist on Thursday, but I really want to wait for this other Dr. I will keep you posted…pray this medicine works…I try to have hope…

May 2, 5:57 p.m.
Linda: Thank you, but these drugs are making me worse…I don't know if I want to try anything else…this is the pits… Love, Linda.

May 4, 8:22 a.m.
Linda: Going to get a pedicure today. Dave went golfing, he can't stay here and watch me…It was my idea for him to go. I'm sure it will take a few weeks for me to notice any difference with these pills. He even said it might not until he ups the dose. So far no reaction, but we will see what the next few days bring. Enjoy your day. Love, Linda.

May 4, 8:50 p.m.
Linda: I promise I will tell the doctor everything…you are right! All my reality shows will be coming to an end in about three weeks, I know you will still have the Bachelor to watch…but then Big Brother.
Me: Good, I think that it's best for you! Can't wait for Big Brother, hard to top the last one but we love them all. Nitey Nite, Love, Shirley.

May 4, 9:07 p.m.
Linda: It was nice talking to you on the phone.
Me: Yes it was! And I'm happy to hear you'll start setting some boundaries, you'll see it won't hurt it should actually feel good after you get used to it. It's called Self love — which is more important than anything. Love, Shirley.

~

It was the afternoon of May 5. There was no email today, just a phone call. Expecting to hear Linda's voice, I was surprised to hear a male voice – Dave – Linda's husband.
"Shirley?"
"Yes?" I responded in a small voice.
"This is the phone call I dreaded making the most and I waited as long as I could, BUT Linda went out with a bang."
I think I knew what I was hearing, as my heart sank deep into a place so familiar, and instantly began weeping loudly. I needed to hear it again, as I was momentarily in denial, yet knew this was not some kind of practical joke.

Dave continued, trying to stay calm, echoing his initial message, "Linda shot herself this morning."

I don't remember hearing anything else; I don't remember hanging up or saying goodbye. I just remember crying so hard, virtually nonstop for days.

Suicide is not necessarily a "planned" event. Having had a pedicure just the day before, clearly Linda had no "plans" to take her own life, a mere 24 hours later. Sometimes, the momentary pain becomes so great; so dark, that there is no rationalizing and no way out.

The darkness, during these instances must be so BLINDING.

In the days following the tragic news about MY LINDA, I couldn't stay indoors; I needed to go outside and keep walking. In a completely robotic state, I stopped strangers in the middle of the sidewalk, telling them my best friend had just killed herself. I didn't know any gentle way to say this. Many people I had only met for the first time hugged me, and I guess I needed that. Yet, what felt like an endless dampness in my soul – one from which I could never get warm – the deep sorrow wouldn't go away, no matter what I tried to do.

I called Megsy. When I told her the news, she started crying with me and dropping everything, immediately flew out to attend Linda's service.

Megsy arrived at our house and as soon as we saw one another, we held each other and cried. Knowing full well how much I needed my other best friend, she insisted on driving us to the church in her rented Escalade.

Linda's service reached into my soul and touched it, ever so gracefully. Considering the short time the family had to prepare everything, it was very tastefully done. Rotating photos of her and her lifetime of experiences and friends were projected on a big screen. Needless to say, there weren't any dry eyes anywhere.

I was aware that her brother had singing talent, but I had never met him in all the years I knew Linda, as he lived in Northern California. At her service, he strummed the guitar while singing the song, "If" by Bread, so very beautifully. Many of her friends shared humorous stories about Linda and not unlike Billy's celebration, it brought laughter to the tears that flowed from our hearts.

I couldn't speak; it wasn't even a choice for me.

I knew her daughter well and yet I felt she could barely look at me. She asked only once, "Please Shirley don't even start!" (sobbing) as she was trying to be strong on this day. She had been so very close to her mom and was keenly aware of how close we had been, too. I gave Dave a big hug and with that, no words were needed. There were also hugs for Linda's son.

On the way out of the church, I ran into Linda's grandson. I told him that she lived for him and his brother, triggering him to really start crying. I remembered him as a youngster as if it were yesterday. When they would visit her from out of state, I would bring the boys a tin full of jelly bellies, and they called me Pocahontas.

We were invited to her cousin's house afterwards but didn't stay long. A lot of Linda's other close friends told me they were absolutely shocked at Linda committing suicide. I thought everyone was at least somewhat aware of her intense suffering, yet it did make sense to me that none of us EVER expected anyone to take his or her own life.

Megsy had to fly back that evening as she was swamped at work. I was very grateful she came out to be with me. Eric remained very supportive and respectful that day, and all the days after.

I mistakenly thought Linda's service would bring some closure, but I was wrong. I cried constantly on Eric's shoulder and just didn't know how, or what, would make this pain go away. Even my daily walks and reaching out to strangers didn't help.

The loss of someone from the physical world is one of the most painful experiences one can endure, in their human life. Suicide of a loved one is particularly agonizing. I wasn't mad at Linda, not in the slightest, but I just missed her beyond comprehension. I was also coping with Mo's continuous "ups and downs" and was myself, in a very fragile place.

It crept up on me slowly, but noticeably: I was having a small nervous breakdown. I too, saw my doctor and what did he prescribe me? Xanax – which I barely took any of. How could I look at the bottle of pills and not be reminded of Linda, and her battle with depression! The doctor also advised me to see a psychologist in order that I could talk with a professional. I made an appointment but went only once, as I felt it was an intrusion upon my personal life, and honestly, digging into my childhood wasn't helpful for this at all.

My German way was to be strong and to battle things naturally.

Although my mom recovered well, a second stroke slowed her down. Suddenly, she wasn't as lively anymore, nor was she as focused as she had been all her life.

It took me a full five months of deep grieving, when the sun started to beat its warming rays into my soul. Slowly, I started to feel a part of the human race again. The sadness persisted, but my survival Spirit knew I had to function again. Most of all, I knew that Linda would have wanted me to. Still, I cannot visit Dave because of the reminder and loss of Linda – it's just all too vivid. Even now, I continue to, and always will miss her in her human form. She was almost 65, presently my own human age.

It gives me tremendous peace today, knowing that we don't die, and at the precise moment of our death, we simply disconnect from our invisible "silver cord" that holds both body and spirit together. It's the same thing that ensures we always return to our bodies, after our Spirits wander far and wide during our dreams. I know for a fact that Linda still watches over me, and that she is no longer suffering or in pain.

Nobody goes to "Hell," as there is no such thing. Hell is simply a state of mind, whether one is in human form, or in Spirit. I believe that when one takes their own life, they are stuck in living HELL, here on earth. In Spirit, Hell is merely the lowest level, where forgiveness has not been reached. But the opportunity for redemption is always present, where even such souls as "evil leaders" stuck in the dimension of Hell can graduate from.

I cannot emphasize enough the seriousness of mental illness. Clinical depression is a form of mental illness, with so many people suffering in shame and silence. The consequences of this can be severe and permanent, as in the case of Linda.

I dedicate this chapter to you, dear Linda, and promise never to stop fighting for this cause. I love you.

# 57 SKY DIVING ON MY 60TH BIRTHDAY!

Mo was again released from the hospital, under the care of Pathways Housing. She was so happy to have received an apartment, this time, without any roommates. Tiff was in the process of getting divorced, and needed me more than ever now. Both of my children were somewhat taking my mind off Linda, but her passing had only occurred eight months ago and was still very fresh.

Tiff informed me she was flying out to spend my 60th birthday with me. I was so excited to see her, but it wouldn't have mattered what we did, as long as we got to spend time together. It is a fact that she enjoys going "all out" for special occasions like these, and although she doesn't have to, I still LOVE her love and attention!

It was January 18, 2008, one day before my birthday – and the date of my 6th wedding anniversary. I was pacing the floor looking out the window, eager for Tiff to arrive. In just moments, I saw Tiff pull up and not one to sit still, went outside to greet her with lots of hugs and kisses.

We went inside and just as we were sitting down, I heard a knock on the front door. Wondering who in the heck it was, and not wanting to be disturbed as I was too busy with family, I swung open the door, not bothering to look first in the peephole.

To my UTTER SHOCK, there stood Mo in the doorway, with a huge smile on her face! I was about to pass out as I screamed her name!

I turned to look at Tiff while an enormous smile grew on her face, knowing how happy she had made me. Then I turned back to my other child, hugging Mo as tightly as I could. All the while, she had been hiding in the back seat, waiting until we had gone inside to spring this BEST SURPRISE EVER! I thanked Tiff profusely. As far as I was concerned, I had just celebrated the best birthday I could possibly imagine. That's MY TIFF!

Tiff not only made all the arrangements for Mo's travel, but also prior to coming here, took her to Vail snowboarding, buying her new ski clothes in the process.

Pure joy literally filled the room. As I looked into the faces of those sitting around the kitchen table, I was also filled with a sense of pure love.

"Happy birthday, mom," Tiff grinned a little sheepishly, while handing me an envelope.

My birthday wasn't until tomorrow, and I momentarily wondered why she gave it to me one day early. I opened the envelope and inside was a gift certificate, redeemable tomorrow for – SKY DIVING.

I had no thinking time; nor very little preparation time, but isn't that how most dreams manifest? I started to laugh and scream with delight, not believing my eyes.

Tiff interrupted, asking me if this had REALLY been a dream of mine, as Mo told her it was. Still laughing, I responded, "YES, YES!"

With relief, Tiff shared that she, Mo, Eric and me were all going to sky dive together the next morning, and it was all her treat! Mo reminded me that she distinctly remembered me telling her this on more than one occasion, while spending time with me during college breaks.

There are moments in life when the energy of an emotion simply isn't translatable into words, and this was truly one of these moments. Not only was I finally going to sky dive, but I was also going to do it with every single one of my loved ones! Unbelievable, and in every way a blessing. I had the best little family I could ever ask for.

At the crack of dawn on January 19, my birthday morning, we all piled in the car to drive to Perris, in Lake Elsinore, about a 90-minute drive from Long Beach.

During our drive up, I called my mom, telling her about my birthday surprise. She tried sounding excited for me, but I could detect fear in her voice. All of us reassured her that everything – and everyone – would be perfectly fine.

As we arrived to Perris, we were all pretty pumped up. In truth, my great desire to do this had lessened a little through the years, but there was NO WAY I was going to wimp out now! I still wanted to do this, and I couldn't wait.

Once we finished "signing our lives away" in the office, we were all given instructions. In a huge hanger we started assembling our gear, with each of us being assigned an experienced instructor that would jump with us – this being called a "tandem jump."

My instructor had a real sense of humor, telling me with a straight face, that HE was excited to do HIS first jump. Being a little gullible, I thought he might be telling the truth, but when the other instructors broke out into laughter, I joined in on the joke! Another instructor asked where the "duct tape" was for me; I was the first one to laugh. Seriously, I wasn't frightened at all!

Tiffany treated me once again to the cost of getting my jump burned onto a CD. Just like on a movie set, the photographer started giving me some hints as how to look best for the camera, while in the air.

Ha! I thought. We'll all be lucky if I don't pass out mid-jump!

I noticed Tiff's excitement was building the closer we got to the jump, while Eric and Mo were getting quieter.

We boarded a funny looking plane that had an open back, which would take us up high into the blue. Calmly, Eric sat across from me, Tiff was behind me smiling, while Mo was now looking extremely serious.

We were given last-minute instructions before jumping. Eric was first, and I watched as my husband leapt into the sky. I turned to Mo, and saw that she looked as if she had seen a ghost. I mouthed to her that everything would be just fine. Tiff kept smiling at me and the open door in anticipation, since I was the next one to jump. My funny instructor was strapped onto me from behind.

Later, Mo confessed when she saw me jump, she thought, "Oh no, there goes my mom!" It scared her to death, hoping she would see her mom – me – in the flesh again!

Perched on the edge of the plane, I was ready to jump, leaving my life behind in a very literal leap of faith. I refused to look down; instead, I held my head up towards the sky while reciting a silent affirmation:

*I surrender to you, oh Heavens.*

And suddenly I was in the air.

It was so unexpectedly loud, and as I spun non-stop, thought I was going to throw up. I felt sicker than ever and stupidly confessed my age in mid-air, warning the instructor I was about to be sick. He politely asked if I wouldn't mind doing it under my arm, as not to hit him in the face. I did everything in my higher power to hold it all in, and luckily for us both, I succeeded. Was I ever glad the camera never had an opportunity to catch a moment like THIS! Now that would have been some film!

Feeling sicker beyond imagination, I forgot to push THE red button that I was expressly instructed to push – the one that opens up the parachute! Thankfully, my instructor dutifully remembered and did it for me, ensuring a much smoother and less-messy landing!

Without a hitch, I experienced a perfect landing, and was beyond grateful! I was totally stoked by this entire experience.

We all met on the ground safely, with Mo throwing her arms around me, in a sweet and touching moment. Eric was excited, having completed another adventure under his belt. Tiff looked like a total expert, and when she walked towards the camera with her comments, looked exactly like a television reporter.

More fun came in the months to follow as we shared with everyone that we had sky dived!

This was the best and most memorable birthday I had ever experienced, in my entire life.

Thank you my Tiffers! You too, made a dream come true for me! I LOVE YOU!

# 58 I JOINED FACEBOOK, AND WHAT A TRIP THIS HAS BEEN! IT OPENED UP MY LIFE SO MUCH!

One day I received an email invitation from Tiff to join what is called "Facebook." At the time (2009), I had no idea what this was, but whatever Tiff sends me is in my best interests, so I completed all the required information. It seemed a bit strange to me at first, because I didn't know exactly what to do with it. Tiff only explained the basics, telling me with use, I would soon catch on.

Immediately, I received 15 friend requests, so I clicked the "Accept" button, still not knowing why. I had really wished Linda were here so she could be on this thing with me. I knew we would have had some serious fun while figuring out the ins and outs of Facebook! I asked Megsy if she would join, but laughing, she told me she was too busy (being an attorney) and besides, it would probably be too addicting.

That evening, I noticed the "What's On Your Mind" field, and typed that I was eating a delicious, salmon dinner, then taking a sunset bike ride. Suddenly, I saw Tiff and a few friends comment that it sounded great; others pressed a "Like" button.

I was actually getting the hang of this! I felt proud, and for the next few weeks, I tried posting a little something each day about what I was doing. But with only 20 friends on my "Friend List," I noticed their comments were becoming less frequent.

Then, as quickly as I felt good about Facebook, I started wondering what the point of all this was. Then, out of the blue, I received a friend request from a complete stranger living in Australia. I wondered how in the world this guy, Dennis, found me.

Not one to over-analyze, I thought, what the heck and accepted his friend request. I read his posts and figured he must have been some kind of

238

guru, really enjoying what he had to say. Every day he posted something spiritual that really hit home for me. I thought Tiff might enjoy these posts, too.

I became quite excited, re-energized about Facebook once again, and emailed Tiff, asking her to friend this guy as well. Tiff ignored my suggestion, telling me later she doesn't friend anyone that she hasn't had some kind of contact with, or that she doesn't know personally. I looked at her friend list and saw that she had over 500 people listed there and it blew me away!

Suddenly a light bulb turned on in my mind and I thought, I could write these sorts of uplifting and inspiring messages as well. Seeing a "Share" button, first I copied and posted most of what Dennis wrote, hoping Tiff would see them in turn. I knew Mo was also on Facebook once in a while, so she might be able to appreciate them as well.

It didn't take long for many other strangers to ask me to friend them, but I still never figured out how they found me from all parts of the world. Nonetheless I accepted their requests.

I soon noticed a link called "Friend Suggestions" on the right-hand side of the screen, so I started to look at other people's profiles. The ones that sounded interesting or I felt some sort of connection with, I would send them a Friend Request. Sometimes I was intrigued by someone's look or face – after all, it was called "FACE-book" right?

I noticed some people shared common interests with me, including someone who liked Elvis Presley! I couldn't wait to send them a friend request, and when they accepted, I was thrilled.

I had no idea Elvis was still so popular, even amongst younger people, and slowly, this started to make more sense. I was locating lots and LOTS of Elvis fans, from all parts of the world. Not a day would go by that I wouldn't see a "Wall" filled with Elvis news, photos and songs. This was, and still is fun, but I wanted to venture out even further.

I was getting pretty familiar with some of the great spiritual leaders such as the Dalai Lama and Gandhi, loving all their quotes I read. I began to Google all kinds of spiritual passages, posting the ones that resonated most with me, and subsequently, received more and more friend requests from like-minded people. This was just plain old fun now!

I kept telling myself that once I reached 100 friends, I would stop accepting or inviting people. But, before I knew it, I had 200 people on my Friend List. At times I would feel a little overwhelmed by having so many new Facebook friends, realizing I wanted to give each a little attention, but still, I kept reaching out.

Facebook helped to fill an empty spot in my heart which Linda used to fill. After I lost her, I really had very little interest in going out and making new friends. I didn't want any more "real life" best friends.

I can really feel people's energy on Facebook and naturally, felt closer to certain individuals than others. What I was truly enjoying now was connecting with people all across the world, not believing I could be in England, Norway, France and India all at the same time!

I didn't turn anyone's friend request down, unless they became rude or negative. In these instances (they were few and far between), I only had to hit the "Unfriend" button and poof-be-gone! Most everyone was fantastic, and I enjoyed seeing the "good" in so many of my friends.

Through the years, my own spirituality started to grow, simply by reading and contemplating other's posts – including my own. To-date, I have gathered over 1000 wonderful friends, and relish in appreciating the genuine love shared online here.

There were a few European friends that I became especially connected to, keeping me close to my roots. Some individuals I literally felt as if I had known forever.

I have an interesting take on the concept of Facebook, believing that everyone I had invited to become friends with, or accepted as friends was spiritually connected with me from other lives I have lived. Just think for a moment: Out of all the people in this world, and the approximate 1 billion people on Facebook, how is it that only THESE were chosen to connect with me? That's NO coincidence!

Facebook is still a huge part of my life. I would like to pay tribute to my friends, a partial list including: Kenny Wise, Deborah Long, GiGi Sosnoski, Alisha Skylstad, Ann Christin Magnusson, Heiki Losoa, Michele Parker, Susan Slamka, Lucille Seiffer, Dominique Fruh, Alejandro C. Garcia, Ann Rizzuti Standhardt, Julie Ann Cooper Clawson, Megan Boyden, Joanna Podbierezki, Jeanne Oakwood Schuette, Linda Munday, Louis Eckersley, Robin Solano, Elisabeth Trolle, Daniel Lawrence, Kimberly Silva, author of "Life at the End of the Tunnel," Geoffrey Jowett, Author and Medium, Hanne Bay, and Cara Sands. Many more helped inspire and cheer me on to write this book. My profound gratitude to all.

This cherished list includes Gail Cooley, Laura Fuino and Vivian Madrigal – my "real life" and Facebook friends.

Most of all, I thank my daughter, Tiffany, for bringing such a wonderful gift to my attention. At the time, I am sure she had no idea it would become such a major part of my life and a wonderful vehicle to communicate from!

I contacted a dear Facebook friend Cara, aka Lan Mara and asked for her help in editing my chapters, as I had remembered her comments and posts written so eloquently. She kindly said yes to edit my book and I then learned she had a degree in English and Scriptwriting!

Spirit was once again, guiding and assisting me. In the beginning, we were drawn together by our mutual love for Elvis. But now, not only are we working together but also our friendship is blossoming, to say the least.

She has had the intense job of becoming "me" while editing, and without a doubt there is no one else that could have been this magnificent!! Spirit picked Cara – not me!

Her main passion in this lifetime is acting as a dolphin and whale advocate, working tirelessly to improve the lives of our cetacean relatives. She loves the fact that I live at the ocean, and am able to enjoy the occasional wild dolphin sightings. Living in Toronto herself, we plan on a visit in the not-too-distant-future in person, here in California. I know I've made another best friend for life!

This is just another one of the magical gifts of Facebook. Thank you Cara Sands! I love you!

# 59 BACKSTAGE AT THE U2 CONCERT

Megsy was, and is dating the Production Manager of U2, and invited Eric and me to attend the show with her at the Rose Bowl.

We jumped at the chance, first, because I love their music, but most important, I wanted to spend some time with my best friend! With Megsy living in Sacramento, we weren't getting together as often as we would like, although we did continue to email on a regular basis. It always feels like only yesterday whenever I do see her – time has simply stopped for us!

It was the end of 2009, and Megsy told us to drive up to Los Angeles and meet her at her hotel, so we could all ride up together in the crew bus for the U2 360 Tour!

It was so amazing to see her again, and the hotel was absolutely exquisite, although we didn't stay long. Many streets were blocked and heavy concert traffic was everywhere. Of course, for us, security opened all the barricaded streets, which was very cool!

Hanging out in the office, full of the crew for U2, Megsy introduced us to everyone, including Jake, her boyfriend. But in typical Shirley fashion, I beat her to the punch. I spotted Jake instantly, and in all my excitement, ran up to him, just dying to hug him. Not waiting to be formally introduced, I couldn't wait to thank him. Jake started to hand us all sorts of different passes, including tickets for first class seats!

Finally, it was show time, and we were all very excited to be here. The Black Eyed Peas opened for U2, with Fergie looking and sounding pretty hot. I cannot recall the last time I had been at such a huge concert, and both Eric and I were getting in the groove.

We looked around and spotted several celebrities, including Paul Gasol from the Lakers, Cindy Crawford and her husband, and, walking right next to me – Paris Hilton and her own security detail. I loved her reality shows and, excited to see her, tapped her very lightly on the shoulder. She looked at me, smiling, and said, "Hiiii." I returned the very sweet greeting.

At long last, the energy shifted, and U2 came on stage. Enjoying such a close-up view of Bono, I must say he really had his moves down to a tee. And what a voice! The band's performance was fabulous, and as I knew most of the lyrics, had fun singing out loud. We never even got to sit in those first-class seats, as we were standing right next to the stage. Especially since watching Bono up close, is never tiring!

After the show, we took the crew bus back to the hotel, still on a natural high from all the excitement and from U2's fantastic performance. Talking to the driver, we learned she was from Long Beach. For two days after, we actually ran into her again, once at Best Buy and then at the SSI building. Long Beach isn't a small town and we all found it strange that this would happen, with us never to see her again.

It was late into the evening when we thanked Megsy for such an amazing night. As we waited for the valet to bring our car, we noticed a man next to us, also waiting for his vehicle. It was none other than Pierce Brosnan, from the James Bond movies. Graciously, he smiled at us and said hello, this being the perfect ending to our very memorable night.

I practically hate asking for favors from anyone at all, but HAD to ask Megsy if Jake could hook Tiffany up with U2 tickets, as this was her all-time favorite band. No coincidence here! Megsy checked with Jake and told me it was no problem! I was screaming with excitement, feeling so wonderful to be able to have the right connections to make my daughter absolutely ecstatic.

Attending the U2 concert provided an unbelievable and memorable night for her, one that will stay with her forever. She told me that her pass allowed her to be right up front next to the stage, practically touching Bono as he performed right over her cute, little nose.

I was over-the-top happy when she shared all this with me. I could relate, remembering back when I was next to the stage where Elvis Presley performed. Memories like these aren't easily forgotten.

# 60 LEARNING ALL ABOUT "MEDIUMSHIP" AND MEETING "THE" JAMES VAN PRAAGH

In September 2010, Eric's 100 year-old, very sweet grandma passed away, as did her son, Ervin, a mere 11 days apart.

During one of our daily walks, we discussed all things about life and death. James Van Praagh came up in our conversation, with us both wondering what had happened to him, as he no longer had his television show.

Eric later looked online, and discovered that James lived relatively near to us, in Laguna Beach, and held what he called "Spirit Circles" on a monthly basis. Both extremely curious, we were excited to learn more and decided to purchase tickets to attend one of these circles.

The evening of James's event came and we both hoped that one of our deceased loves ones would come through. Little did we know at the time, that was only scratching the surface of communication with the departed, and there was so much more. We arrived to the venue to see approximately 100 people seated. We loved this smaller gathering, figuring our chances to be read would be that much higher.

James came out like a little ball of fire, and one could not help but smile and love him instantly! We immediately noticed his wonderful sense of humor, too. Before giving any readings, he would mention things like, "We are ALL Spirits, having a Human experience." Right from the get-go, we couldn't get enough of what he had to say. He told us there is no such thing as "death" and again, Eric and I looked at one another, wanting to hear why.

James continued, "Life is Eternal: At the time of death we just shed our human body with Spirit continuing on." We perked up in our seats – although I had always believed in the afterlife, hearing the way James explained things was phenomenal and resonated strongly with us both.

I knew I personally found complete "truth." I understood why religion had always felt uncomfortable to me, with the various rules and threats. James himself mentioned he was raised Catholic, but then received a much higher calling.

Before long, after a meditation session was held, James told us the Spirits had been patiently waiting, anxious to reach their loved ones in the room. He explained he himself played no part in choosing who got read, since his own Spirit Guides chose for him, while protecting him. We watched this entire process unfold, and were truly amazed, no pun intended, that the readings were quite literally, "out of this world!"

Real personalities with full descriptions and details came through for others, giving them needed confirmation. Important and healing messages were imparted, answering so many of their questions. I found myself crying at one point, and spontaneously hugged the lady in front of me, as she seemed to be in shock after her reading.

We both felt this was truly enlightening, temporarily forgetting about having a reading for ourselves. We clearly observed that night, the ones that "needed" readings most, were precisely the ones who received them.

After three hours of miraculous observations, James remained until the end, signing his books and taking photographs with participants, if requested, and we waited to do both.

We drove home, sharing our insights with one another. I believe that this night changed both of our lives and us forever.

During the following year, we couldn't get enough of James, attending many more Spirit Circles. Each and every time, we learned something different and were exposed to more insights from Spirit.

I would be lying if I didn't have hopes, deep down, that someday, I would get a reading myself. But the gifts I did receive were plentiful, and we considered ourselves extremely fortunate to have lived so close to James and be able to learn what we did. In fact, attending these events were our favorite evenings out!

James got to know us pretty well and started calling us by our first names. One night as he spotted us in the audience, he announced he loved looking into the crowd, seeing us there with our smiling faces. He also hoped we would attend one of his special outings or cruises, which we plan on doing, one day very soon.

Eric was constantly ordering spiritual books from Amazon, reading them cover-to-cover. In a small way, I was a bit envious, as I didn't read much at all. I was also feeling a little guilty that I hadn't actually read any of James's books, although I knew full well of his messages.

But Spirit works in funny and miraculous ways, and my relationship with printed text was about to change in a big way.

*"When we are aware of the power and magic of the universe and life itself, extraordinary occurrences or miracles are natural." ~ James Van Praagh*

# 61 THE HILARIOUS STORY THAT GOT ME READING

Both my children and Eric enjoy reading, and I continued making excuses as to why I wasn't. I told others that if I read, I would be lulled to sleep within minutes, and came up with other excuses, too. Truth be told, I really thought I simply didn't like to read!

Being on Facebook practically on a daily basis, I read many short quotes and in the process, learned a lot. When it came to reading a full book however, I couldn't imagine opening one. I was convinced I would be bored, and that the level of concentration needed to actually focus on such a large chunk of text just wasn't for me.

*"It is through our 'thoughts' that the world can be filled with either magic or misery, and our thoughts direct everything in life." ~ James Van Praagh*

As usual, one day I was on Facebook and found an awesome post. I must admit that it's important for me to see that I have touched others in some way, even possibly helping my friends as a result of certain messages or posts. I call this my daily, spiritual affirmations.

Anyway, I was especially excited about one, particular spiritual message I had posted, picture and all, because it was powerful and great! I couldn't wait to see how many "Likes" I would get, with responses generally coming in immediately after posting, and more over a 24-hour period, due to the different time zones in which friends live.

All I can say is that I waited – and waited – and while the crickets chirped, felt more and more rejected. I thought maybe I had lost my touch, as there wasn't a single "Like" or "Comment" on the post. It was unbelievable actually, because I had established so many nice friends that liked pretty much everything I posted.

I tested this rather miserable "new" reality, deciding to publish another good post, and the same thing happened – nothing! Being a very sensitive soul, it actually brought me to tears.

"Is there some kind of sudden conspiracy against me?" I wondered. Honestly, I had no clue what I could have done to make everyone ignore me like this.

A couple of days passed, and I noticed some sweet messages on my wall. Friends were posting messages, saying they were thinking about me, and hoped everything was okay! It felt good, but I thought to myself, of course everything is okay, BUT if they were that concerned, I wished they would just "Like" my last post!

At this point, I would have been happy to receive one, single "Like" on the greatness I felt that I had posted, and would have been grateful to touch even one soul!

A week went by with many heartfelt messages of love and concern populating my wall. I was totally confused. It was comforting to know my friends still cared, but I guessed they no longer felt my posts were of any value. Still, something wasn't right, I reasoned.

My husband was getting pretty tired of me complaining about Facebook. I felt since he was not on the site, he just didn't understand the concept. In my opinion, it's sort of an unspoken rule that people do seek the "Likes" and "Comments," for some validation that what they are doing matters. Otherwise, why would one bother to have a public presence in the first place? It's like an actor performing to no applause!

I went from being very busy on Facebook, interacting with all my friends to someone who suddenly felt very lost. I had a voice and wanted to use it, yet for some reason, had suddenly been silenced.

I knew an immediate intervention was required, so I decided to pick up one of our James Van Praagh books and give the "reading thing" another shot.

As my desk and work space is set up so I can "walk while I work," so to speak, allowing me to add many miles to my day, I got into my normal Facebook stance (literally standing) and started to open the pages of James's book. And I found I enjoyed everything I was reading!

As a matter of fact, I could barely put the book down!

I was beyond happy about this, and feeling pretty wonderful about my newfound achievement, ended up reading every, single one of his books. Very satisfied and hungry for more, I ordered more books, favoring authors such as Eckhart Tolle and Gary Zukav, to name a few.

Still, I missed my Facebook friends and one day, out of curiosity, looked again at my posts, seeing if anyone had ever left any "Likes."

I noticed something, right then and there that I had never seen before: The last two posts on my wall looked different than all the others. I looked even closer, trying to grasp what the anomaly was, as there were light blue markings around the picture portion. Suddenly, I saw the posts were visible to "ONLY ME."

Only ME? I clicked on the post and discovered one could choose many different settings when posting content onto Facebook, specifying who could actually see the posts. Somehow, I or something selected myself as the "only person" able to lay eyes on, and read my writing!

Wanting to double-check this bizarre finding, I saw that sure enough, all my other posts were set to "Public!"

I cracked up laughing, as this was the answer to my mystery! I was so very relieved, and recognized that this gift had been "hand-delivered" – literally – by Spirit, as I would have never known to change this setting myself.

If the posts hadn't been set to "Private," I wouldn't have had the time or interest to pick up a book and start reading. But now that I've started reading, and loving doing so, I have been awakened to yet another one of my life's purposes – writing my autobiography. Yes, the one that YOU are READING!

Aho! (Amen)

# 62 THE END OF MY MOTHER'S LIFE, AND THE "MIRACLE" OF ALL MIRACLES

My mother suffered two minor strokes, and also developed some slight dementia; and just wasn't the same anymore. It was extremely sad, as she had always been a little spitfire; now, she could barely respond to me on the phone. Needless to say, this took some time getting used to.

By an invitation from my half-sister, she moved to the mountains of Colorado while still in her 50's, living a fairly secluded life, yet making some very special friends in the process. I was busy living my own life, but was still sorry to see her leave northern California.

I was always worried for her wellness and safety in the wintertime. A few winters saw her completely snowed in, with her electricity going out for days, and once, for an entire week. I learned later all she was able to do was huddle underneath blankets, in an attempt to stay warm. I don't know how she survived and remained sane while in her 80's and alone, weighing no more than 100 pounds.

Although my oldest half-sister lived nearby, she herself couldn't get to her in those periods of harsh weather. Even if she could, my mom and she never enjoyed a close relationship, going for months and sometimes years without speaking. My mom told me she would never, ever move in with her, choosing instead, to stay independent as long as she possibly could.

But when my mom was faced with yet another total snow-in during the winter of 2010, my sister told her, "You're moving in with me." In some ways it seemed ideal as she, too lived alone in a beautiful, large home with plenty of room.

My mom on the other hand, felt completely defeated, but agreed to move in with her.

At first, it seemed to be working out better than I expected, as she bounced back a little. I started to think her move might have been positive, but the progress I had hoped she would continue to make didn't happen. Not long after, once again, she started to go downhill.

In July 2011, Eric and I took a trip to Colorado, staying at Tiff's house. I was a little scared to see with my own eyes my mother's deterioration, which I knew had taken place, in such a short time.

We went to visit my mom, surprising her as we entered through the back of the house. She was sitting alone in the living room, with only a cleaning lady present. As the three of us made our way into the room, I smiled at her, holding my arms out.

"Momsy," I said softly, not wanting to startle her as I approached, knowing how delicate she had become in her advanced years.

Her mouth opened slightly, forming a smile, as she couldn't believe her eyes. She looked so very adorable as she perked up so much that day – my sister later telling me how very rare that was.

She was so happy to see Tiffany and Eric but focused mainly on me, as she always did. We sat and talked for a few hours, when I suddenly began reminiscing about my wonderful memories of growing up in Germany with her; unusual, as this wasn't something I did often.

Completely out of the blue, my mom asked Tiffany about her dogs, even though she didn't like dogs; fearing them, yet remembering how much Tiff loved them. She asked Eric a couple of questions as well.

Not long after as we drove off, I looked up at the balcony to see my mother standing outside and waving at us. This really surprised me as she was very fragile and her balance, very precarious. Instantly, tears welled up, and I quickly snapped a photo, waving back and throwing as many kisses as she could catch.

And in these last moments, I knew; somehow, that this would be the last time I would probably ever see my mother alive. Part of me wanted to run back upstairs, inside the house, and just hold her.

Four months later, I received a phone call from my sister, giving me the sad news that my mom had a heart attack and another stroke, telling me she would not survive.

My mom was in the hospital for a couple of days, and both my sister and I agreed not to put her on life support, knowing that this was her wish. She was immediately transferred to hospice for the last few days of her life.

I felt numb in every way, yet had to think seriously whether to immediately fly out to see her, or whether I should remember her in the wonderful and very special way that I last saw her. I was so torn, with my mind going back and forth; this being one of the most difficult decisions I would ever have to make. One thought I had: I didn't selfishly want my presence influencing my mother to hold on any longer, as I believe this is possible.

As well, my mom and I had such an extremely close bond in our lives, that the thought of seeing her, knowing she could die at any moment, was unbearable. Right then I felt that this was not the last impression I wanted to have of my mother. I knew I was "with her" in Spirit now.

I struggled with my decision on a daily basis; at one point, feeling I may want to spend "alone" time with my mother in hospice, after her other children left. At that point, I would jump on the next plane to be with her, since it was only a 2+1/2 hour flight. With my mind so terribly confused, I was leaving this once again to faith, knowing Spirit would guide me through this very emotional time.

I called hospice every single day, grateful at how extremely loving and caring they were. They would place the telephone to my mom's ear so I could talk to her. I gave her all my love, but she was no longer able to speak or answer me. The hospice workers told me that by her slight expression, my mother knew it was I.

By no coincidence, we purchased tickets some time ago to see James Van Praagh in a spiritual fair in Orange County, and felt it was the perfect time to attend such an event. James spoke with me at the fair, advising me to use my heart chakra and my deep, conscious level to communicate with, and help her, at this time.

During the morning on her fourth day of hospice, my niece, Chrissy called from my mother's bedside. She told me to prepare myself, as my mom would not make it through the day.

In that moment, I myself became lifeless. On their own accord, tears streamed down my face at this profound reality – that my mom would truly be gone physically from this world – TODAY. It was all too surreal.

Chrissy asked me if I wanted to speak with my mom. She held the phone on my mother's ear, telling me to take my time. I had to hold every-single-emotion together, as I had much to tell her and didn't want to break down. This was so, much more difficult than I could have ever anticipated.

In the most gentle and loving way, I told my momsy that her time had come and to not be afraid; that she must not hold back, and that she must surrender to the light. I also said not to be surprised when she finds herself "alive" again on the other side (I didn't want this to be a shock to her.)

I told her – amongst many, other things – that I would see her again.

In a simple and condensed version I told her everything that I believed in, and all that I had learned myself. I was shivering inside. I wanted my words to fill her with the sweet fragrance of "new life" which would continue on, even more beautiful than she could ever visualize.

I could feel Spirit so powerful right here with me, right at this moment; crawling inside of me, giving me more strength than I ever imagined possible.

All her life my mom had been afraid to die, thoroughly believing it was the total end of everything. I wished nothing more than to help her cross over and not be afraid. This was the last thing I could do for my mom – to give her peace and love to send her off.

I hung up and sobbed.

Later, functioning in a trance-like state, I logged onto Facebook and interacted with some dear friends that held me in their hearts, at such a heavy time. Thankfully, Eric was home, which helped me so much as I was unable to leave the house for any reason.

I truly have no words for the feelings I felt during this time of just – waiting – waiting for my mother to die.

A few hours later, at 1:42 p.m. on November 5, 2011 I suddenly got a strong urge to post a gospel song by Elvis for my mother, called "Peace in the Valley." I debated at first as she was absolutely in love with Dean Martin, but I loved this song for the spiritual message it held.

After posting, I played the song again to listen myself. More teardrops rolled down my face, and still lightheaded and shivering, I sang along with Elvis, in barely a whisper. I was truly submerged inside the cradling beauty of this song when suddenly it STOPPED.

I was irritated, naturally, at the abrupt interference, but instead of trying to make it play again, I couldn't help notice the picture that it had stopped on.

It was truly the most amazing picture, and I was in awe. The colors were out of this world – such a soft, pale yellow with some white clouds above. And from the clouds came a big arm with a hand reaching down, as if it were God's arm.

The hand was picking up a little dot, surrounded by four more dots off to the side. The dots themselves almost seemed out of place, as they were dark and the picture was colored so softly; so beautifully softly.

I ran into the kitchen to show Eric and a voice blurted out, "What if my mom just died?" Eric looked at me the moment I released these words, then back at the picture, which he found strikingly beautiful, too. I attempted to explain what I saw in it, but Eric felt I was understandably emotional and possibly looking for an explanation, so that the agony of waiting would finally stop.

Although there were a few brief moments of resignation, I started doubting this was THE DAY. Thoughts of losing my mother in the physical were almost impossible to conceive. But I wrote down the exact time all this had happened: 1:45 p.m. I looked once more and then finished playing the song. I realized that the other four dots were my mother's four children, which she would leave behind on earth.

A half hour later my sister called, telling me that my mom was gone.

I could barely speak, asking only what the exact time of her death was, thinking she had died that moment. My sister's response?

2:45 p.m. her time – 1:45 p.m. MY TIME.

This was the EXACT time the song stopped – and the moment God had taken my mom back home.

This was the posting I did on the day my mom went to the light. You can clearly see the time of 13:42. It was here where the miracle of all miracles happened, as I was playing this song for my mother.

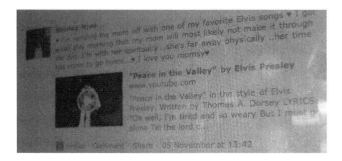

I needed some silent time, and quietly thought about the mother that fought to give me life; the mother that was the very best mother in the world to me; the mother that had sacrificed so much, and the mother which I loved – and LOVE – more than any words can ever express.

A short while later, I wanted to look again at that particular photo, so I went back to my post and I played Peace in the Valley on my iPad. Yet I could no longer see the picture – it was GONE! I was really shocked and played the song over and over, yet there was no brilliant picture with the arm of God coming down.

I told Eric and he said he would find it for me, as he too, saw it, and thus, it must still be there. Yet he couldn't find it either. My husband is THE sanest person I have ever known, and I was thankful I had shared the picture with him, as I could now never doubt that I myself saw it. I looked for it every day for about a week, stopping the song at one-second intervals, yet I never saw it again. It was really gone.

It was a miracle enough to have stopped the song the exact time my mother crossed, but to have a non-existing picture so brilliant was the miracle of All Miracles.

*"'Coincidence' is God's way of staying 'Anonymous.'" ~ Albert Einstein*

Suddenly, I knew it was a "miracle" and a gift from my beloved mother. I learned that Spirit is capable of manipulating things like this, yet I had never in my life been blessed with this type of miracle. It gave me so much strength in the days, weeks and months to come, and because of it – including everything I learned about the afterlife – my grieving process was lighter.

*"Miracles occur naturally as expressions of love, the real miracle is the love that inspires them. In this sense everything that comes from love is a miracle." ~ Marianne Williamson*

There are no wrong decisions in life, only lessons, and in my case, if I had gone to be with my mother, I would not have experienced this particular wondrous miracle. I felt strongly that my mother wanted it this way.

According to what I have learned, there are seven different levels in our dimensions, right here; and not anywhere far away. At the time of death most of us enter the third level, this radiant dimension being visually most like earth, except that it's filled with pure love and exists in the absence of sickness and aging.

As we become even more spiritual, we can graduate to higher levels, or we can choose to return to earth to master more lessons. This process is commonly referred to as "reincarnation" and the choice is entirely up to us.

It's all so mind blowing and fascinating, yet I don't have all the answers, still living inside my own human costume. I do know that life IS eternal, and my mother will be there smiling and jumping up and down to greet me one day.

My mother's wish was to never have a funeral or service; but rather, to be cremated, something she arranged for while still alive. She specified that I was to keep and receive her ashes. When she first told me this, she would smile, asking me to take her for rides once in awhile on the dashboard of my Mercedes. I promised her I would.

I asked my half-sister to please let me know when she was shipping me her ashes, so I could mentally prepare myself. A couple of weeks later the mailman knocked at my door handing me a package. Thinking it was something I ordered from Amazon, I opened it and found the parcel contained my dear mother's remains.

I broke down, as there was no warning, no note – nothing.

I became creative, taking some of her ashes and a younger photo and putting them in a tiny clear 1+1/2 oz. bottle, calling it my travel size "mini mom." This allowed for me to take a physical part of her wherever I went, knowing that she would be smiling and getting a serious kick out of it!

I was just happy to have my mom's remains right here with me, exactly where she wanted to be. I also took her for that nice, long drive she requested.

There is no wrong or right way to grieve; there are no rules of what to or what not to do. I believe we must all do what feels best to us, allowing our hearts to guide us.

Eric and I stood on the beach and released a lavender balloon with writings of love, high into the sky as my mother's little memorial. We will do this on every anniversary of her death in honor of her life and crossing.

You will continue to exist. It doesn't matter whether you define this as Spirit or just "continuing on." Energy does NOT die, it only changes forms. We are Eternal Beings.

# 63 MY VERY OWN AMAZING AND PROFOUND READINGS WITH TIM BRAUN AND OTHER FANTASTIC MEDIUMS

I have many loved ones on the other side, including Christian Brando, who crossed over in January 2008 at age 49, from a coma with double pneumonia.

I felt the time was now to gift myself with a spiritual reading.

I knew James Van Praagh maintained a list of very good mediums, so we looked and made an appointment with Tim Braun, for February 2012.

The following are selected excerpts, taken from transcriptions of our readings.

~

We drove to Costa Mesa, where Eric and I received our readings together. The moment we stepped into his beautiful office, I liked Tim immediately.

One of the first things he told us was: Transitions to death are no more than walking from one door through the next.

Linda and Bill

Tim started the reading with Eric, and soon moved to me, telling me there was a woman in the room directly behind me. She wasn't immediate family and had died in 2007. When he stated her approximate age and provided additional validations, I knew immediately that it was Linda.

Linda and I used to make a big deal about how thick our hair was. Now, she was bragging that her hair was still very thick. She also said how much she loved mine in this new style, and tugged at my blonde braid. There was not a single doubt in my mind, it WAS Linda!

Her funny sarcasm came through, with Tim repeatedly saying that she was a real "pistol." After the fourth time, I couldn't stand it anymore and volunteered that she had shot herself. This was HER humor!

She wanted to acknowledge Eric and putting her arms around both of us, said that she had known he was a good guy but that she had no idea just how good he was. This was exactly what Linda would say and do. She also brought Eric's dog through for him, never having known his dog in real life, or that he even had one.

Linda asked me to take more beach walks on the sand and to just "talk to her." She said, "I- MISS –US."

Tim asked me if I took beach walks. I told him I live on the beach, but prefer to walk on the boardwalk versus the sand, explaining I don't like the feel and mess of sand between my toes any longer.

Linda interrupted, "Sit there – get a bucket of water – put your feet in = problem solved!"

Unbelievable! This was her sarcastic humor! Eric and I cracked up laughing AND naturally, I did start walking in the sand, once again.

She then affirmed that she's still really sharp with names, dates, details etc. and that she hadn't lost her photogenic memory. Tim said she had a good mind and that it was an attribute while here. It's what made her excel! He then gave me another example: Some may use their big smiles and big breasts such as how Dolly Parton marketed herself. No coincidence as Dolly Parton shares the same birthday as me, January 19. Linda knew this and we used to joke about!

This was all truer than true! I used to say I needed her memory if I was to ever write my life story, since she would remember every single detail. Her mind was that sharp!

Linda added that she doesn't know how she stayed in her body for the last three and-a-half years of life, as it was emotionally unbearable. She said she had several very close friends, close to a pack of five, and that she was the first one to leave the pack.

Tim said that Linda was tearing up about missing her two boys, and I immediately knew she meant her grandsons – she adored them! She mentioned she really loved her daughter as well, and how difficult it was to leave them in the physical. She said she was extremely close to her daughter and loved both her son and daughter very much. In Tim's presence, I had the most wonderful visit with my "siSTAR" once again. Tim said that we were more like sisters than friends, and he couldn't have been more spot on!

Bill Bates, my young love who was killed on his motorcycle by a drunk driver, came through as well. He said that he wouldn't have missed this for anything! Tim described him exactly, saying he was in his late 20's when he was killed, and that he still looked "real good." He described him as having had a sensitivity not often seen in men, and a very loving soul.

Tim smelled alcohol very strongly and sensed it wasn't either of us or him. We knew instantly it was a message from Bill – that he died at the hands of a drunk driver. Coming in SO strong now, Bill also explained in detail how it felt to be thrown off his bike, and that it was a complete shock for him as he spun out. We learned several more disturbing details about his accident, but Tim reassured us that Bill wasn't trying to put a downer on the reading.

Bill continued to embrace me in his gentle and loving way and as sweet as he always did in life, wrapping his arms around me – so very tight, directly from behind, his cheek touching mine. Tim said that when Spirit does this, it's the ultimate and most intimate way of showing love, more so than hugging from any other angle.

Bill then placed laid a soft kiss on my lips, as a tear ran down his face.

Tim exclaimed, "Shirley you are really loved! You've had so much love in this life."

I agreed – and this is EXACTLY why I am able to give so much love.

I was also told that Bill was a continuance from a past life, and a continued, eternal soul mate. In this life, it was very quick; very brief, and then he was gone. Very, very powerful!

Although Bill displayed his love for me once again, he was extremely respectful towards Eric. He put his hand on his shoulder, sincerely thanking him for taking care of me. This was all so heavy, but it was exactly how both Linda and Bill were, while still alive in the physical.

Bill then stepped aside to let Linda back in, as she was still waiting. Tim noted that Spirit didn't have to do this, and that it's a very kind and sincere gesture – comparing it to someone having given up their spotlight to another! Bill joked and replied that there was no way he's messing with her! (Linda.) Laughter once again filled the room.

Linda told Tim from the beginning that he better get this right or she's-not-leaving! Tim clearly registered fear on his face as he adjusted his posture to sit up straight, while the three of us laughed. He said he didn't want to be on her bad side, and that he would give not 100%, but 110% with her, assuring us that he does his very best and gives his all in every single session.

Linda then said, "They need to know I-AM-FINE!"

As Tim records all his sessions, giving them to his clients, one can listen again and again at their leisure, digesting more details each time.

We experienced two extremely powerful and wonderful sessions by Tim. In the second session, Linda once again came through, as did my mother. The session was held in July 2012.

At this time, I was told that Spirit, via Tim, was pointing out I had more

"Untapped Talent." Tim continued to impart Spirit's message that I needed to go to the next level, insisting that there was still something untapped. (Honestly, I thought, YEA RIGHT! I'm retired now! My talent days are done!) Spirit continued to show Tim there IS a NEXT thing!

As in authoring my very, first book? Who would have "thunk" it!!

In this session Tim told me, that he saw a complete "VOID" on my father's side.

He suddenly asked me, if my mom ever told me that my birth father was significantly older than her. He was blowing me away when he added, that she met up with him on the other side and forgave him. Tim also told me that she did not CHOOSE this older man, it just happened! And, that bad things do happen to good people.

Looking directly into my eyes, he said, "It was meant to be; it brought YOU into the world." I was choked up at this profound truth.

Tim is priceless!

Tim has also done work with Mother Theresa in India.

Tim was taped for a television episode in Las Vegas for TLC's *SIN CITY RULES* scheduled to air on December 16, 2012 at 10:00pm PST. We ask that you, your family and friends view the show and send your comments to TLC asking for more episodes, and the creation of a show with Tim Braun.

Eric received several good family readings too, since he has many older family members that have passed.

Overall, both readings left me an even bigger believer than I already was. They brought me closure and validations, but most of all, they were really fun. AND THE BEST PART? They felt exactly like a direct visit to Heaven.

## My Mom

We both received several more readings from other mediums, too. My mom came through often, dancing and jumping up and down; clapping her hands just as she always did in "real life."

In November 2012 my mother went as far as to contact a Facebook friend, Medium, Donna Hartt. My mom insisted that Donna gift me with a reading, telling her I do so much for others, that it was my turn now. I was beyond surprised and extremely happy, with the intensity of the reading balanced with much-needed laughter, something that flowed the entire time.

Donna started out in the very beginning with a TA-DAAA and instantly I knew it WAS my mom. She continued by doing the happy–clappy dance, being totally ecstatic that she orchestrated this reading. Donna affirmed that my mother is very animated, strong-willed and determined. Bragging, my mother exclaimed that she's still skinny "over there" and likes to dress up while tooting her own horn (just as in life).

Donna also told me that I was the most "free spirited one" out of all my mom's children. (Very true.) My mom showed Donna she felt a sense of pride where I was concerned, and then said that I am "living the way I am supposed to be." After more than an hour, Donna finished with, "that I did no wrong." I was really blown away, as that's exactly how mom felt towards me in life, although I beg to differ with her.

My mother's message of "thank you" continued, as she always thanked me in life, for what I felt were little things. Loving my mom was easy and NO thanks were ever needed.

I will be forever thankful and very grateful to both of them for this magnificent gift.

## Billy

Donna brought Billy through as well – and he kept apologizing to me as he displayed his love. Billy remembered our trip to Hawaii very fondly, as Hawaii was his "big thing." Billy stated he was very broken here in this life, and that I was more gracious than he could handle. He felt so much remorse, and wanted me to know that nothing was my fault. He thanked me for all I did, and especially, for staying with him and loving him until the very end.

During a separate telephone reading for Eric, Billy walked by, lingering and interrupting, until he was able to express and thank Eric for taking care of me now.

It was really wonderful to hear from Billy. He helped in fulfilling some of my dreams, giving me more gifts than he could ever have known while here on earth; and I'm so very grateful to him. He knows all this now and can clearly see how very "majestic" he really was in my life. He also knows how very much I loved him!

*"No one comes to you by accident and life is not by chance; it was all mapped out this way before we were ever born."* ~ *Shirley Njos*

Donna also gifted me with a beautiful, angel reading. These cards indicated the following:

I allow myself to let life unfold, instead of pushing doors down. The age of ascension is upon us and I see the light; I'm in THE ZONE. I have a good relationship with myself spiritually, physically and emotionally, creating a life of no worry. I honor my Spirit, creating a trickle-down affect that becomes contagious for those around me. I have done a lot of clearing and have created an environment of love. My ability to feel for others has really opened up, leading to more adventure, and a continuous, unfolding journey. And finally: I set my intentions, and allow myself to be guided by Spirit. I absolutely loved this truth!

When Eric and I first met, we had a very strong feeling of "familiarity" towards one another. We talked about this and came to the conclusion that both Billy and his good friend, Greg both had a hand in putting us together.

We have had further confirmation regarding this from a total of four different mediums: Michele Fletcher, Al Barrera, Donna Hart and Tim Braun. Michele instantly and flat out said Billy put Eric and me with each other. Tim not only agreed about Billy, but also added that Bill Bates put Eric in my path.

It's no coincidence that all three of these men are Taurus's, with birthdays only two days apart: Eric's birthday being smack in the middle.

I couldn't have possibly asked for more, with all my readings leaving me with even more love in my heart. Most important was the knowledge that ALL of us would be together again, one day.

We are ALL in the same soul-mate family! And without any form of separation in all living things, WE-ARE-ALL-ONE!

My Whole "Life" – and connection to the "Afterlife" is, and has always been – NO COINCIDENCES ONLY MIRACLES.

# AFTERWARD

*"Living in fear stifles your actions and blocks your personal growth. I'd rather simply give my life – than to fear it! Fear is merely a "thought" – one which needs to dissipate so you can live the life you were born for – a life of love." ~ Shirley Njos*

The passages you have just read – and experienced alongside me – have been recounted in a most honest and honorable way. I took care to respect those involved, both living and dead. There are no fabrications or exaggerations in any of my words. My life is too much of a miracle for embellishments!

I wrote my book with Spirit's guidance every step of the way, purely using my "heart-brain" to share my life, with love and gratitude.

*"As spiritual beings, we are on an eternal journey and we have to learn and grow from all our experiences." ~ James Van Praagh*

I wrote this book for many, many reasons, some of which I will summarize here:

I want to leave a legacy for my children. I also wish for my story to inspire others, as I have touched on so many delicate, yet pertinent, subjects. And finally, I want to entertain, as many aspects of my life are quite simply, a riot, to say the least!

If after reading this book, you felt strongly towards a particular event or moment, recognize this is your own spiritual power speaking to you. Spirit ALWAYS recognizes Spirit.

Life is our Earth School, with certain lessons being more difficult to master than others. Everything had to happen to me exactly as it did, in order that I be brought to this most amazing and perfect time in my life. Each moment I experience, I strive to do so from a place of unconditional

265

love.

Love forms the basis of every lesson we are here to learn, and everything we think and do has its roots in love.

I have been blessed to have so much love in my life, and as I've mentioned in many ways throughout my book, this is the EXACT reason I am able to give love so freely.

Love attracts Love!

THANK YOU to all that have loved me!

# A NOTE TO MY CHILDREN

I have the most wonderful relationship with my daughter Tiffany. You are a precious and beautiful child, inside and out. You have been extremely loving and generous to me in every fathomable way, and I couldn't have asked for a more special daughter in my life. I still learn from you and I am forever grateful and honored you chose me as your mother. I love you Tiffany! You are my present in this lifetime. Keep shining your beautiful light. Thank you for so many very special and amazing memories.

Eric and I enjoyed celebrating Tiff's 2011 BIRTH-day in Laguna Beach at Splash restaurant. I know there are many more fantastic and memorable times ahead for us. It was an amazing night; absolutely perfect!

I have the greatest relationship with my daughter, Mo.

We have come such a long way together. You have been there for me so many times throughout my life, when I really needed someone, and I treasure you. To experience your sweet and innocent kindness, along with your wisdom, absolutely warms my heart. You were born with a very spiritual essence, and I have learned so much from you; you being a very special gift to me. I love you Mo! Thank you for choosing me as your mother, and thank you for being YOU!

Eric, Mo and me at a fantastic Italian restaurant in New York, celebrating our visit in February 2013.

# ABOUT THE AUTHOR

Shirley Njos has such a passion for life, that nothing ever seemed too impossible or daunting for her. Her life story has touched the glamour of Hollywood and Italy, as an actress. She found herself sharing kisses with Elvis Presley. She dated Marlon Brando's son, Christian. With no formal training, she taught herself fashion design and living her life as an artist, enjoyed a successful career designing suede and leathers for both the stars and for the general retail market.

And yet at the core of it all, Shirley found her beliefs and values aligned directly with Spirit. From experiencing the suicide of her best friend, the loss of her former husband and her mother's passing, to being a mother to the most wonderful children; Shirley invites you into her private world.

In her first book, she shares the raw intimacy of these experiences in her compelling life story. Her journey starts out in post-war Germany and takes the reader "across the pond" to Long Beach, California.

Sometimes brutal, sometimes exciting but always absolutely magical, Shirley's honest storytelling is bound to grip you with every emotion possible.

Shirley presently still lives in Long Beach with her husband of 11 years, along with the hundreds of sea gulls that make their home on the beach.

Made in the USA
San Bernardino, CA
23 July 2013